THAT'S ANOTHER STORY:
THE AUTOBIOGRAPHY

With her talent, infectious spirit and self-deprecating humour, Julie Walters has been described as the nation's most popular actress and comedienne. Now she tells us the story of her extraordinary life: Born in fifties Birmingham, daughter of an Irish Catholic mother, she left convent school and went into nursing to appease her mother. Soon after, however, she joined The Everyman Theatre in Liverpool. When *Educating Rita* became a West End success, she replicated that success on film, playing opposite Michael Caine. Julie's collaborations with Victoria Wood have given us the unforgettable 'Mrs Overall' in *Acorn Antiques.* Starring in many films including *Billy Elliot, Calendar Girls* and *Mamma Mia!,* Julie has now charmed a new generation of fans playing Mrs Weasley in the Harry Potter films.

JULIE WALTERS

◆

THAT'S ANOTHER STORY
THE AUTOBIOGRAPHY

Complete and Unabridged

CHARNWOOD
Leicester

First published in Great Britain in 2008 by
Weidenfeld & Nicolson
The Orion Publishing Group Ltd.
London

First Charnwood Edition
published 2009
by arrangement with
The Orion Publishing Group Ltd.
London

oı(lᴄ

British Library CIP Data

Walters, Julie, *1950 –*
   That's another story: the autobiography.
   1. Walters, Julie, *1950 – 2.* Motion picture actors
and actresses- -Great Britain- -Biography. 3. Television
actors and actresses- -Great Britain- -Biography.
   4. Large type books.
   I. Title
   791.4′3′028′092–dc22

   ISBN 978–1–84782–885–9

Published by
F. A. Thorpe (Publishing)
Anstey, Leicestershire

Set by Words & Graphics Ltd.
Anstey, Leicestershire
Printed and bound in Great Britain by
T. J. International Ltd., Padstow, Cornwall

This book is printed on acid-free paper

For Maisie

Acknowledgements

Firstly, my brother Tommy for introducing me to the sheer pleasure of reading and for his encouragement, enthusiasm and delight in my early 'literary' efforts at school. My sister-in-law, Jill Walters, for putting me right on the geography of my home town, bits of which I had long forgotten; and Professor Carl Chinn for putting her right on the bits that she'd forgotten. David Thompson for providing me with precious photographs and memories.

Paul Stevens for getting the whole thing off the ground so brilliantly and my agent Paul Lyon Maris for his tremendous support, inordinate good sense, but especially for his words of wisdom.

Alan Samson, for whom 'thanks' just doesn't seem enough and without whose Albert Hall-sized knowledge of just about everything, gentle encouragement and necessary sense of humour, I would never have had the courage to write this book in the first place.

And last but by no means least, my husband Grant and my daughter Maisie for being there and listening patiently to my fears, moans and long, protracted readings of roughly written passages from this book; in short, for being who they are.

Contents

1. 'Five Years Ago Today' — The Beginning 1
2. 'This Old House' — 69 Bishopton Road 5
3. 'Don't Go Out Too Far' — Holidays.....61
4. 'A Fine Figure of a Man' — Dad.........69
5. 'At the Third Stroke She Will Be 78' — Grandma 78
6. 'Mixing with Doctors' Daughters' — Junior School....................................90
7. 'I Thought You'd Failed' — Senior School 106
8. The Little Nurse — Work 138
9. 'So You Want To Be an Actress?' — Manchester.....................................171
10. Foreign Adventure.........................201
11. Learning to Teach 210
12. 'Can We Still Go on the Honeymoon?' — Breaking Up...........................224
13. Life at The Everyman — Liverpool 230
14. *Funny Peculiar* in London 255
15. 'We're Missin' *Brideshead* for This!' — Victoria Wood.................................275
16. *Ecstasy* with Mike Leigh 289
17. Rita on Stage and Screen 294
18. The Two Alans..............................326
19. 'I Love to Boogie' — Oscars and BAFTAs 331

20. 'Something There to Offend the Whole Family' — *Personal Services* 344

21. The Arrival.................................361

Epilogue — Another Beginning..........372

Filmography................................374

1

'Five Years Ago Today' — The Beginning

'Five years ago today . . . '

It's my mother's voice. She is at the foot of the stairs, calling out the story of my birth, as she did on so many birthdays.

'Ten years ago today . . . '

It is Irish, a Mayo voice worn at the edges, giving it a husky quality, which, she told me once, some men had found alluring.

'Fifteen years ago today . . . '

Now it is soft with memory and buoyant with the telling. I was the fifth and final child to be born, each delivery producing its own particular trauma.

The first, my brother Tommy, arrived during the war in 1942. He never slept and continually scratched at his face, until eventually he was taken into hospital where his tiny hands were bandaged to prevent further harm. When Kevin, the second, was born three years later, my mother's screams of 'Put him back!' apparently reached the outskirts of Birmingham. This, according to my mother and much to our amusement, was due to the inordinate size of his head. The third, a girl called Mary, was stillborn, and in order to get me to eat eggs my mother had told me that it was Mary's refusal to do so

1

that had caused her demise. This went on for some years until one day I challenged the assertion, pointing out that a dead baby wouldn't have been able to speak let alone have much of an appetite. And anyway, I went on, where is she? Where is her grave? My mother went quiet. I was beginning to think she had made the whole thing up, that there never was a Mary, until my father chimed in with awful innocence, 'Well, she was incinerated, wasn't she? She didn't have a proper funeral. No! That's it! She was buried in, like, a job lot.' That was the first time I ever saw her cry and I didn't understand her grief, at least not for about another thirty years.

The penultimate birth was a late miscarriage, a boy, of which very little was said. Then after she was told it would be too dangerous to have any more children, I came along in 1950 on 22 February, apparently at three o'clock in the afternoon.

'My waters broke . . . ' A slight vibrato begins. 'Your father and I got on the bus.' She knows I need to know and that she needs to recount it; again and again. 'I was passing your motions.' Well, perhaps I don't need to know this, but I'm not sure, and no matter how many times I ask, this last detail is only ever explained by further increasingly impatient repetitions of it. Now, of course, I know and see its significance: I was shitting myself. 'They should never have given me that big fish dinner . . . ' I am now standing in the room in St Chad's Hospital, watching my mother, the said fish dinner having been thrown up over the pale-yellow counterpane. She is

2

huge, about to give birth. 'The cord was around your neck.'

'God, Mum, I know this so well I feel as if I was actually there.' She ignores this.

'They got in the priest.' I can see him, well, not really. I cast Father Sillitoe in the part, our parish priest from St Gregory's church, round and avuncular, his red face testament to his fondness for altar wine. My brother Tommy, an altar boy himself, tells how Father Sillitoe would slip a hand under his elbow, forcing him to pour a lot more wine into the chalice than the usual mouthful. 'They could save only one of us . . . Your father had to choose.' My mother's incomparable sense of drama now removes all vibrato from her voice and this last statement is made with a terrible flat resignation. Like the best of actors, she knows that less is more.

'I chose you.' My father chipped in on this only once that I remember. His voice is gentle and unassuming with a big, full, Birmingham, inner-city accent. He is sitting, his hair full of plaster dust, exhausted and weathered far beyond his years, in the kitchen at 69 Bishopton Road, wet shirts dripping from the pulley above him, smelling of turps and house paint and years of cigarettes. The cigarettes weren't just in his clothes; they were in his skin, in his sweat. He had smoked since he was ten. Even though he died in 1971, I can summon up that smell in an instant.

'He chose you.' Her voice is that of a sad, bewildered child. My mother's father never chose her.

'Yes but it doesn't matter. It was all right in the end,' my father soothes.

'The priest had to give me the last rites.'

'Yes but you were all right in the end.'

'Extreme unction.'

'Yeah but — Oh blimey . . . ' He knows when to give up and does so with an ironic, forgiving little laugh.

'They took you away. I didn't see you for a whole week.'

No one speaks.

'Happy birthday, Julie.'

2

'This Old House' — 69 Bishopton Road

Number 69 Bishopton Road was a big, draughty, end-of-terrace house. There was a song around in the fifties called 'This Old House', with lyrics like, 'Ain't got time to fix the windows, ain't got time to fix the floors.' Whenever it was played on the radio my mother sang along with such gusto and empathy that as a small child, whose universe began and ended at our back gate, I presumed that it was being sung specifically about our house.

Similarly once, whilst I was watching *Watch with Mother* on my own, aged about three, a kindly lady sat there holding a teddy bear and waving its paw straight at the camera, saying, 'Look, Teddy, there is a little girl watching us and she's got a teddy just like you!' I was off that sofa and into the kitchen before you could say Andy Pandy, screaming at my mother that the lady on television could not only see me but she had spoken to me and she knew about Teddy as well, and there might be a damp patch on the sofa; but that was Teddy, not me. My mother simply replied mysteriously, 'Don't listen to Grandma.' It was only when I asked my father why, when there were Tom cats, were there not any Kev cats, and he explained that Tom cats were not named after my older brother, that it began to dawn on me that the sun didn't shine out of my arse.

At the far end of Smethwick's Bishopton Road, about two hundred yards down, was Lightwoods Park, right on the border of Bearwood, which is part of the Black Country around Birmingham. As a child I was forbidden to go to the park unaccompanied because of 'strange men', the park keeper himself being quite possibly one of the strangest. Lightwoods Park, which covered about ten acres, had a bandstand with a large, domed roof, kept aloft by several spindly-looking, wrought-iron pillars, whose top-heavy nature sent my brother Tommy into a panic when he was small, with tearful claims that it was 'Too big up there'. There were a set of swings, a couple of roundabouts, a see-saw and a defunct witch's hat. This last was a conical roundabout in the shape of a witch's hat, the top of which was balanced on top of a tall pole and, because of this shape, it not only went round but veered crazily up and down as well as from side to side. Next to this play area was the pond, about an acre of water, upon which people sailed their model boats and suchlike, whilst in hot weather it became a muddy soup of children and dogs, paddling and swimming. At the edge of the park stood (and still stands) Lightwoods House, built in 1791 for Jonathan Grundy, a Leicestershire maltster. It was eventually donated to Birmingham City Council in a philanthropic act by Alexander Macomb Chance, one of the Chance glass-making family of Spon Lane, Smethwick. In my day it had been downgraded to a

6

café where teas, ices and suchlike could be bought.

Never were my mother's warnings to keep out of the park fiercer than during the summer holidays when the annual funfair came for a week. I found the smell of hot dogs, diesel and candyfloss, the garish colours, the loud pop music, half drowned out by the noise of generators, totally alluring, and I loved rides like the dodgems and the bumping cars where swarthy, muscle-bound young men, in dirty jeans and covered in tattoos, would take your money and jump on the back of your car, or better still on the waltzers, where the more you screamed the faster they would whip your car around. The fair-ground was always full of groups of adolescent girls careering drunkenly about in a whirl of light-headed hysteria and something closely akin to post-coital relief. According to my mother, 'The fair attracted the wrong sort and no decent girl would be interested in boys like these; they were low types from God knows where,' and were to be kept away from. Needless to say I went every year, mostly avoiding being found out. The fairground boys — the waltzer boy in particular, so poignantly described in Victoria Wood's song 'I Want to be Fourteen Again', 'The coloured lights reflected in the Brylcreem in his hair' — played leading roles in an early fantasy of mine about living in a caravan, working on a stall involving goldfish and smelling of petrol.

Our end of the street formed the junction with Long Hyde Road. Only about a hundred metres long, it was short and there were rarely more than two or three cars parked in it at a time, one of them being my father's, when it was not parked in the garage at the back. Dad always owned a car except for when he first started his business, when he pushed around from job to job a wooden handcart laden with ladders and tools. On the side it had THOS. WALTERS Ltd, builders and decorators and the address, painted by a signwriter. This, however, was before I was born. The first car I remember was in fact a small, bright-yellow van, which my father referred to as Sally.

Sally had no side windows at the back, just two little square ones, one in each of the back doors, and so her rear end consisted of a fairly dark space that was always full of tools, paint, bits of wood and the odd paint-spattered rag: the general requisites and detritus of my father's work life. Yet if we went out in Sally as a family, she would be transformed; Dad would shift everything out of the back and sling in an old bus seat for my brothers and me to sit on. I can see it now and not only see it but feel it. It had a silky, soft pile if you ran your hand one way across it, although this became quite uncomfortably rough and prickly if you had the misfortune to run it the other way. It had an abstract, jazzy, brown and green pattern against a dull, beige background and the whole thing was edged in creased brown leather. This bit of 'necessity being the mother of invention' thinking on my father's part worked really well unless we had to stop suddenly for any reason, such as at a traffic light or a pelican crossing or when arriving home again. The seat, having no support at the back of it, would abruptly tip over backwards, sending all of us sprawling into a chaotic backward roll. So any journey would mainly be spent scrambling about in the semi-darkness, getting the seat upright again just in time for the three of us with a mighty, united scream of 'Daaaaaaaad!' to be sent flying once more. In fact every journey ended like this as we pulled up outside the house, accompanied by my grandmother's declaration, if she was with us, of 'We've landed!'

Sally was eventually replaced by a far superior and very 'modern' Ford Esquire estate. It was a sedate grey colour and its main advantage was that the estate bit at the back served as extra passenger space for small persons when the car was at capacity. Of course this was long before seatbelt laws and would be illegal today. The small person was inevitably me and it meant that not only could I travel staring out of the back window at the car behind, possibly making faces or breathing on the glass and writing fascinating back-to-front messages, like 'ylimaf neila na yb detcudba gnieb ma I !!pleH' for the driver behind to ignore, but I could also avoid being poked or teased by my brothers.

The other advantage of this new acquisition was that it soon became clear that Dermot Boyle, the boy who lived opposite, with whom I played on a regular basis, was envious. As may be obvious from the name, the Boyles were an Irish family. Mr Boyle was a builder's labourer who came from Kerry and, as my dad would say, liked a drink. He had very red, permanently wet lips that appeared to work independently of the rest of his face and, indeed, independently of anything that he might happen to be saying. They flopped around clumsily, an impediment to the words that came pouring through them in unintelligible strings. These were buoyed up on clouds of alcoholic breath and always accompanied by blizzards of spit. The whole thing was pretty hard to avoid for, once buttonholed, Mr Boyle would always address a person no more than three inches from their face, due to his poor eyesight. He was severely short-sighted, which meant he was forced to wear glasses with lenses so thick that it was like looking down a couple of telescopes the wrong way, his eyes becoming tiny, blue, distant dots. We often stood giggling at the upstairs window, behind the nets, watching Pat Boyle wobble up the street on his pushbike and stand swaying for a good ten minutes, trying to get his key in the front door lock, his face jammed right up against it. Then, eventually, the door would be opened by the long-suffering Mrs Boyle and Pat, with key still in hand poised to slip it into the lock, would go lurching forward like a pantomime drunk, Mrs B berating him as he stumbled in. The irony of the whole Boyle saga was that Mrs Boyle, who never took a drink in her life, died of liver cancer and Mr Boyle, who was rarely sober as far as I know, died of natural causes.

I am ashamed to say that I exploited Dermot's envy of our car to the maximum and with relish. If he happened to be out playing on the street by himself, and the car was appropriately parked, I would sit provocatively on the front bumper, caressing its shiny chrome with one hand, the other stretched backwards across the bonnet, occasionally fingering the Ford insignia, one leg crossed over the other, swinging my foot nonchalantly back and forth, chatting inanely on whilst secretly clocking Dermot's reaction. He would sit on the kerb by the side of the road, usually eating a piece of his mother's home-made cake, squirming and covering his eyes. At last he would run off, mid-conversation, down the entry that led round to the back of his house, shouting 'Stop it!' and spraying cake crumbs, as he went.

A couple of years later we went up several rungs on the status-symbol ladder of car ownership, acquiring a two-tone Vauxhall Victor estate, in green and cream. I couldn't wait to torment Dermot with it. In fact my father had hardly got out of the front seat after bringing it home than I was draped across its warm bonnet, in true motor-show fashion, while the hapless Dermot, caught innocently chalking on the pavement opposite, tried not to look, his bottom lip thrust out and his face turning cherry red in an attempt to control his rage. My father never ever told me off, but that day, on his way into the house, he wheeled round when he realised what was going on and shouted, 'Wharaya doin'? Gerroff, ya daft cat, you'll scratch the paint-work!' Whereupon, out of the blue, like a missive from the gods, a bird shat on the bonnet right next to me, splattering the fingers of my left hand. 'Now, look! Come on, gerroff!'

I jumped down and ran into the house, feeling vaguely ashamed of the excrement as if it were my own, while Dad whipped out an old handkerchief from his pocket and began to lovingly wipe the bonnet clean. I guess Dermot and I were even stevens after that and years later, on a visit home, I remember asking my mother to whom the flash car belonged that was parked opposite. I think it was an immaculately kept Cortina but can't be sure of the make, only that it was extremely shiny, with a bigger aerial than most and enough headlamps for several cars. 'Oh, Dermot is home to stay.' And I felt my own little dart of envy; I wasn't to pass my driving test until I was thirty-seven.

It was here on Long Hyde Road, which ran along the side of our house, that during daylight hours and sometimes later, weather and school permitting, I would spend my time playing with any neighbourhood children who happened to be around. My first crush developed here when I was about five. Or, perhaps more accurately, I experienced my first feelings of loss. I'd been playing regularly with a boy called Robert, who had pale blond hair and lived on the far corner of Long Hyde Road. Suddenly he was going away; the family were moving house. He stood there, I can see him now, eating a piece of bread and butter, or a piece as we called it, whilst kicking the bottom of the garden wall opposite as he broke the news. I remember him not looking at me as he spoke and then running off, leaving four little crescent-shaped crusts on the top of the wall. Somehow it was the sight of those crusts that sparked off the grief of this separation. I picked one up and ate it, but couldn't continue to eat the others as the damp edges where his lips and teeth had touched it brought a lump to my throat. I kept the other three pieces in one of my father's old Senior Service cigarette packets until they dried out and went a bluish-green colour. I don't remember much else about this boy's family, except the reporting some years later of the death of Robert's older brother whom I never really knew. He was killed in a climbing accident on Snowdon. And again the image of the small blond head with the blurred face, the foot kicking against the wall and the sweet taste of those damp crusts, slid into my head like a frame of film, as it has continued to do on the odd occasion ever since.

Long Hyde Road was almost permanently marked out with white chalk for rounders or hopscotch, and a couple of times the whole length of the pavement, a good hundred yards, was marked out into four wobbly lanes for an athletics tournament organised by my brothers. Tommy and Kevin, at least in my eyes, were the cocks of the neighbourhood, heroes who made other boys look pitiably inadequate. To say I was proud of them could not be more of an understatement. It was unimaginable to me that anyone could possibly be cleverer or stronger or wittier or braver. They were the very best at everything and I as their little sister basked not only in their glory but also in their protection. They were knights in shining armour. This is best illustrated in an incident that occurred when I was about seven.

There was a boy in the next street who, whenever I walked past his house, would leap out and attack me with his big, black-and-chrome plastic space gun. He would hold me there for what seemed like hours but was probably about twenty minutes or so, his great, long gun pinning my chest to the wall while my head and shoulders were stuck uncomfortably in the privet hedge above. On some occasions he was accompanied by Benji, the family boxer dog, which he would whip up into a frenzy so that it would leap about, whites of eyes flashing and long, jellied globules of saliva stretching and swinging from its jaws. He would then pat my shoulders so that the thing would jump up at me, its pink shiny willy out and fully ready for action and then, with an onslaught of slimy licks and fetid, wheezy breaths, it would attempt to mount me. It was rape by proxy. Needless to say I would walk miles out of my way to avoid this awful boy and his oversexed dog but one day, mistakenly thinking he was on holiday and that it was safe, I got caught again. It was a particularly lengthy session and, arriving home upset, I blurted out to my older brother Tommy what had happened. Within minutes, so legend would have it, he went round to the child's house and not only soundly thrashed him but did so in front of his astonished parents. The boy never came near me again.

Our house was north-facing and we didn't get central heating until 1963. Climbing the stairs to go to bed at night was often likened to scaling the north face of the Eiger, and ice on the inside of the bedroom windows was usual throughout the winter. On the coldest nights my parents would simply pile the beds with coats and the resulting weight would make turning over in bed a feat of strength that just wasn't worth the effort. This, of course, meant that the seat nearest the fire in the kitchen was fiercely fought over by the three of us and, once won, it would be given up only for the direst of emergencies. I remember my brother Tommy managing to stay put for a record-breaking length of time, eventually jumping up with a howl of expletives to find that his wellington boot had melted with the heat and had welded itself on to his leg. He still bears the scars.

The house was on three storeys and there were three doors to get into it: the front door, which was rarely ever used, the middle door and the back door. The front door opened on to an oddly shaped hallway, one wall of which was almost all window. This was because the previous owner had an electrical shop and had built the hall on to display his radios. There were two doors off it, one leading into the front room, which was my father's office. It smelt of tobacco and ink and him, and in the corner was his big roll-top desk, from which he ran his building and decorating business. It also contained the piano, upon which he could vamp anything by ear, and upon which I wrote hundreds of songs, all sounding very similar and which I sang at the top of my voice, over and over again, with my foot hard down on the loud pedal, hoping distantly that someone would say, 'My God, that's brilliant!' instead of 'For Christ's sake, shut up! Your voice is so piercing!' or my mother's warning anthem of 'Shut up or I'll crucify you!' which tended to persuade me to stop.

The other door led to the sitting room, which held the television. We were one of the first houses in our road to have one and on important occasions like the Grand National, the Cup Final or the Queen's Speech, various neighbours would be invited in to watch. It was a similar story with the telephone, which was also in this room. Most people hadn't got one and so if there was an urgent need for a neighbour to contact someone, they would come round and use ours, always offering to pay. This would invariably result in the same scenario: my mother and one of her friends sitting at the kitchen table with cups of tea, pushing a couple of a coppers back and forth, with 'No! No! I couldn't take it from you!' and 'Yes! Now don't be silly, Mary, just take it!' This could go on for up to half an hour, broken every so often by little flurries of gossip and then taken up again with renewed vigour: 'NO, no, I won't hear of it!' and 'Yes! Yes, or I will never ask again!' until eventually and with much tutting my mother gave in.

However, the most important feature of the sitting room was the three-piece suite with its sofa, the back of which was the perfect height for saddling and mounting. Most nights after school I would jump on its back and go for a hack: my school satchel the saddle, its strap the bridle. I can remember a teacher once asking me why some of my exercise books seemed to be bent in such a peculiar way. 'Have you been sitting on them?' I went red, inwardly horrified that someone might have a clue to my after-school, imaginary life on the range, and said that I thought the leather of my satchel had a natural warp in it, a bit like wood. After this incident I made sure my satchel was empty before saddling up. In my imagination I was the boy from *Champion the Wonder Horse*, trekking across the prairie and then sitting down to beans and coffee with the folks from *Wagon Train*. Eventually it was necessary for me to become the twin sister of the boy from *Champion the Wonder Horse*, when, after he rescued me from the Indians I married Flint McCullough, the scout from *Wagon Train*, with whom I had been in love for many years.

It was on this sofa that my addiction to *Coronation Street* started back in December 1960, watching the first episode with my mother. I am slightly ashamed to say that when my own daughter was born and I brought her home, that very evening I was sitting in front of the television, holding her, and when the theme for *Corrie* came on she turned her little, week-old head around towards the television in what was obviously recognition. She remembered it from the womb, where hearing is the first sense to be developed. Sitting watching TV with my mother was a rare occurrence, her television viewing being confined to the Saturday-night variety show of the time and *Sunday Night at the*

17

London Palladium. It was on that sofa that I would lie on a Saturday afternoon, the curtains drawn, watching the afternoon film. They were generally films from the thirties and forties, with Bette Davis being my favourite. I loved her in absolutely anything, although the ones that instantly come to mind are *Now Voyager, Jezebel* and *All About Eve.* She was unique; there was an exciting, un-Hollywoodish reality and lack of vanity in her performances, and she always played strong women who had to be reckoned with, who were not there simply to function as a fantasy to attract and please men. Now occasionally on a Saturday when no one is in, I try to re-create the Saturday afternoon of my childhood, the curtains closed, lying on the sofa with toast and jam, hoping that Bette will appear, brave and insolent, brazenly cutting a swathe through life, but more often than not finding that, although there are many more channels nowadays, the options are disappointing.

I can still feel the rough, bobbly texture of that sofa with its maroon and grey upholstery, and smell its musty, ubiquitous aroma of stale tobacco and the unique essence that was us, as it warmed up on a winter's night in front of the four-bar, Magicoal electric fire. We were allowed to have this on, and just the two bars only, if the weather was really cold; anything warmer than arctic and my mother's voice would shoot up an octave, reaching a note she reserved solely to register panic and shock at the thought of an upcoming, potentially colossal bill. Her ancient and irrational fear of being without and in debt, and her resultant husbandry to the extent that she would walk several miles to save a halfpenny on a pound of carrots — meant that no bill ever went unpaid. In the latter part of her life the penny-pinching took a slightly different turn when she took to regularly trawling through the local charity shops, filling her wardrobe and drawers with tons of musty-smelling, second-hand clothes, most of which she never wore. She would often turn up on a visit to London, well into the 1980s, dressed from head to foot for a seventies night: in jackets with huge, pointy collars and blouses with Laura Ashley prints, all with the same stale aroma.

The door leading out of the sitting room opened on to a little hall, on the left of which, down a couple of stone steps, was the pantry. It was a small dark room under the stairs, cool even in summer, with shelves laden with tinned food, a constant supply of my mother's rock cakes and, on the floor, a huge basket full of clean, unironed laundry. I loved my mother's rock cakes but their springy texture was the endless butt of jokes. I can remember my father up a ladder, mending a hole in the roof and shouting down to me in the garden, 'Oh blimey! Hand us up one of your mother's rock cakes.' Or when the back door kept banging in the wind, my father suggesting that we shove one of Mum's cakes underneath it. Once, my brother Kevin and I decided to put their robust quality to the test by playing a game of cricket with one. It lasted for several overs before the first currants began to work loose and it wasn't until my brother hit a whacking great six that it finally disintegrated into a cloud of crumbs.

The reason that the pantry is so significant is that it was brilliant for pretending to be Mrs Waller, who ran a small grocery shop over the road. Mrs Waller was a queen amongst shopkeepers; she didn't so much run the corner shop as reign over it. A handsome woman in a pristine, pink, nylon overall that shushed every time she moved, she had beautifully waved, honey-blonde hair and perfect make-up. If there was ever more than one customer in at a time she would throw her head back, as if for all the world she was about to sing an aria, and call, 'Trevaaaaar!' Trevor was her shy, rather awkward, teenage son with whom she appeared to be endlessly impatient and disgruntled. If Trevaaar was not available her husband would be summoned. A quiet, bespectacled, careworn man would appear through the multi-coloured plastic strips of curtain that hung across the doorway and stand there, mutely, often unwittingly wearing a few of the said strips draped over his head and shoulders, like an Indian chief's headdress. Then without deigning even to look at him, she would bark instructions: 'Mrs Jordan's ham, please.' The men in Mrs Waller's life were a burdensome source of regret to her and she had a particular tone of voice reserved only for them. It was strident, posh and imperious and every syllable screamed, 'I am too good for you and I'm here only under sufferance!' But when I walked into the shop, her face would lift into a pretty pink smile and I would have penny bars of chocolate and twopenny chews thrust into my hand, along with whatever purchase I had been sent there to get. Poor Trevor! If only he'd been a Tina.

I would spend hours in the pantry, by myself, serving shopful after shopful of customers whilst acting out the Waller family drama, except that the Trevor in my fantasy grew into a bit of a hunk, so much so that he couldn't possibly be called Trevor any longer and I was forced to change his name to Tony, at which point we became husband and wife. This could not, in any sense, be construed as bigamous, as the scout from *Wagon Train* operated in an entirely different universe to the one Tony and I inhabited in the pantry.

It was in the pantry, some years after I had left home, that I mysteriously came across a copy of the *Kama Sutra* whilst looking for a clean towel in the laundry basket. It was hidden in the washing. I felt uncomfortable and a little shocked at the find. Where on earth had my mother got it? Surely she wasn't attempting any of these Olympian postures herself and, if so, who with? My father had died some time back. I never did find out and in some ways I'm grateful for that but it did go partway to explaining something that my mother had said a little while before the discovery. We were sitting in the kitchen, discussing the new husband of a friend of hers, when she suddenly announced in a rather baffled but thoughtful voice, 'I don't think your father was very good at sex.' End of conversation.

Next to the pantry were the stairs, which like the little hall itself were covered with the same brown carpet, enlivened by a small, abstract motif in black that was repeated at regular intervals. Not long after my father had laid this carpet, my mother and I went into Freeman, Hardy & Willis on the Bearwood Road to buy me a new pair of shoes and there it was, our new carpet, all over the shop!

'Mum, I — '

That's as far as I got. I was dragged outside, my arm only just remaining in its socket and my mother's hot, urgent breath steaming up my ear, her voice like something from *The Exorcist*: 'Don't mention the carpet!' My father was the shopfitter for Freeman, Hardy & Willis.

At eighteen months I had trodden on my nightdress whilst going up these stairs to bed and put a tooth through my lip, which still sports a tiny hairline scar today. These stairs were where I had tested my mettle by jumping down, first two, then three, then four and five steps at a time. They were where, on dark nights, heart pounding, I had shouted endless 'Goodnights' to my parents, stopping each time to wait for the comfort of their reply, and where I sang nonsense lyrics to made-up songs as loud as I could so that any menace hiding behind the dark crack of a door or waiting to pounce on the other side of a billowing curtain would know how unafraid I was. They were also where I prepared for a possible career in bus conducting, charging up and down them wearing my father's old Box Brownie as a ticket machine and a shoulder bag

22

of my mother's for the money. I wanted to wear that fitted, black, military-style trouser suit they all wore; I wanted to chew gum, stink of cigarettes and jingle with money as I leapt, gazelle-like, up and down the bus stairs, shouting 'No room on top! Fares, please!' I wanted to wear that ticket machine slung low across my hip, discharging tickets with expert ease and issuing that gorgeous metallic sound that almost made my mouth water. My conductress would wear loads of make-up and have lashings of lustrous, black hair, and she would always be accompanied by the same bus driver who would bear an uncanny resemblance to the scout from *Wagon Train*.

Opposite the pantry and the stairs was the middle floor; this opened at the side of the house on to the garden, which ran around to the back of the house. The middle door was also opposite the back gate, which in turn opened out on to Long Hyde Road, and it was where everyone who knew us called; only strangers knocked at the front door. It was at the middle door that the milk was delivered and where the milkman called for payment of his bill every Saturday, his milk cart being pulled by a big brown and white horse. My mother would shout, 'Get out there with a bucket and shovel, the milkman's coming' then she would keep watch from an upstairs window and shout, 'Too late, SHE'S got it!' thus referring to a neighbour who was already scooping the steaming heap of horse dung into her own bucket with a satisfied smirk. There was talk at one time of a small boy, a few streets away, who stuck a straw up the horse's nose, resulting in the poor creature rearing up on to its hind legs, which caused the cart to overturn, smashing every single bottle, both full and empty, to smithereens.

Our coal was also delivered by a horse-drawn cart. Mr Charlton of Charlton Brothers, Coal Merchants, would call at the middle door throughout the winter for his money, after lumbering up the garden path, followed by a couple of his minions, to the coalhouse, each with a hundredweight sack of coal on his back. He would dump his load, the larger pieces of which — and some were a couple of feet in diameter — were smashed up by my father using a sledgehammer, then march silently back to the lorry for the next one. He was an almost Dickensian figure, sporting a nautical-looking black cap, shiny with grease, that was pushed back at a jaunty angle on his head, and a thick black jerkin that looked like leather. On his feet were a pair of huge hobnailed boots, dulled from layers of coal dust, and the bottom of each trouser leg was tied with a piece of filthy string. He was completely black from head to toe, while his face was like an amateur actor's, blacked up to play Othello. The only bits that escaped were two pink crescents, one behind each ear, his pale-grey eyes, made dazzling by their smudgy black surround, and his pure-white hair. This last was only visible when, in a gentlemanly gesture, he would remove his hat to receive payment of his bill. Our coal fires were eventually replaced by gas ones in the mid-sixties and, although they were far more convenient with their instant heat, for me they could never replace the bright, ever-changing energy and cosiness of a real fire, nor the sense of achievement that I still feel today from getting a fire blazing away in the grate.

Next to the middle door was the door to the kitchen. This was the room in which we mainly lived, as a family. My earliest memories are of this room; of clambering out of my pram, down on to a sofa, which the pram was parked next to, and finding Nelly, our black and white cat, in fighting form, buried beneath copies of the *Daily Mirror* and the *Reveille*, the latter probably being the equivalent of the *Daily Star*. One of the few times I saw my mother cry — apart from after the conversation about her stillborn daughter, at the death of her own mother and finally the death of my father — was when Nelly died of cancer. I suppose you'd call it breast cancer, as it first appeared as a swelling in one of her teats. She was at least twenty years old, but no one could be quite sure as she was already adult when she turned up out of nowhere and muscled her way in at number 69, ejecting the then resident and cowardly tomcat in the process. During her twenty-year reign with us she had over a hundred kittens, mostly delivered in the bottom drawer of my mother's dressing table. Mum, cooing like a proud grandmother, fed any weaklings with an eardropper full of warm milk. There were times, when the births were at their most prolific, that the kittens would disappear soon after delivery and it was announced that Nelly had suffocated them by accidentally sitting on them, but I remember furtive conversations in the scullery, and my father coming in from outside with an empty bucket, and my brother Kevin getting it slightly wrong and telling me that Dad had flushed the kittens down the toilet. It was never discussed.

Nelly wasn't an affectionate cat that would snuggle up, purring, on your lap. On the contrary, too much stroking and the claws would be out like a flash and the old yellow teeth would be sunk into a girl's hand before you had time to say 'lethal injection'. When I was a child my hands and arms were permanently striped from Nelly's bad-tempered lashings, but Mum adored her and reserved a special voice with which to address her. It was high pitched and squeaky with delight, framed in a language all of its own and warm with affection that none of us could ever hope to excite.

As an adult I myself developed relationships, mainly with pet dogs, of a similar nature to the one my mother had with Nelly, although in my case they were often to the detriment of whatever relationship I was in at the time. '*No*, not the baby talk, *pleeeeease!*' has been quite a common cry in my various households over the years. One day about eight or nine years back, a visiting friend overheard me talking to our Cairn terrier in my 'special language', which was barely intelligible to an outsider and would just bubble up out of me on a wave of elation, with no thought involved whatsoever. Full of strange Brummyisms and speech impediments, it was performed in what was to my ear the tiny voice of a child. 'Comala Babala Momola, 'er wants a bit of lubbin' is an example. My friend stared at me aghast and then said, 'How does Grant put up with that?'

I said, 'Well, he didn't for a long time but now he's just given in.'

She replied, 'You do know this is your sickness, don't you?'

'What do you mean?'

And she told me that this was the lavishing of the love and affection that I myself missed out on as an infant. There seems to be a grain of truth in this because one of the constant phrases that comes up in these streams of consciousness that the poor dog is subjected to is, 'Love the baby . . . love the baby . . . '

Once, whilst standing in the queue for the checkout at the supermarket, I heard my daughter, who had engaged a complete stranger in conversation, say that her sister 'was a dog', to which the woman replied, 'Oh, you mustn't talk about your sister like that.' Maisie answered, 'No, she is a dog.' I felt slightly ashamed of this and later felt compelled to explain to Maisie that no dog could ever begin to rival her in my affections and that I didn't see her in the same light as the dog at all. She replied, 'No, I know, well, I should think not, I don't go around sniffing strangers' bottoms in the street, do I?'

Strangely, the kitchen was not a kitchen at all. The real kitchen, which was called the scullery, was a tiny room next to it. The 'kitchen' was a smallish room; with the sofa now long gone, it was crowded with three easy chairs, one of which, of course, was Grandma's, their thin foam cushions usually balanced on top of a heap of newspapers that had been stuffed underneath, an attempt at tidying up. There was a large Singer sewing machine on elaborate, wrought-iron legs, upon which our mother made all the curtains as well as a lot of our and her own clothes. In one corner stood a large kitchen cabinet with a flap that dropped down on which we made golden syrup or jam sandwiches when we came in from school, and in the other corner was a big, old-fashioned radio.

This was of great fascination with its list of exotic-sounding locations like Luxembourg, Lisbon, Hilversum, all printed on a little rectangle of glass on its front that lit up when it was switched on. I loved turning the tuning dial and being plunged into some fuzzy foreign world called Hamburg or Bordeaux, to catch scratchy, distant voices speaking in unintelligible tongues that came and went, as if on the wind. It was a link with far-flung places and yet it was safe and cosy with its walnut fascia and its warm, yellow glow. It was a comfort to hear its familiar drone from other parts of the house. It meant that you were not alone, that life was being lived, and the velutinous voices of the BBC Light Programme or the music from the likes of *Whistle While You Work* promised that somehow, somewhere, we were in safe hands. The first sound of the day, as I lay in bed, was invariably the low drone of the shipping forecast vibrating up through the floorboards as my mother got ready for work. On

Sundays our lunch, or dinner as it was called, was eaten to *The Navy Lark, Round the Horne, Beyond Our Ken* and *Hancock's Half Hour.* We took our meals around the Formica-topped table that was stuck snugly into the bay window, but as we grew older we simply collected our plates and took them off to eat elsewhere, watching television or doing homework, leaving my poor mother, who had invariably cooked the food, to eat by herself, as my father always came in much later. She never complained and was probably glad to be left in peace. My sister-in-law tells of how she came round to be introduced to the family for the first time and to have tea with us. She says that once the meal had been served up suddenly there was no one in the room but herself and my mother and, with my mother nipping in and out of the kitchen, she virtually ate alone.

The real kitchen, the scullery, was where as small children we stood in the big, old Belfast sink and washed. Water would have to be boiled up on the gas stove as there wasn't a hot tap. It was where my father shaved. I would stand on a little table next to him so that I could watch at close quarters the very pleasing process of shaving foam and bristles being removed in sharp smooth tracts, revealing the weathered hollow that went from cheekbone to jaw. I can still smell the soap and I cannot deny that to this day a whiff of Old Spice does cause a distant thrill. It was where my mother did her nightly ablutions, shouting high-pitched warnings not to come in as she crouched over a washing-up bowl on the floor, and it was generally where we all washed and brushed our teeth.

The bathroom upstairs was used only once a week when the immersion heater was put on for the briefest possible time, closely monitored by my mother; otherwise it offered no hot water and was a room in which from November through to May you could see your breath. Lying in a hot bath during these months meant lying shrouded in steam so thick and opaque that you could barely make out the taps at the other end. However, once a week, it was an oasis of isolation. Unlike today, when it seems that most children's bedrooms are a haven of warmth and privacy, furnished with both a computer and a television, when I was growing up the bedroom, its hypothermic temperatures aside, was purely for undressing (in winter, pretty quickly), sleeping and dressing again. It never occurred to anyone then that people might 'need their space'. So apart from the lavatory, where there was always the threat of someone banging on the door, wanting to get in, the only other room with a lock was the bathroom. Once ensconced in the warmth of the water, the clouds of white steam softening and for the most part concealing, albeit only briefly, the cold, functional and often messy nature of the room, a girl could be transported for at least half an hour. With its echoey acoustic, a girl could all but fall in love with her own voice and hone to near perfection her impersonations of the likes of Sandie Shaw ('Always Something There to Remind Me'), the Ronettes ('Be My Baby') and the Supremes ('Baby Love'). And then, of course, the water would become tepid and the steam would turn to condensation. I can recall the mild pall of disappointment that would descend as the bleak old bathroom would gradually reveal itself out of the mist. It was lying in this bath, aged eighteen, knowing I was to embark on a nursing course in a matter of weeks, that I felt safe enough, under cover of the hot tap running at full tilt, to say, in a small voice to the palm of my hand, held very close to my mouth, 'I want to be an actress.' Words I had never spoken before. To anyone.

The scullery led in turn on to a sort of outhouse extension, which was called 'the back place'. In the corner there was a drain and there was always a smell of soapsuds in the air from the seemingly endless rounds of washing and washing up. In winter it also smelt of geraniums and coal dust, whilst in the summer the soapy freshness of the drain often turned a tad fetid. It was built on before our time to incorporate the coalhouse and the outside toilet, the latter often being referred to by my brother Kevin, for some unfathomable reason, as the Lah Pom. I preferred the upstairs toilet and rarely used the Lah Pom as it was often home to at least a couple of large house spiders. I was terrified of the creatures. These days, having lived in the country for many years, I am less so, but back then and well into my twenties and thirties I could not bear to even look at a picture of one, let alone be in the same room.

This is amply illustrated by an incident in 1979, when I was working on a play at the

Hampstead Theatre Club and was renting a basement flat from a friend. One evening I went to run a bath only to find a spider the size of a Bentley attempting to climb up the side of it, in order to get out. After letting out an unstoppable scream and trying, without looking at it, to flush it down the plughole from whence it came followed by an unsuccessful attempt to enlist the help of a neighbour, I ended up phoning the director of the play I was doing and asking whether he would be so kind as to come and get rid of it, otherwise I wouldn't be able to sleep that night, never mind take a bath. After coming some way across town, and with much ribbing and hilarity, Mike Leigh humanely disposed of the thing and then went back to finish his tea.

The back place acted as an overflow to my father's garage, and it was here that, on coming in late at night as a teenager, I would reach up and blindly scrabble about on a dusty old shelf — amongst a jumble of plumbing items, heaps of tools, my mother's geranium pots, a selection of old shoes and anything else that people saw fit to sling up there — in order to find the key to the middle door and let myself in. It was also home to a succession of pet rodents that I kept when aged about eleven and where I attempted to breed a couple of my best mice for business purposes. I pinned an advert on to the garage door for passers-by to peruse. It read: FOR SALE, ATTRACTIVE DOMESTICATED BABY MICE, TWO SHILLINGS EACH, OR TWO FOR THREE AND ELEVEN, PLEASE APPLY AT GATE ROUND CORNER. The breeding programme went rather better than I had anticipated and within a couple of weeks there were eight or nine tiny brown mice, no bigger than a thumbnail but able to jump at least three or four inches in the air. Before I could separate them they had bred and bred again. I remember only one small girl and her friend calling at the middle door and enquiring about the mice. However, when they clapped eyes on them they wanted a reduction in price, claiming, 'They'm brown! They ent proper pet mice. Pet mice am white.'

'Yes they are. Pet mice can be any colour.'

'No they cor. I bet ya caught them in your house. I'll tek two for a bob.'

Needless to say there was no sale. I then became increasingly desperate as their numbers grew and soon the advert was changed to: FOR SALE, ATTRACTIVE DOMESTICATED BABY MICE. TWO FOR THE PRICE OF ONE, A SHILLING A THROW. APPLY THROUGH GATE AT SIDE. But no one did and to add insult to injury people kept crossing out bits of my advert to alter the meaning. We had: FOR SALE, ATTRACTIVE DOMESTICATED BABY MICE, A SHILLING TO THROW THROUGH GATE AT SIDE. Another was: FOR SALE, ATTRACTIVE DOMESTICATED BABY, A SHILLING, or we will THROW THROUGH GATE AT SIDE.

Finally I came down one morning to find that the babies, whose multiplication was now way out of control, had eaten an escape route out of the little wooden box in which they were being kept, presumably because of overcrowding, and had disappeared into a very convenient, tangled heap of assorted piping that my father had dumped on the shelf next to them. Despite my not inconsiderable attempts to capture the little creatures — time after time, blocking both ends of a pipe, only to find that there was another pipe leading off it, out of which they had escaped — I managed to catch only two or three. For years whenever we went out into the back place there was the sound of tiny scurrying feet across the stone floor or up over the wooden shelving.

Upstairs, there were three bedrooms. My parents' room was at the front corner of the house and it looked down on to both Bishopton and Long Hyde Road. In the corner stood a large, mahogany wardrobe where our Christmas presents were hidden every year, so a quick recce in about the third week of December would usually give the game away. It was where I came across my beloved red and yellow scooter, upon which for years I went everywhere. Most people eventually graduated to bicycles but I was not allowed one as my mother thought they were 'death traps'. I think if I were young today I would definitely be one of those kids hanging round city centres with the crotch of my jeans dangling at mid-calf, a good three inches of bum cleavage showing at the top, and a skateboard permanently welded to my person.

My parents slept in a creaky old bed with a dark, walnut headboard and it was into this that I would creep every Saturday morning, once my mother had gone out, to cuddle up to my dad and, much to his annoyance, check his back for spots. On several occasions, seeing him get out of bed, I thought I had caught a glimpse through the flies of his pyjamas of something odd hanging around his nether regions. I subsequently asked my mother whether he was 'the same as me down below' because it certainly didn't look like it and this needed clarification. She instantly looked away and, with what seemed like not a little irritation and impatience, but what I now see as total embarrassment, she said, 'Yes, yes, yes, yes, yes, yes, yes . . . Yes.' I thought the yeses were never going to stop and, in my innocence, regarded them as simply an expression of absolute confirmation. You can therefore imagine my surprise when, around the same time as this odd little conversation, I came across my brothers playing about in the bedroom before getting dressed one morning. They were in fits of laughter, having put elastic bands on their willies. In complete confusion, I could only deduce from this that the willy detached itself and fell off at some point before boys grew into men and that perhaps the elastic band had something to do with it. This conundrum took a while to clear up; in fact, I remember fiercely debating and defending this theory with several of my contemporaries, thinking how out of the loop and uninformed they were.

It was under my parents' bed, aged about eight, that I found what looked like a kind of greasy, deflated balloon. I could see from its colour that it wasn't a festive balloon, one that you might hang on a gatepost to indicate the location of a person's birthday party, and that it might possibly have some sort of medical connection. I sat on the floor to examine it further; first stretching it this way and that, then finally blowing it up and holding it up to the light. Inside it was a kind of gloopy liquid. I stared at it and, piece by piece, snippets of overheard remarks and conversations that I had hitherto no understanding of, began to connect. The realisation of what it was that I had only seconds before held to my mouth and tasted sent me rushing downstairs, the thing held away from me at arm's length, rudely deflating and spitting globules of the liquid as it did so. Once out in the garden, I couldn't when it came to it jettison the thing into the wilderness behind the rockery, as had been my intention. Instead I held on to it for a few seconds more and the revulsion that I had felt just moments before melded in with something else, something like a sadness I couldn't quite place.

I could spend a whole afternoon in this room, going through the bottom drawer of my mother's dressing table, leafing through the personal things of her past with frozen fingers. In my memory it was always arctic in there, the big faded rug cold and slightly damp underneath me. It was where I felt I could find her, touch on her history, discover clues to her, like a detective: clues to the girl she once was before we came along and disappointed her, before she became anxious and tired, when she was excited by life, optimistic, when the world was her oyster. It was full of old photographs of her as a young woman: dark and handsome. It is said that a lot of people living along the west coast of Ireland have dark complexions and this is attributed to the fact that the Spanish Armada crashed on the rocks there. My mother, with her dark hair and eyes and olive skin, could easily have passed for Spanish, but when questioned about this she was mildly outraged, claiming that 'The Irish met them with pitchforks!' To which my father replied, 'I think the Irish met them with something else, Mary!'

In these photographs her dark, strong features were set in an unsmiling, no-nonsense face, against an alien, sepia background that looked more like the moon than anywhere on earth. The images were peopled by worn, dusty-looking folk, staring pale eyed at the camera with a self-consciousness that now touches me but then enthralled me and drew me in. There was a shabby leather handbag full of letters and postcards, from close friends and distant relatives long ago, from California and Australia and, of course, Ireland: friendly, chatty, intimate letters to a girl we never knew, who didn't yet know us. I couldn't get enough; I would read the same letters over and over again, and stare at the same photographs, at the same faces, often employing a magnifying glass, as if that would take me closer into them, into their eyes and through into their heads, hoping against hope that I would discover a vital secret. Also in the handbag was a faded, pink crêpe handkerchief that, as I read the letters and pored over the photographs, I would hold to my nose, breathing in the musty traces of a once-sweet perfume.

Up until about six or seven I slept in the room

next door to my parents, the door of which was just down the landing that ran the full length of the house. I shared it with my brothers; they slept in a double bed and I in a single. It was in here that on God knows how many Christmas Eves my brothers called me to the window with great excitement, claiming that Father Christmas was just at that moment crossing the night sky on his sleigh, and each time I believed I'd had the misfortune to have just missed him. It was here, sleepless with anticipation of his arrival, that I lay under the covers pretending to be asleep, like millions of other children, and holding my breath as the door creaked open and in he came. And it was here that, one Christmas, before the discovery in my parents' wardrobe, I saw Him, at least the red tip of his hood, but it was Him.

And it was here during the Christmas of 1955 that I shared my brothers' double bed with my Auntie Agnes who was visiting from London. Auntie Agnes was my mother's younger unmarried sister. In her youth, with her high, wide cheekbones, flawless skin, lustrous hair and pretty mouth, she had been quite beautiful. We were told that she was once pursued by the actor Trevor Howard and was never short of admirers. As a young girl, however, she developed an abscess on her hip that resulted in crippling arthritis and she ended up with one leg being several inches shorter than the other. This plus regular and severe migraines served to completely incapacitate her in late middle age. She would have no truck with men, my mother said of her rather disparagingly, 'Ah, no one was ever good enough,' and she lived alone in a bedsit in Shepherd's Bush. I can't help but link her antipathy towards men to the rather cold, dismissive attitude that my grandfather, Patrick O'Brien, took towards the women of the family. He had time only for the boys, my uncles, Joe and Martin John, doting particularly on the latter. My mother responded to his cold, domineering nature by choosing my father, a gentle man who simply adored her and thought her to be a cut above himself.

She seldom saw her sister, once a year at most, and when she did come to visit us, the visit was usually cut short by some sort of argument between them, resulting in Auntie Agnes flouncing out and, in an act of outrageous extravagance, taking a black cab to New Street station to board the train to London. My mother would no more take a cab to New Street station, let alone get on a train, when the coach was so much cheaper, than boil her own head. In fact the only time a black cab was ever seen in our street to my knowledge was when Auntie Agnes came to stay.

Their relationship was beset by a petty competitiveness. My mother once sent her a silk scarf for Christmas. Needless to say, she had not bought it; it was a gift that had been given to her by a work colleague. My mother rarely kept anything that was given her. All presents were recycled in this way. On receiving it my aunt sent it back immediately with a curt little note saying that she never wore silk next to her skin. During a visit one Christmas to her sister's flat, my mother, noting the paucity of cards that Agnes, 'the poor lonely thing', had received, asked in her best, innocent, little-girl voice, 'Oh, you've got a nice few cards. How many did you get?'

'Oh . . . ' my aunt began, but that was it, my mother came straight back with 'I had eighty-two!'

And so it was here, in this big sagging double bed that couldn't help but conspire to throw its occupants together in the middle, that I have my earliest memory of wetting the bed. It wasn't the first time, for I had never stopped; it was simply the first time I had felt ashamed. Bed-wetting for me was a nightmarish saga that lasted — although in the latter years it was rarer — through to the beginnings of puberty. Every night I begged God to spare me the usual morning humiliation of having to confess to my mother that I'd 'done it again' and met with her angry, exhausted despair. 'Oh Gaaard, she's done it again!' she would repeat to no one in particular. Every night I stretched my pyjama bottoms to bursting point with a raggedy old towel or sometimes an old pyjama jacket of my father's as a makeshift nappy, which more often than not I managed to circumvent, only to wake up in my own wretchedness at the familiar stench of ammonia and the cold, soggy tangle of pyjamas and sheets. How my mother managed, going out to work full time as she did, with three children, Grandma and no washing machine, is simply unimaginable to me. Today the sheets would be whipped into a machine, then into the tumble-dryer and be back on the bed before a person could say 'incontinence pad'. Instead they had to be boiled in a bucket on the gas stove, rinsed, put through the mangle in the back yard and then transferred to the washing line, in all weathers, maybe taking days to dry.

The whole thing made staying at friends' houses out of the question unless my mother had words and this brought its own shame: the whispered conversations in the hallway as we were about to leave; the little laugh that served to cover my mother's own shame; the friend's face as she greedily cottoned on to my deep, dark secret and then no one mentioning it, culminating in my not daring to allow myself to sleep at all and so returning home exhausted. The only time my bed-wetting didn't provoke my mother's wrath was that Christmas when Auntie Agnes came to stay.

At the opposite end of the upstairs landing from my parents' bedroom, past the stairs to the attic and the bathroom, was the back bedroom into which I moved after my grandmother passed away, the scent of her skin hovering long after she had gone. It was an L-shaped room and, with the airing cupboard in the corner and the toilet next door, there was a continual and somewhat comforting sound of dripping, whooshing and ticking of pipes. There was a sash window looking out over the back yard, the garage, and across into Waller's shop on the other side of Wigorn Road, a windier, longer, busier road than either Bishopton or Long Hyde Road, which ran along the back of the house. It was here that I lay in the very dark, wood-framed single bed that my grandmother had died in, listening under the covers to Radio Luxembourg on my father's big blue Bush transistor radio, until late at night when a hand smelling of Boots soap and fags came and retrieved it from down beside my bed.

It was here one awful autumn in 1967 that I lay for a whole month in mourning and disbelief at my being 'packed in' or 'dumped', as they would say today, by my first love, a chap called Bob. Not turning up for work, I endlessly pored over his letters (he had gone away to college), which I kept in an old sewing box under the bed, called my Bob Box. It was a relationship that was never consummated, its physical side consisting of a lot of snogging to the Beach Boys' 'God Only Knows' and well-mannered groping in Bob's front room, either when his parents weren't in or were keeping a discreet distance in the back kitchen.

In fact the only time we could have done the deed was when a group of us from school, who my parents thought were all girls, spent a weekend in a caravan on a windswept site somewhere in mid-Wales, the boys turning up later after our dads had dropped us off. Bob and I spent hours in frenzied snogging on a very narrow bunk once the lights went out but in an act of gallantry he placed the sheet between us, so that should his passion reach uncontrollable heights there would be this crisp, white contraceptive to save the day. However, it wasn't to be the sheet that eventually cooled our ardour. It was the sound of whispering coming from the bunk opposite ours, where one of my friends was sleeping with a boy who was new to the group. The whispering then became more urgent.

'No! No! No!' And then, 'No, please, you're hurting me.' And with every 'No' I remember that Bob squeezed me to him as if I were the one calling out. For what I think was several minutes, while the rest of us held our collective breath, this poor girl's pleas hissed out into the silence, punctuated by pitiful sobs, which eventually died into whimpers and then finally stopped. What was chilling about it was that there was no utterance whatsoever from the young man, just the lonely, frightened sounds of the girl. No one spoke or moved. I know that, were my adult self to be miraculously transported back there, I would have spoken out in the darkness to that girl and put a stop to what was going on. But back then, we weren't sure and, indeed, one of the boys the next day, when his girlfriend had expressed her concern, was reported to have said, 'Oh, she was all right. She must have wanted him to or she wouldn't have got into bed with him.'

Bob and I lasted only the length of the summer holidays but in my memory, like all summer holidays from childhood, the time was idyllically stretched. I have no photographs of Bob, but in my blurry memory he is tall, dark and handsome, with a bit of a Roy Marsden look about him, easily outclassing the normal run of suitor. So I thought myself lucky. There had been two or three before him, but they felt more like practice until the real thing came along. My dates with them involved mainly writhing about, while trying to keep straying hands out of my bra in case they should happen upon the handkerchiefs stuffed therein, as we sat in the back row of the Princess Hall Cinema on Smethwick High Street, on seats scarred with cigarette burns, black and shiny where thousands of bottoms had worn away the once plush-red upholstery. Some of them had large holes gouged out of the front so that when you sat down a great gust of air would be expelled, sending your dress flying up.

It always seemed as if very few of the audience had actually gone to see the film. People would be talking at normal volume, running up and down the aisles, fighting, or throwing things. I was once hit on the head by a flying shoe and another time, bizarrely, I saw half a grapefruit fly through the air and land ever so briefly on a chap's head like a chic little hat. On one occasion someone actually set fire to his seat and we were all evacuated, but generally when the anarchy reached a certain pitch there would be a complaint, prompting the manager to storm down the aisle to the front and scream at the top of his voice, 'All right! That's it! All the one and nines out!' And those in the cheap seats would be shown the door.

But my dates with Bob were on another plane. He had just left school, grammar school to boot; having done A levels, he was going to teacher training college; my brothers didn't sneer and, most importantly, my mother approved. So when he came home for the weekend after being away at college for about a month and told me in his

44

front room — the room in which we had rolled about, copping a frenzied feel in painful and awkward positions on the tiny sofa; the room that I had left on so many occasions with my lips and chin raw from kissing, relishing the soreness of the hot, angry beard rash as I lay in bed at night, dizzy with romance and lust — that he thought it was best that we perhaps finished, it was as if he was suddenly speaking Urdu and, indeed, everything in that familiar room instantly became unfamiliar. He too became unfamiliar; gone was the warm, crinkly-eyed, only-between-us look and here was the awkward staring-down-at-shoes-and-carpet look and body language that said, 'Don't make yourself comfortable, you won't be staying long.' He walked me to the bus stop. I don't know what was said and I probably couldn't have told you then either, overwhelmed by the terrible need to get away and cry.

As I sat on top of the bus as it bumped and swayed its way along the Bearwood Road, the tears began and they never really let up for about a month. My parents never once challenged my red-eyed silence or my staying off work for four weeks, dragging myself around the house, my eyelids swollen and puffy, and I had no inclination to discuss it with either of them, thinking that neither would understand or realise the magnitude of my feelings. I was bewildered: under any other circumstances my mother would have harangued me for taking to my bed and not going to work, and at the time though I didn't understand it I was grateful for her silence.

I questioned her about it much later in my

thirties, wondering whether she remembered and what on earth she had made of the whole thing.

She said, 'Oh yes, we knew what had happened. We guessed that you had a broken heart, but we didn't like to say anything. We thought it best.'

I'm not sure why I was immensely touched by the fact that they had known all along. I know that their silence was born out of an inability to deal with 'feelings', as it wasn't the done thing to talk things out then, but it was also born out of recognition, sympathy and, of course, wisdom.

The main advantage of the back bedroom was that just below the sash window there was the roof of the back place. This could be seen very clearly from both Wigorn and Long Hyde Roads, and as the Boyle family were not only devoid of motorised transport but also lacking such a roof, it was another useful source of agony to be heaped upon the unfortunate Dermot when so needed, simply by doing a bit of sunbathing. However, this was not easy nor, may I say, comfortable as not only did the roof slope at quite an angle but it was also corrugated. There once existed a photograph, long since lost, of me lying flat on my back on this roof, my eyes tightly closed, my mouth clamped shut, lips pressed together in a thin line, arms and legs straight and rigid, a picture of endurance; instead of lapping up the sun, I looked as if I was braced for a cold shower. But I'm sure that if we were able to widen the shot out to the left and down a bit, we would come upon Dermot sitting in the gutter of Long Hyde Road, eating his mother's cake and trying not to look. The roof joined on to the garden wall, which was about six feet high and separated us from number 68. This meant that it was possible to get out of the back bedroom window, down over the roof, on to the wall, down on to the dustbin placed conveniently beneath, and out into the world. It was also possible to do the thing in reverse if, as sometimes happened, the key to the middle door hadn't been left out amongst the jumble of junk on the shelf in the back place.

At around sixteen or seventeen, I started going to clubs with Chris, my best friend from school. She was strikingly beautiful, with a mane of dark-brown hair and blue eyes fringed by almost doll-like thick lashes, causing male heads to whip round to look wherever we went. My mother knew nothing of our Saturday-night forays into town and thought that I was just spending the evening round at Chris's house, watching television or listening to records. We would head to Birmingham, dressed and made up to pull, or at least impress, the thought of pulling a stranger in a nightclub being a little too scary for either of us. Once on the number 9 bus, we would go straight upstairs and, if it was free, on to the back seat. Then a small, silent ritual would follow whereby Christine would open her handbag and take out a bottle of Estée Lauder's Youth Dew. She would first spray both of our necks just below each ear and then, employing a huge circular movement, she would totally enshroud us in a cloud of the stuff. Next out of the bag came a little pack of Beechnut spearmint chewing gum, out of which two tablets would be dropped into our waiting palms and tossed with practised ease through the air on to our similarly waiting tongues. Then to finish off and complete the 'style queens of the number 9 bus route' image, out would come the Peter Stuyvesant's or Consulate menthol cigarettes. We were good at the silences and expert at communicating solely by gesture or look. This was mainly down to the fact that Chris had a not insubstantial stutter. Conversations would go like this:

'J — J — J — Julie . . . have you s — s — s — s-s-seen m — m — my b — b — b — b — '

'Biro?'

'N — n — n — no, m-my b — b — b — '

'Brush?'

'N — n — n — no! M — m — m — my b — b — b — '

'Bum?'

'N — n-no. Errr, . . . s-s-s-stop i — t! M — m — my b — b — '

'Bag?'

'Yes.'

'No.'

And so it went on, with me finishing off by guesswork whatever sentence she had started. On the day of her wedding, not many years later, she went through the whole ceremony without a single stutter.

We both purported to be Mods, which meant that we wore leather jackets over twinsets and pearls, below-the-knee pencil skirts and clumpy shoes, usually brown suede Hush Puppies, which would nowadays be worn by sensible old ladies with bad feet. On our nights out in town, however, we donned more slinky evening attire and Chris would often do our hair. One of the hair fashions of the day was a soft set of bubbly, bouncing curls and on a Saturday night Chris made a valiant effort at achieving this look for the two of us with the help of a set of rollers and a couple of litres of cheap hair lacquer. This sticky, sickly-smelling liquid set the curls into rigid little pompoms all over the head, so that not only was the soft and bouncing quality of the style never quite brought off but the whole thing was also rendered highly inflammable. There were terrible tales of girls bending their heads to light a cigarette and their whole hair catching alight instead of the cigarette, burning it down to the scalp and reducing it to a frizzled, stubbly mass.

There was an occasion once, after I'd started work, when I went out to one of Chris's dos on a Sunday night. As a result there wasn't time on the Monday morning before I went to work to comb out the stiff curls with their solid lacquered finish. After I had slept on it for several hours, my hair had taken on a very odd shape, completely flat on one side, whilst wildly frizzing out in all directions on the other. At the end of about twenty minutes in the toilets I felt, after much tweaking and despite its having a certain Brillo Pad quality, that my hair was in an acceptable state, so I slipped into the office at the insurance company where I worked — my first proper job on leaving school — and sat at my desk. Within minutes the boss was at my elbow,

49

hissing in my ear: 'You're late! And take that silly wig off your head!'

On these nights out we frequented several different clubs: the Rum Runner, La Dolce Vita, Club Cedar, the Metro, but we would most often end up at the Locarno, a large club in the centre of Birmingham. In my memory at any rate, it was enormous and was divided, I think, into several bars and a couple of dance floors, each playing a different kind of music and so each appealing to a different age group, one of them for what we thought of as middle-aged people but who were most likely folk in their early twenties. Here the music was live and the band, usually something like a five piece, tended to play rock and roll, Elvis Presley, Frank Ifield, Tom Jones, the Beatles. No matter what, it always seemed to finish off at the end of the night with couples, some the worse for wear, draped over each other, in various stages of pre-coital foreplay, moving slowly round the room to 'I Remember you' by Frank Ifield and, later, 'Hey Jude'. These were played solo by a bespectacled chap, sitting on a low stool, with a huge red-and-white electric guitar. At some point midway through the evening we would usually look in on our way to the toilets but mainly with the intention of mocking the 'aged' dancers.

On one of these occasions I was asked to dance by one of them, a tall, gaunt-looking Irishman with an engaging smile. After a few minutes jigging around he started to have a coughing fit and during the course of it something flew down the front of my dress. Whatever it was had gone down with complete ease of passage and had disappeared. Then I remembered the cigarette in his hand and, seeing that it was no longer there, began to jump up and down, frantically shaking the front of my dress. By this time the man was on the floor, flailing about amongst the feet of the nearby dancers. I shouted down to him not to bother about his fag, that my friend had some, but he was having none of it, eventually getting up and rudely lurching out of the room without a word. I thought no more of it. Later that night on the bus home, I reached down to adjust the handkerchief padding of my ill-fitting bra and entangled in it was a pair of false teeth on a little pink plate. The poor bloke must have gone home, his engaging smile disfigured by a big black gap in the front of his mouth, and talking with a lisp to boot.

The other room at the Locarno was presided over by a DJ and was dark and crowded. In here they played mainly Tamla Motown, the Four Tops, the Isley Brothers and the Supremes, which was our kind of music. 'This Old Heart of Mine' by the Isley Brothers along with 'The Harlem Shuffle' by Bob & Earl never fail to summon up the Locarno for me. We would throw our bags down between us and, fag in hand, coolly shift from foot to foot, our shoulders lifting and dropping to the beat in a kind of lazy shrug.

Christine was a good few inches taller than my five foot three and a half, and could easily peruse the periphery of the dance floor over the top of my head, where groups of young men lurked and perused us back. I would watch her face and await the signal that meant we were being approached by two eligible contenders; this would be an excited widening of the eyes and the hint of a smile with the tip of her tongue literally in her cheek. If, on the other hand, we were being approached by two chaps that she considered inferior in some way, she would throw me a look of horror that befitted the heroine in a silent movie, then drop her head and look to one side.

She was very conscious of her height and of the height difference between us. If, for instance, we were walking along a pavement that sloped to one side, she would drag me across to the higher side, in order to lessen the gap. However, it was guaranteed that if two blokes came over, one tall and the other short, it would be the short one that made a beeline for Chris, as if her height was a challenge, something to be scaled, like Mount Everest is to a climber. She would generally ignore them by staring imperiously into the middle distance above their heads.

On one occasion, however, a particularly small man suddenly appeared from nowhere, right in front of her, and started to cavort about in a horribly frenzied fashion. It appeared to be some sort of awful homage to Mick Jagger, with much leaping up on to the toes of one foot, bringing the other knee up and clapping his hands above his head in a completely abandoned way, and all done side on to Christine, like a matador with a bull. It was as if he were trying to show how physically liberated and virile he was, yet at the same time proving the exact opposite. 'I am anally retentive, probably an accountant and don't get out much,' was writ large in neon above his head (no offence to accountants, especially mine). This, of course, we found irritatingly uncool and embarrassing, and Christine, who could blush for Britain, went purple. Then finally, having had enough, she stopped dead and stood there, staring down at him, arms folded across her chest; but to heap insult upon insult, the man didn't notice, too wrapped up in his hip-thrusting, bottom-shaking, toe-curling dance. Finally he threw his hands up into the air above his head in order to clap them together. Christine caught hold of them with one hand and shouted directly down into his face, 'Can't you see I'm taller than you!' And, in unison, we turned and left the floor, cackling cruelly as we went.

On these nights we would most likely get home somewhere between midnight and one o'clock. My parents, having gone to bed at about ten-thirty, assumed, because it is what they were told, that we had got in not long after that and that, after a night spent listening to records at Chris's, she had walked me home and stayed the night. On many occasions when they had forgotten to leave the key out I scaled that wall up on to the roof and in through the bedroom window in evening clothes and high heels, having downed several rum and blacks. My mother never questioned why I had got so dressed up, just to stay in. I still don't know whether she thought it was innocently done for the sheer pleasure of dressing up, as little girls do, or whether she secretly guessed but didn't want to know. I suspect an exhausted mixture of the two.

Across the yard from the back place was a double garage, built by my father, that opened by way of a set of yellow sliding doors on to Wigorn Road. It housed my dad's car and that of Reg Wood, his sometime partner who lived up the road. There was a poignant little echo when, twenty years later, I teamed up with Victoria for the Granada television series, *Wood and Walters*. As well as the cars, the garage was home to the guinea pig, which after much thought and debate was imaginatively named Guinea.

Guinea lived in an open cage; that is, with no front on it. This meant he was free to wander wherever he pleased. He pottered around the garden and grazed on the lawn during the day, going back into the garage at night, usually when my dad came home from work. Indeed, my dad missed him after he died because Guinea always ran out and watched as my father drove his car in, returning to his cage when the parking was complete. My father said that had Guinea lived much longer, he would have started shouting, 'That's it! Left hand down a bit! You've gorrit!' For six years he led an uneventful, peaceful life until we introduced him to a female guinea pig called Janet. He went berserk, making a hitherto unheard-of noise, chasing and trying to mount this poor creature in a very agitated fashion.

After only a few hours during which I left them, thinking that things would calm down in due course, I went in to check on them, only to find Guinea stone dead and Janet lying exhausted and spent in the corner. (My father said there was a lesson in that for all of us, so that when he died in 1971 of a heart attack whilst in bed, purportedly chatting to my mother, I did wonder whether he had quite taken that lesson on board.) However, it was a good long life — the guinea pig's, that is, not my father's — and goodness alone knows how long it would have gone on for, had it not been cut short by Guinea's frenzied lust for Janet.

Many years later my daughter had a couple of guinea pigs of her own, a large grey male called Robin, named after the decorator, and a tiny chestnut one called Rosette. Remembering my own experience of Guinea's right-to-roam lifestyle, I suggested that Robin and Rosette should also roam free and graze to their hearts' content, on the little lawn at the back of our house. It seemed to make sense, as Robin wasn't a sex pest as Guinea had been. They got on fine for at least half an hour, whereupon Maisie came screaming into the house, 'They're dead! They're dead!' I ran out into the garden, expecting them both to be prostrate from shagging, only to find that Plato, our big, gentle, black-and-white tomcat, had savagely attacked them, having Rosette for first course and Robin, which he couldn't quite manage all of, for second. Of course I was wholly responsible for this and suffered many years of 'You saids' from Maisie, but I honestly thought all would be well. It remains a mystery to this day how Guinea survived all those years unmolested when he was surrounded by a neighbourhood full of cats, not to mention our own formidable Nelly.

The garage was also the venue for my first theatrical triumphs. These were shows, for want of a better word, put on by my brother Tommy with me very much in a supporting role. We bullied local children into getting threepence and some sweets from their mothers, then proceeded to lock them in while we terrorised them with our made-up dramas, mainly inspired by some television play or other and involving a lot of my mother's old lipstick and a couple of her cast-off dresses.

It all came to a stop during one of my brother's magic acts. He would stand there, in a magician's cape and hat that he had been given for Christmas that year, and tell the audience that he was going to make me disappear by putting me in the special cabinet. This he had made himself out of bits of old wood that were stored in the corner of the garage. We had rehearsed and rehearsed, and all that I was required to do was to step into this cabinet. Whilst waving his wand about, Tommy would declaim in a high, moany sort of voice some mysterious incantation, which generally involved the words hocus pocus and abracadabra. Then touching the top and sides of the cupboard with the tip of his magic wand, he would close the door. After this there would be more incantation and magic-speak, rising in speed and volume to increase the dramatic tension. Meanwhile inside the cabinet I was simply meant to slip behind a bit of old red blanket that was hanging down at the back, so that when my brother at last opened the door I would have 'disappeared'. The blanket was supposedly there as decoration, but of course its real function was to conceal a secret chamber or, in lay person's language, a gap between it and the back wall of the cupboard.

However, one summer holiday after a long and successful run of the magic show, the act did not go to plan. We had gone through the usual procedure of my brother talking up the sensational nature of the act, then introducing me as his assistant, whereupon I would leap out and parade about with much waving of arms, dramatically indicating the various facets of the 'amazing magic box' and, at the same time, hopping from foot to foot and pointing my toes. Of course I wasn't allowed to speak and was given a good whack once when I had offered — for just a few extra pence or, if people were short, sweets would do — to tell them where I had actually gone during the period of my magical disappearance. On this particular day, I dutifully got into the cabinet as usual. Whether my brother was rushing matters too much and I simply didn't have time, or whether I was feeling mutinous, as the whacking incident had rankled, I don't know, but I suspect I was simply bored and the thought of pricking the bubble of my brother's theatrical pomposity as he preened and strutted about the 'stage' was terrifying, exciting and, above all, funny.

The door was duly whisked open with a grand flourish, Tommy announcing with great assurance that, as everyone could see, I had vanished. He didn't notice for what seemed like an age that I was still standing there, rigid, in the same stiff pose as I had held when he had closed the door. It was only when the children began to titter and point that he cottoned on. He wheeled round on the spot and I can still see his face to this day: the shock in his little brown eyes, somehow made more vivid by the bright-red hieroglyphics painted on his cheeks and forehead with my mother's lipstick. I can still feel that sublime surge of power as I watched him. Then the look of shock changed briefly to one of hurt, followed, in a second, by a flash of anger as almost in slow motion he came towards me. I jumped out of the box and ran, cutting a swathe through the audience, children falling off boxes this way and that, out across the yard and into the back place, where I locked myself in the dreaded, spider-ridden Lah Pom.

After the children had been dismissed, my brother came to find me and having been given several assurances that he would not hit me I opened the door. He was still wearing the red lipstick but the hieroglyphics had smudged into a vague, greasy redness, which, whether he was or not, made him look very angry indeed. He said, 'It's all right.' And I could see that he wasn't in fact angry at all. 'Why did you do it?' His expression was one of bafflement. I had betrayed him and I guess it could be said that this was an early lesson in stage trust, but there was something else and I think it was a little touch of respect. I had rebelled and he had caught a glimpse of the future actor in me, creating the drama and grabbing the limelight.

A year or so after our flurry of garage performances a man knocked on the middle door with a script in his hand. He was from our parish church, St Gregory's, and having told my mother that they were doing a play at the church hall, he asked whether I would like a part in it. He gave me the script, retired with my mother to the sitting room, and I scurried off upstairs to the bedroom, like a dog with a bone, to read it. I have little memory of it, except that my character had quite a few lines in the form of a single speech and the play was vaguely religious in that it was a bible story of some sort. My mother made this man a cup of tea, and by the time he had drunk it, I was downstairs again, performing my part, the script held behind my back, the speech having gone effortlessly in, purely from the thrill of acting it alone upstairs and the thought of acting it on a stage in front of an audience. When I did come to perform it, it was my brother Tommy who rushed backstage to congratulate me and to tell me, with wonder in his voice, that not only was I really good but that I was the best! It is something he has done ever since.

In between the garage and the back place was the yard, with a high wall that separated us from next door at one side and a little strip of garden running down the other. It was crossed at wonky angles by a couple of washing lines and until about 1960, when we acquired a washing machine, up against the garage was the mangle. There were many gory tales regarding mangles, mostly, I suspect, coming from my mother's imagination, in order to keep us away from it, stories of squashed fingers and, in one blood-soaked saga, the painful loss of an entire digit. This had to be tested out and obviously the use of my own finger in such an experiment was out of the question. So with the help of a wodge of plasticine, I constructed the nearest thing to my own forefinger as was possible and put it through the mangle. The sight of it coming through the other side completely flat made my stomach give a little lurch. I hadn't allowed for the fact that there are bones in a finger, of course, but the totally flattened strip of plasticine furnished my imagination for many years to come with a graphic image of my bloody, mutilated and, naturally, flat forefinger, which actually made the said finger throb.

3

'Don't Go Out Too Far' — Holidays

It was in the back yard that I got my first suntan during a heatwave in 1966 when I was preparing for my GCEs. I sat out on a kitchen chair, head back, eyes closed, revising for my geography exam, the only subject that I ever really revised for. When after a couple of hours I went back into the house, I found, on looking in the mirror, that my face had turned a bright, not unattractive, brownish pink. And there began an addiction, which I still have, albeit in a less desperate form, today. It made everything look better. My hair, which was still vaguely blonde, looked blonder; my eyes looked browner, and my skin looked even in tone, brighter and healthier, with a tight, warm glow, but above all I looked as if I had been somewhere exciting and exotic. It was in the sixties that people started to take holidays to Spain and so gradually suntans, which were very rare after a holiday in an English seaside resort, began to be something of a status symbol. In our own street, the first people to go abroad on a regular basis were a family at the bottom end of Long Hyde Road. They were an attractive lot, in a flashy, television-advert sort of way, living in a largish corner house with a big, yellow Ford Consul parked outside, a pretty blonde mother and daughter and a darkly handsome father and son. But what set them aside from the rest of us was that at least once a year they would go off somewhere, looking similar to everyone else, and return a couple of weeks later as another species: bronzed, relaxed, transformed into world travellers.

The Walters, however, took their yearly week away within the confines of the United Kingdom and came home looking much the same as when they left. We holidayed in Wales and, like a lot of Birmingham folk, we went to Tenby and Saundersfoot, camping with a couple of other families. We had caravan holidays in Weymouth, Margate and Weston-super-Mare, and even now the smell of Calor gas takes me right back there, snuggling down under the covers on a narrow bunk bed, in the cosy, farting, giggling intimacy of a night spent in such close proximity to the whole family.

My earliest holiday memory, when I must have been about eighteen months old, was in the west of Ireland, visiting friends and relatives on my mother's side of the family. We stayed at a farm where there was no electricity and my memory is of my mum getting me up to wee, hovering over a big jam jar in the middle of the night, by candle light, and it not being a great success, but the holiday location I most remember was Blackpool. We would save up for weeks, collecting coppers in an old biscuit tin, and then all five of us would pack into our Ford Esquire car, the roof-rack piled high with a motley collection of suitcases, wrapped in an old piece of tarpaulin and tied on with rope. We would head off on a journey that probably took about six hours as there were no motorways. I always had to sit in the middle, my two brothers on either side, and Kevin, who was generally on my right, was invariably carsick.

There were a couple of mysterious remedies employed to stave this off. One was a small chain that was suspended from just underneath the rear bumper, on the right-hand side, and the other one was Kevin having to wear a brown-paper vest. As neither worked, the smell of vomit, petrol fumes and cigarette smoke was the perennial olfactory accompaniment to these journeys, my brother insisting on the last — the cigarette smoke, that is — claiming that it would prevent the first. So my father, having been given the excuse to smoke continually, did so. We spent the whole journey in an eye-watering fug, my brother with his head stuck in a carrier bag, retching and belching, and the rest of us playing I Spy through the smoke, and eating the cheese-and-tomato or ham-hock-and-salad sand-wiches that my mother had made before we set out, handing them out to my father as he drove and over her shoulder to us in the back. The game of I Spy would stop on the approach to Blackpool, if it hadn't been stopped already by a fight or boredom, and would be replaced by 'The first one to see the tower!' and then, 'The first one to see the sea!'

We holidayed in Blackpool three times during the latter part of the fifties and we always stayed at the same place: number 26 Empress Drive, a bed and breakfast that was run by a Mrs McGinn. Empress Drive was a quiet, residential street, each side of which was lined with neat, terraced, Edwardian houses, mainly with bright-white fronts, well-kept privet hedges and gleaming windows, and where nearly every other house was a B and B. Inside, number 26 smelt of fresh paint, clean carpets and lavender furniture polish. Every object, nook and cranny was dust-free and polished to a military shine. On one occasion, having returned in the evening with fish and chips for our dinner, we were told, 'Don't bring chips in th'ouse, they'll make th'ouse smell.' Once inside, we were encouraged by my mother to speak in little more than a whisper. Breakfast was a self-conscious, almost silent ritual, where the crunch of toast was deafening, the only other sound being the restrained scrape of knives on plates, the careful clink of cups on saucers and the occasional swallowed murmur of voices. It was as if we were guarding some terrible secret, the secret being, I suppose, us.

After breakfast we would gather our things for the day, because we were not allowed back in until the evening. If the weather was fine — that is, if it was not actually raining — we would walk down to the North Shore and my parents would ensconce themselves in a couple of deckchairs, both of them, whatever the weather, fully dressed, my father on occasion wearing a suit, albeit with sandals and socks. I would strip down to my stretchy, ruched bathing costume, having underdressed back at the B and B, in order not to have to go through the embarrassing palaver of trying to change on the beach and not show your nether regions to hundreds of other people. It was bad enough at the end of the day, wobbling about on one foot as you tried to remove a sodden swimming costume, then pulling your knickers on, dragging them up over damp, sand-coated skin, made sore from the salt, and all this whilst attempting to keep an inadequate towel wrapped around your vitals.

I would run off to the sea, dodging in and out of deckchairs, with my mother's cries of 'Don't go out too far!' hanging in the air after me. A few years previously, before I was born, my brother Kevin, who would have been two at the time, had nearly drowned in a deep pothole at Saundersfoot, but was saved by a family friend, himself only a boy at the time. He had held on to Kevin after seeing him in trouble, until my father reached them after running flat out without a thought for himself across jagged rocks and stones, cutting and scraping his feet and shins as he went. Then, with terrible irony, when he was a young man my brother's saviour was himself drowned, after being swept away by a freak wave whilst on holiday. So my parents were ever vigilant when any of us were in the sea, my mother sitting awkwardly, with her neck craned, a squinting, hawkish look on her face, and my father sitting up straight and shielding his eyes, watching continuously until we came out. Then Dad would half get up and wave frantically so that we could spot them amongst the heaving throng.

The Blackpool sea was always grey, even on the odd occasion when the sky was blue, and during our last holiday there I found little brown particles floating in it. Luckily it was on the way home that I brought this up and my brother, his head as ever in his carrier bag, informed me in a muffled voice that the said particles were in fact shit. I don't think I've ever swum in the sea without first checking it for excrement since.

In the event of inclement weather we would walk down the Golden Mile. In a small bag slung across my shoulder would be my spending money, saved from pocket money, and gifts at Christmas and birthdays from aunts, uncles and friends of my parents. The Golden Mile was an exciting string of shops selling tacky tourist trash: 'Kiss Me Quick' hats, sticks of rock, plastic miniatures of the tower, all sorts of incongruous items made out of sugar, such as bright-pink, giant baby's dummies, false teeth, or women's breasts. I remember on one occasion, whilst we were taking our late-afternoon stroll along the prom, seeing an elderly woman sucking, I presume innocently but nevertheless with great enthusiasm, on a pink phallus, wrapped in a bit of cellophane. I had never seen anything like it, but instantly knew from my giggling parents' reaction that it was somehow lewd. There were shops selling every piece of crockery imaginable with 'Blackpool' plastered all over it. It was thrilling to my seven-, eight-, or nine-year-old self and I believe that at one time or another I bought all of the above, excluding, that is, the body parts.

The very best, though, was the funfair, the terrifying, wonderful, sick-making funfair. We visited this only once during the whole holiday because it was deemed too expensive. My abiding memory is of the Mad Mouse, a small bullet-shaped carriage built to hold two people sitting one in front of the other. The track along which it went was high up over the water. It started, as most of these rides do, going teasingly slowly up a steep incline until it reached the top and the first corner, around which it would abruptly swerve at breakneck speed, making the passenger feel that the little car simply won't make it and that the whole thing is going to career off the edge and plummet into the water below. It was heaven! After going on it the first time, I was so gloriously terrified that when the ride finally came to a stand-still my right arm was paralysed. I had to go on it again, several times, to get the feeling back.

I went back to Blackpool in 1995 when I was filming a BBC Television film called *Wide-Eyed and Legless*. I was thrilled to find that I would be staying at the Imperial Hotel on the front, because when I was a child whenever we drove past it my mother would suck in a deep breath, her accent becoming what she imagined to be refined, and with a wistful little laugh she would say, 'Oh, the Imperial.'

And my father would chime in, imbuing his voice with a deep respectful resonance, 'Oo ah, I'd love to see inside that.'

As I stood at reception, checking in, I felt a lump gather in my throat and at the earliest opportunity, when I found that I had a morning off, I went in search of Empress Drive. As always happens when you revisit a place you frequented as a child, everything was smaller. The street was narrower and shorter, and the houses cowered back from the road, lower and less substantial, the proud glow of immaculate seaside white now a little chipped and bashed, a little grimier, poorer, less cared for. I walked back to the hotel feeling as if the sight of that road was an assault on my little, perfect bubble of memory; but the memory is robust and the Empress Drive of the 1950s is still preserved within it, in all its bright, optimistic glory.

4

'A Fine Figure of a Man' — Dad

I notice as I write down the memories of my life that I tend to constantly refer to my mother and far less to my father. This is because my mum was the emotional driving force and centre of the family, whereas my dad tended to hover, unsure, on the edge of our life.

Thomas Walters was born in 1909. The family lived in Ickneild Port Road in the Ladywood area, a poor inner-city suburb of Birmingham that was widely regarded as a slum. He was the second youngest of five children, comprising three older sisters, Rachel, Amy and Betty, and a younger brother, Reg. His father was killed in the First World War, during the battle of the Somme in 1916. He often told us how he was sent to the headmaster's office and how, aged seven years, he stood there in the presence of this terrifying and often cruel man, holding the hand of his five-year-old brother, to be told, bluntly and without an ounce of compassion, 'You'd better get off home to your mother, your dad's been killed.'

I think it is significant that he himself didn't have a father for much of his growing up, for he seemed ill at ease with some of the requisites of fatherhood. Dealing with my brothers, who were lively, combative, intelligent boys, he seemed to shrink back and it was my mother who was always at the forefront when it came to family discussion, or discipline and its consequences. If a fight or argument were to take place, he would disappear. There was one incident between my brother Kevin and myself, when he was about eighteen and I was thirteen, where I hurled an ashtray at him. I missed Kevin and hit my father on the knuckle. Dad, instead of intervening, simply said, 'Oh, I'm getting out of here.' And he left the room. He seemed to have little connection with his sons and, although he was proud, I believe he felt reduced to some extent by their academic achievements. However, it was his sense of humour that was the basis of his survival. When my brother Tommy won a scholarship to Cambridge to study for a PhD, and announced it to my parents, my father was sitting reading the *Smethwick Telephone*, our local rag, and without looking up he said, 'I can't see any adverts for philosophers in the Situations Vacant.'

He was a slightly built, wiry man with thick, dark curly hair, swept back and tamed by a daily dose of brilliantine. Both of my parents being small, dark eyed and dark haired, they were often, so my mother said, mistaken for brother and sister. Dad always, especially towards the end of his life, looked older than his years, his face hollow-cheeked, weathered and deeply riven with lines. Even when he was smiling, there was a permanent expression of worry etched deep into his face; across his forehead and between his brows were lines of anxiety and bewilderment.

I was his favourite and was in no doubt whatsoever of his love for me. My love for him, however, felt more like pain; it hurt and was suffused with pity. As a child, I fretted about him and for him. I feared somewhere that he wasn't up to the task of life. This, I think, was in part because of his physical appearance. His smoking habit, having started in childhood, kept him very thin. When questioned by us as to why he never went into the sea whilst on holiday, he said, 'Last time I went swimming, everyone thought it was a pair of braces floating in the water.' In the later years of his life I would say that he was emaciated; his pulse didn't need to be felt, it could be taken simply by looking at his outstretched arm and counting the twitches in the radial artery that ran the length of it.

But it was also due in part to the way my mother related to him. She constantly referred to him as 'your poor father' while commenting favourably about other, bigger men: 'Oh, he's a fine figure of a man.' She spoke in reverential terms about men in professional positions, with the usual little gasp that would precede statements like 'He's a bank manager!' or 'He's a doctor!' Her breathy, wavery voice, lowered in register, indicated on these occasions the deep respect she felt for such a man in such a position. I don't think these things were said with any malice towards my father. I think they were born more out of insensitivity, together with frustration about her own position in life and her own lack of self-esteem; but they fuelled the fear and pity that I felt for him and my brothers took much pleasure in whipping up these feelings with merciless teasing.

One incident has stayed with me. I was about five and there had been a snowstorm with high winds that had brought our garden fence crashing down. I watched, helpless and sobbing, at the kitchen window as it began to grow dark and my dad struggled alone, in the driving snow, with the six-foot-high fence as the wind lifted it and tossed it this way and that, its force sending him staggering under the weight of the big wooden panels. He looked small, David against the Goliath of the elements, and there was no one to help, all three of us having been told that it was dangerous and to stay indoors. I felt wretched watching this pitiful little scene, while my brothers, amused by and seizing on my misery, cranked it up several notches: 'Oh poor Dad, look, he can't lift the fence. Ahhh, poor Dad.' I was conscious of the fact that he was a lot older than other people's dads, forty-one when I was born, and this was a source of embarrassment; I felt guilty that I didn't want friends to see him drop me off in the car anywhere and that I changed the subject when the age of people's parents was being discussed.

He met my mum whilst drinking in the Leebridge Tavern on Dudley Road in the Ladywood area of Birmingham, where she was working as a barmaid, the job she landed when she first came to England. He set her on a pedestal instantly and proceeded to adore her, I suspect feeling that he had been lucky to catch this attractive, intelligent, driven woman who was a cut above those around him. No one could make my mother laugh as my father could. There was many a time that I would walk into the kitchen and find her doubled up, face bright red, unable to get her breath, to the point where I thought she might even be sick, because of some story or some joke that Dad had relayed to her. He would be laughing too but his laughter was more to do with the pleasure of watching hers. They courted for six months and then married in 1941. My father was never called up into the army, he said because, after his initial interview, they moved house to number 69 and they never contacted him again. Instead he worked at Lucas Electrics, making munitions.

His great pleasure in life was a pint with his cronies at the Dog Inn on the Hagley Road or the King's Head, also on the Hagley Road, about three-quarters of a mile further down towards town. Which one he chose to go to depended on whom he was meeting. The Dog Inn was a place for a quiet drink with other regulars and friends, whereas the King's Head was where Dad went to 'see a man about a dog', which presumably meant he was meeting a business associate. My mother continually complained about this, 'Oh, your father's down the pub again,' and related to us in front of him how she had seen people ruin their lives by drinking their money away in the Leebridge Tavern, while claiming that her own father 'never went into a shebeen in his life'. Eventually Dad developed some kind of intolerance to beer, resulting in urgent trips to the lavatory after consuming just half a pint, but after barium meals, enemas and every other medical test under the sun, nothing was found to be wrong with him.

His other love was horse racing. Before the First World War his father had been an illegal bookmaker. Some years there would be what he laughingly called a works outing to Ascot, where he and a couple of workmates would go to the racecourse for the day. He studied form and was often to be found in front of the television, in a smoke-filled sitting room, fag in mouth, with a couple of blue form books open on his lap, watching the racing on a weekday afternoon when my mother thought he was at work. He had several large wins, which paid for cars and holidays and suchlike, but I think there was never much money in his account; in fact when he died it was pretty much in the red.

When the war was over he started his decorating business. Although he was wholly uneducated, leaving school at fourteen, he had an eye for colour and form, and a strong visual sense. This could be seen in the way he dressed, as he was dapper and knew how to put clothes together, and in the few oil paintings he did, two of which were hung in a local art gallery, in an exhibition of local people's work. He started late in life, in his fifties, and generally liked to paint portraits, having less success with still lifes, his only attempt, I remember, being a rather stiff, lifeless painting of a vase of daffodils. His paintings of people, on the other hand, had an

74

energy and an honesty. He did a telling self-portrait; a portrait of me at about twenty-one, which I found embarrassing at the time, because it touched on my adolescent awkwardness; and a beautiful, oddly touching painting of three children, a black girl, an Indian girl and little ginger-haired girl, eyes fixed on the painter as if they were staring down the lens of a camera.

In his decorating business he employed one man full time. This was Leonard. My father was fond of Leonard, but he was often the victim of Dad's sense of humour, once being asked whether he would drop in at the ironmonger's on the way to work to pick up a box of bubbles for the spirit level. This he dutifully did, still not getting the joke when he arrived for work and reported that they had run out. He was a small, sickly, rather slow individual, with a tiny ball of cotton wool always shoved into each ear, his eyes forever watering, and his nose runny and red. He was constantly afflicted with ear, nose and throat infections and never had enough money to support his ever-increasing family. My father used to say that, every time he went down to see what was 'up' with Leonard after yet another period off work, he could swear there was another 'nipper' that he hadn't seen before. My dad had several talks with him about perhaps cutting back on the procreation, pointing out that the number of children they had produced — I think six at this particular point — did have a bearing on the amount of debt they had accumulated. One time Dad said that Leonard had tried to conceal the latest addition to the family behind the door and that he, Dad, had nearly crushed the child on entering the living room.

My father's work life seemed to take a huge toll on him and he appeared battered by it. His hands, always cut and misshapen with bruises, were yet another catalyst for my pity. As a child I would hold them, moved and pained by their appearance, and Dad would just laugh, basking in and amused by my concern for him. He became increasingly tired as the years went by, unable to get up in the mornings. During the school holidays, my mother used to ring up every morning from her office in her tea break, having by then graduated from packing chocolates at Cadbury's to being a clerical assistant at the General Post Office, to see whether he had gone to work. At night he would fall asleep in the chair after tea, head back, mouth open, snoring.

He broke his ankle whilst painting a ceiling, aged around fifty, falling off a wooden plank that was suspended between two ladders and catching his foot on a metal bucket as he fell. He had a spell in hospital where pins were inserted, but it took a long time to heal and afterwards he always walked with a limp. This, plus a heart attack when he was fifty-two, blamed largely on the forty Park Drive ciggies a day that he was by then smoking, aged him terribly and he looked a good twenty years older. One day he walked into the local GP's surgery, thinking he was suffering from indigestion. The doctor listened to his heart and wouldn't even allow him to take off his own overcoat, sending him straight to hospital. The heart specialist who attended him said it was imperative that he give up smoking. My father refused point blank, stating that smoking was 'the only pleasure I've got left'. The heart attack simply confirmed what I feared as a child, that my 'poor father' hadn't the strength to withstand the blows that life seemed to be dealing him, and it sent my mother's anxiety about money and poverty up to new levels.

A couple of months before his death I was sitting with him in front of the kitchen fire drinking a cup of tea, having come home from college for the weekend, when he said, 'I don't think I've got a lot longer left, Bab, but I want you to know that it's all right because I've had a good life and I'm tired now.' He died, aged sixty-two, in 1971, of another heart attack, this time a massive one that killed him more or less instantly. He was lying in bed with my mother, chatting. She asked him a question and he didn't answer, just hiccoughed and died. It had been a beautiful July day; he had been up on the roof, mending it; but, more importantly, he had won on the horses.

5

'At the Third Stroke She Will Be 78' — Grandma

And so there were the three of us: Tommy, Kevin and Julie, and that is what I was always called: Tommy-Kevin-Julie! My mother would fire off the three names in quick, stressful succession, each name a hasty and frustrated correction for the previous one, and each one gaining in emphasis so that Kevin became 'Tommy-*Kevin*'. Only Tommy was ever really called immediately by his correct name and, even then, in times of extra stress there was likely to be a debate: 'Tom — , Kevi — oh *Tommy!* — ' I think it must be a family trait because I simply cannot mention an alpha male member of my family or circle without putting my husband Grant's name first: 'Grant-Tommy or Grant-Kevin'. Similarly, I know my brother, Tommy, calls his eldest daughter Julie-Anita and me Anita-Julie.

There were the three of us and then there was Grandma. Bridget O'Brien, my maternal grandmother, had come to live with us towards the end of the war after the death of my grandfather, having found the farm they ran together just outside Castlebar, County Mayo, too much for her alone. 'Not enough soil to feed a man. Not enough soil to bury a man.' None of her four

78

children, of which my mother was the eldest, was prepared to take it on. Because my mother was arguably the cleverest of the four, her parents had earmarked her to run it and look after them in their old age. Having plans of her own, she ran away, aged twenty-six, telling them that she was just going to visit England, and she never came back. Then when she announced just six months later that she had met and was going to marry my father, a builder, a letter came from her mother, demanding in no uncertain terms that she should 'come home at once!' and then commenting, disparagingly, 'marrying a man in overalls indeed!'

I don't think Grandma acknowledged my father once during the whole fifteen years she was with us, except for the odd, sneering lift of her nose into the air in a pantomime expression of her snobbery. My brother Tommy also got short shrift where my grandmother was concerned, which was generally felt to be due to the fact that he was born before she arrived, and also — and more likely — because of his resemblance to my father. My brother Kevin, born not long after she arrived, was her out-and-out favourite. This, I think, was because he looked like her favourite son, Martin, and, more importantly, her late husband, Patrick. I fell somewhere in between, and feel now that I was probably lucky to be neither loved nor hated by her.

She had suffered a couple of strokes even before I was born and my brothers used to say, 'At the third stroke she will be seventy-eight.' It turned out that she had in fact suffered a whole series of tiny cerebral bleeds, which had an effect similar to Alzheimer's disease. She was never quite with it and at times got very confused. She would frequently get up in the small hours, dressed only in a pair of truss-pink, knee-length, interlock-weave bloomers and a pair of brown, fluffy, zip-up slipper boots, looking for all the world like some bizarre geriatric football player, and she would disappear into the night.

The first we would hear of it would be a phone call from the local post office where, for some unknown reason, she would always end up at a godforsaken hour, banging on the door. My father was duly summoned by a fairly pissed-off postmaster to go and pick her up. Then there would be a bit of a scuffle where he, the postmaster and the postmaster's wife would attempt to get my grandmother into her brown plaid dressing gown. This was no mean feat as Grandma's strength was legendary. I once came home from school to find a piece of coal the size of an armchair sitting in the middle of the sofa. How she had managed to hoick it from the coalhouse and lift it on to the said sofa is a mystery equal to that of Stonehenge. The whole post office debacle would invariably end, after my grandmother's repeated claims that she had no idea who my father was, with her giving in and getting into his van with her usual imperious lift of the nose, accompanied by a little, thin-lipped sniff.

Things seemed to take a turn for the worst, as far as I can remember, when a pigeon shat on her head in Trafalgar Square. We had gone on a day trip to London to visit Auntie Agnes, my mother's unmarried sister, in my father's Ford Esquire estate. The M1 had just been built and I must have been about nine. Things were fine on the way down but after the pigeon incident she became rather quiet. Then when we were about halfway back up the motorway she announced that she was going to 'get up now and make the tea', whereupon she attempted to get out of the moving car. My mother instructed the three of us to sit on her, which we did, but every few minutes, like *Groundhog Day*, she would start again: 'I'll get up now and make the tea.' Eventually we managed to distract her with a pile of magazines that our aunt had given us for the journey. She threw a cursory glance over a couple of pages and then began slowly to shred them into neat, thin strips. By the time we reached home, the car was like a giant hamster's nest.

I can still remember us getting out with strips of paper flying off us into the wind and my mother's face, livid, some of the strips trapped amongst the curls of her newly permed hair: '*Now* you can get up and make the bloody tea!' My grandmother, her expression at first innocently blank, closed her eyes in a slow, world-weary way, then up went the nose and out she got, an exit worthy of royalty. As she walked up the garden path like a world leader on a state visit, my brother shouted from the car, 'Grandma's wet on the seat . . . Eeeeeew . . . '

From then on she had her own special seat next to the fire in the kitchen. She ate all her meals sitting in it. One evening, when we were all sat around the table having our tea, my mother suddenly exclaimed, 'Oh, may the great God look to me!' We turned round and there was my grandmother performing the delicate task of eating a soft-boiled egg with a huge pair of coal tongs, her face blackened with coal and sticky with yolk. It was like the seat in which she did everything, literally. It made a sound like a full sponge if you poked it with your finger or, God forbid, sat in it, though few did unless they had some olfactory impairment. I can remember the priest once getting up out of it with a damp patch on the back of his cassock and us all staring silently as he waved a jolly goodbye at the gate. So we were on full alert when visitors arrived, especially in summer when the whiff was somewhat reduced by virtue of the fact that the fire wasn't lit. We were ready in a second to head them off at the first sign that they might wish to take the weight off their feet.

My poor mother did what she could about my grandmother's incontinence, but with three children and a full-time job at Cadbury's, she couldn't always give it her whole attention. I can remember feeling very angry seeing her, exhausted after a full day's work, clearing up yet another of my grandmother's deposits.

One day, I saw Grandma walk up the middle of our small strip of garden, which Mum had lovingly planted and tended. I watched as lupins, gladioli, iris and pansies were mashed underfoot and at the same time small, hard turds were dropping out from under her old black skirt as she walked along, just like a horse. I am ashamed to say I ran after her and kicked her up the bottom; I am now pleased to say she didn't notice. My dad then erected some chicken wire around the garden to stop her wandering on to it, but this had to be taken down when one day after returning from the shops we found her spreadeagled, flat on her face on the lawn, with both feet stuck in the chicken wire.

My mother kept chickens for several years after the war. Only a dozen or so, they were kept mainly for eggs and occasionally at Christmas one would be dispatched for lunch, my grandmother doing the honours. These birds would invariably be a little tough as they were rather mature, so one year a turkey was bought to be raised for the following Christmas. However, my mother could not bear the thought of the creature suffering and when it came to it refused to allow it to be put down. So it became a pet.

It grew to an enormous size, strutting and scratching around the garden with its brain growing on the outside of its head and seeing off anyone who had the audacity to come in through the back gate. Tradesmen were terrified of it. When the milkman came in with his daily delivery, the turkey would stand at the top of the garden, his head down, aggressively scratching his feet out behind him, then he would run the full length of the garden and, like an overfilled jumbo, take off just as he reached the end. As the milkman was bending down to put the milk on the step, the turkey would fly at him with a fearsome squawk, its awful talons to the fore. People became too scared to come into the garden but still my mother refused to get rid of him, stating that he was as good as a watchdog. This state of affairs continued until one day my brother Kevin, who was three at the time, came running into the house, screaming in terror. The thing was on his head, flapping and screeching, its talons embedded in his scalp. So Grandma was dispatched to do the dispatching.

Grandma was a whizz at dispatching. Legend would have it that she could dispatch, pluck and draw a bird in about ten minutes. The other thing she was good at was making great sugar sandwiches, something my mother would never allow: lovely squares of white bread slathered in butter and then thickly covered in white sugar. She was always there when I came in from school and these treats were produced not only on demand but with pleasure.

She was also an endless source of entertainment, introducing words into our vocabulary that none of us had ever heard before or since, words that no one has ever been able to explain. 'Ahhh, she's like a maharather in bad weather!' is one example, which seemed to be a derogatory term usually aimed at my mother, and we children were often referred to as 'wee goms' as in 'get up out of bed, you wee gom!' When she sat down to watch television, she never really understood that whoever was on television at the time couldn't hear her. For instance if there was a drama on, she would join in with the dialogue: 'How dare you speak to her like that!' She was hard of hearing and would often shout at the newsreader, inches from the screen, 'What did you say? Speak up, man!' Her eyesight wasn't too good either and once whilst watching a ballet she suddenly stood up and said, 'How dare you display yourself in front of me like that!' and marched out of the room, slamming the door behind her. She had thought that the male dancer, instead of wearing tights, was naked from the waist down.

Grandma was a good playmate too and you could engage her in most games of make-believe. I have one vivid memory of telling her that she had just started school, as I had done in reality only days earlier. She became completely immersed in this. I can see her face now and can remember being quite frightened by its sudden transformation. It became strangely lopsided, the small, brown eyes moist and shining, her mouth stretched wide into a grin I had never seen before, clearly showing that she had but one yellow tooth in the middle of her upper jaw. She began to babble excitedly about learning to read and write, and then she wrote her maiden name in a childish scrawl several times on the paper I had given her. Two or three years after she died this had a rather strange repercussion.

I must have been about twelve at the time and I had decided to move up into the unused attic room at the top of the house. It was a large, cold room with a big sash window, looking down over the street. The wallpaper was faded and torn, and one wall was completely papered with front covers of *Punch* magazine from when my brother Tommy had slept there briefly some years back. Before that the only other time it had been occupied was when my aunt and uncle had lodged with us for a couple of years. It felt wonderfully removed from everything — from the rest of the house, as no one ever went up there, and also from the world outside; it was higher than the houses opposite and you could almost see over the top of them. It was a brilliant vantage point from which to view the world of the street and its goings-on, and the relationships of the various children that played there.

Once a friend and I dropped water bombs from the window down on to a football game taking place below. The bombs were made from balloons filled with water. The subsequent surprise and chaos that it caused — boys screaming in terror and shock, and mothers rushing out on to their doorsteps to see what the commotion was, and everyone looking this way and that but mainly up to the heavens as if they'd been dropped from some alien spacecraft — sent us into paroxysms of fear and laughter. We never owned up even though it was the talk of the street for weeks, my mother's wrath being the chief deterrent.

On the first night that I was to spend in this room, I got into bed, excited by the fact that I had a light suspended above my pillow that I could switch on by pulling a cord. I was sitting up in bed, reading my comic, when the light suddenly went out. I was not too worried as I thought it was probably not switched on properly so I yanked it back on. This happened again several times in fairly quick succession. In the end I gave up and snuggled down to go to sleep. Just as I was drifting off, the light came back on again and I began to be slightly alarmed. I pulled the cord to turn it off and dived down under the covers, but on it came again. This time, my heart hammering, I quickly put an arm out from under the blankets and snapped it off. '*Stop it!*' I shouted and it did. I lay there for some time, unable to sleep, wondering whether the light did this every night, in an empty room, of its own accord, sending out a mystery Morse code to the universe, when suddenly, on what sounded like a huge breath of air, the door to the room was flung open. I can hear it to this day, pushing the tattered old rug back with a mighty squeak. I stayed under the covers sick with fear, my pulse sounding in my ears. I told myself it must be a draught and somehow eventually I fell into a fitful sleep.

When I awoke next day the door was still wide open but the morning light had removed all threat. It was when I got up that I noticed it: a small piece of paper a couple of feet from the bed. On bending down to pick it up, I recognised it immediately. It was the paper I had given my grandmother some seven years earlier, on her 'first day at school'. It read in thin wavery writing: Bridget O'Brien, crossed out, and then her maiden name, Bridget Clark Bridget Clark Bridget Clark. I couldn't work out where it had come from, but then I remembered that outside the door, on the small landing, was the trunk my grandmother had brought with her from Ireland when she had first come to live with us. It was filled with various items of her belongings. But why would this scrap of paper from a game played years ago have been kept in her trunk? Maybe she had treasured it for some unfathomable reason, but even so if it had been put in her trunk, with its heavy wooden lid and its substantial metal catch, how did it get out of there and into this room, which I had cleaned thoroughly the day before, and how did this stiff old door, catching on a thick rug, on a calm night, open with such force? Well, suffice it to say I never slept up there again.

Grandma died in 1960. As she lay dying I would sit by her bed, in the little back bedroom of our house, and moisten her lips with a tiny brush dipped in water, fascinated once again by the transformation of her face, this time with an unrecognisable peace that softened her features, the old yellow tooth, unhampered by inhibition, clearly visible again at the centre of a half-smile, and I saw for the first time that there was beauty in her face.

I'm asked time and time again about why I choose to play people older than myself: Mrs Overall, or Robert Lindsay's mother in *GBH*, or, more recently, Evie in the film *Driving Lessons*. I have always found older people endlessly intriguing, as all actors do. The way they think, the way they speak and move, their faces and clothes, and older people were — and are — even more interesting in some ways, simply because I haven't reached their age and I want to go and explore it. But I believe the main reason that I end up playing so many older women is that somewhere I want to re-create and comprehend both the fun and the calamity that was caused by my grandmother's presence in our house for what was actually almost the whole of my childhood years.

This conundrum was partly solved when I was involved in an *Omnibus* for BBC Television about my life and career. I went back to the West of Ireland in the mid-nineties, to the place where my mother was born. The single-storey, thatched cottage that she, her two brothers and sister had been brought up in had long since been demolished, but I spoke to the people who had lived next door to them. When I asked them about my grandmother, the woman they described came as a revelation to me. She was apparently lively, energetic and funny, loved by the local children and always welcoming with an apple to give them from the orchard. I was shocked, feeling both deprived of that woman that they had all known and saddened when I thought of the poor confused, cantankerous old woman I had grown up with. It made no sense to me and then I remembered the beauty of that face as she lay dying, with its secret smile, and somehow it did.

6

'Mixing with Doctors' Daughters' —Junior School

'Now you're a proper schoolgirl!' I felt my stomach tighten. I was standing in the kitchen, wearing a white blouse, with a navy, silver and yellow tie under a navy-blue gymslip that almost reached my ankles and which my mother was about to pin up and hem. It would have been the beginning of January 1955 and in a week or so I was about to start school at the kindergarten of a convent preparatory school in Birmingham. My years there, up until 1961, were amongst the unhappiest of my life. I had spent a carefree term in the nursery class at Abbey Road Juniors where my only memories are of seeing my name printed in big, black letters on a strip of card, and my taking in the shape the letters made, and of being put to bed in the afternoons for a nap. I am assuming it was carefree because the memories are so scant and the ones that remain are pleasant. Just before I left, the namecard came apart in the middle. What I find most significant about this is that I was not afraid of the consequences.

My mother had talked about my new school in hushed, reverential tones. 'Oh, you'll learn how to speak properly,' whereupon she would launch into an awful attempt at a middle-class, English accent, thick with snobbery: 'You'll be mixing with doctors' daughters and the like.' I was uncomfortable with her talking in this way and even then saw it as some sort of betrayal. Clearly the way we spoke and the fact that I was a builder's daughter meant that I was quite simply not good enough, so I started that school ashamed of who I was.

On the day my own daughter started school, she took a couple of cuddly toys with her and her teacher said, 'Now, where would they like to sit?' I couldn't help but compare this to the reception I imagined I would have got on my first day if I had had the temerity to bring such a thing with me. I imagine it being slapped from my hands and being told in a loud and angry voice that this was a place for learning.

I have a very clear memory of that first day. I was to be taken to school by the older sister of one of Kevin's best friends. Her name was Mary and she lived about three hundred yards from our house. Her mum, a small, dark, sharp-featured woman from Northern Ireland, my mother's friend from St Gregory's church, ran a clothing catalogue whereby people could order clothes and pay for them in weekly instalments. Every Monday night I was dispatched to pay our instalment, or the 'club money' as it was called. Her dad was usually there, ensconced in his armchair in front of the television. He was from Southern Ireland and was much older than his wife; where she appeared harder in both accent and attitude, he was soft and gently spoken.

When I was very small he would take me on his knee and tell me stories of fairies and elves and enchanted horses, in a dark, dramatic voice that could make the hair on the back of my neck stand up, but he would always end in a burst of laughter and a rough, bristly cuddle.

I loved these Monday nights; I would be sat down in front of the television and given tea in a china cup and saucer, plus a piece of fruit cake, while I watched *Bonanza*, a Western series about an improbable family. I don't remember their own children, of which there were three, being there very much; they were that much older than me and were most probably either off out having a life or in another room doing their homework. In fact I can remember feeling disappointed if any of the children were there because their mum and dad might have been distracted from their pampering of me. They were a couple whose emotional dynamic was similar to that of my parents, except that they seemed to have more time and were less stressed.

Mary was their middle child, about seven or eight years older than me, with an older sister and a younger brother, and she was a pupil at the senior school, next door to the prep. She was a pretty girl with long dark hair and a massive amount of good sense. The journey to school consisted in part of a fifteen-minute bus ride down towards the city centre. On that first morning I was just about to step down from the bus at the stop by the school when, with a sweep of her arm, Mary pushed me aside and leapt from the bus. Then with one foot still on the platform and the other on the kerb, and the palm of her hand pressed firmly into my chest to stop me getting off, she stood in the path of a speeding bicycle, thus preventing what might have been a rather nasty collision. Instead she struck a pose like Superwoman, straddling the space between bus and pavement, while the cyclist, with a long skid and a squeaking of brakes, ended up with the unseemly parking of his front wheel between her legs and his handlebars pressed hard up against her tightly belted, regulation, navy-blue, gabardine mac. I can still see his head and shoulders shoot forward with the force of stopping so suddenly, causing his Brylcreem-laden quiff to flop down, in what looked like slow motion, over his forehead. Mary then held the cyclist there, their faces just inches apart, while she waved me and several other passengers safely off the bus behind her. Words were exchanged between her and the young man but I cannot remember what they were, except that his were said with an angry scowl, culminating in 'Fuck off!' What I do know is that, without a doubt, she came off best.

After this act of bravery I was in complete awe of her. She was a heroine, a person in whose company I was not fit to be, and I rarely dared to speak a word to her on our subsequent journeys. On many an occasion, I even put up with her spitting on her handkerchief and then roughly cleaning my face with it, enduring the unpleasant smell of dried spit until I could get to a tap to wash it off, rather than hint that I might prefer her not to do it. So I was not a little relieved when at six years old I was allowed to travel to and from school by myself.

This went without a hitch until one afternoon in year six, my final year at the school. I was with my two best friends and the little sister of one of them. We had been waiting for the number 9 bus and, feeling a bit bored, we decided to play in the huge overgrown front garden of an enormous empty house that was next to the bus stop. All the houses along this stretch of road were massive and had been converted into either hotels or offices. After some time we heard a man's voice shouting at us and coming towards us, through the bushes, from the direction of the house.

'Oi! What do you think you're doing?'

We decided to run for it and scampered out of the garden, a way down the road, into the front garden of another huge house and there we hid in the bushes. We crouched down, hoping the man had gone, but a few minutes later he reappeared. He was tall and thin, wearing horn-rimmed glasses and a grubby-looking mac.

'What do you think you were doing in that garden?'

I don't know who said what, but I think we probably all spoke at once.

'We were just playing.'

'We're really sorry.'

He told us to stand up and proceeded to put a clammy hand up each of our skirts in turn and to feel the tops of our thighs. Whilst doing this he asked us what school we went to, this simple question striking more fear into our hearts than the molestation that was taking place. Suddenly he said that he was going but that he would be back in a couple of minutes and then, jabbing his forefinger at us, he told us we were to stay put until he came back or else. We stood there for several minutes in silence, precious minutes during which we could easily have escaped, but we were doing as we were told out of total fear. I can still smell the damp earth and the rotting leaves around our feet, and I can recall wanting this man to be harmless and telling the others in a frightened whisper that I believed his touching us up was simply him working out our age!

'What would the nuns say if they knew what you'd been up to?' He was back again and strangely breathless.

'Oh, please don't report us! We won't do it again.'

'Well, you'd better come with me.'

And dutifully with hearts racing, we followed. He took us back the way we had come, past the disused house and garden where we had been playing and where several people were now waiting for the bus. We then went round the corner into a much quieter road. He took us a little way down it and then instructed us to stand against the wall and lift our dresses up. I can still see his face as he stared at us and my recollecting with horror that not only was I not wearing my school beret, a reportable offence, but that I was also not wearing my regulation navy-blue interlock-weave school knickers. Instead I had on a pair of shameful, pink nylon frilly ones that my mother had bought off the market. After several seconds of staring, he was clearly becoming agitated and took us back the way we had come, up the road and round the corner, where now there was quite a queue at the bus stop. On seeing these people, one of my friends, God bless her presence of mind, suddenly proclaimed, 'Oh! I've got to go and get my bus now.' And she ran off at top speed in the opposite direction.

This of course attracted the attention of the people in the queue. The man, then clearly panicking, said, 'Yes ... yes ... off you go and don't let me catch you playing in that garden again or I'll smack yer bums.' And with that he scuttled off.

We never used that bus stop again, preferring to walk a quarter of a mile to the next one; nor did we ever speak of the incident. I never told my parents. I didn't want them to worry and I felt them to be powerless. The next day at school the girl who had run off didn't turn up. I was in a complete haze of fear the whole morning until her bright little face appeared around the classroom door. She had been to the dentist. I have often wondered what would have happened if that bus stop had been deserted. The man was obviously looking for somewhere to take us and that empty old house would have been perfect if it weren't for the people waiting for the bus outside it. I also think that if we hadn't been so terrified of being reported to the school, we'd have been more inclined both to stand up for ourselves and to get away from this man, and that we might not have been so afraid to report him.

The school was situated in a middle-class residential road, full of large detached houses. It was a neat-looking, biscuit-coloured, brick building, consisting of two wings at the centre of which was the chapel. One wing was the school itself and the other was the nuns' living quarters.

There was no playground as such; we would be sent out to play on the drive or sometimes, as a special treat, 'down the field'. The field was a green area at the back of the school that stretched a couple of hundred yards down to the perimeter fence, the other side of which was the Edgbaston reservoir. It was not a playing field; there were the odd few trees scattered here and there, and the grass was patchy and rough. No sports were ever taught or played there, although I do seem to remember the odd bean-bag being flung about. So weather permitting, at lunchtime and at mid-morning break we were sent out on to the drive to play. Alongside it was a strip of lawn, about the same width as the drive itself, running along underneath the classroom windows and bordered by a concrete kerb. Upon this grass we were forbidden to tread. Many a child, myself included, had been summarily thrashed about the legs for simply letting the back of a heel touch it. So when I visited the school almost thirty years later I was filled with devilment to find that piece of lawn still there.

It was in the mid-eighties and I was up in Birmingham filming *The Making of Acorn Antiques* for the *Victoria Wood Christmas Special*. It so happened that I had been put up in a hotel just two or three miles from the school and one morning, finding myself with a couple of hours to spare, I decided to go and take a look. The school, as is so often the case, seemed to have shrunk, but was just as manicured and pristine as I remembered it. And there it was, the piece of lawn, the cause and the location of my and no doubt many others' painful and humiliating public slapping. It was with joy in my heart therefore, and a pair of high-heeled boots on my feet, that I tramped up and down the full length of this lawn, several times, purposefully and with relish, digging my heels deep into the turf. I was hoping against hope that one of the Sisters would appear and tell me to get off the grass. Alas, no one came and I'm not sure how I would have reacted if one of them had come along and challenged my behaviour. In fantasyland I know exactly how I would have acted. I would have stood there, feet apart, hands on hips, and said: 'Please, . . . make my day . . . Go on! Try and slap my legs.'

The nuns were of the classic penguin variety, wearing black, ankle-length habits with full skirts and waist-length, black veils that billowed out behind them like giant bat wings when they walked at speed. Under this, tightly wrapped about the head like a surgical dressing, was a starched, white wimple held in place by tiny white-headed pins, and covering their bosoms a stiff white scapular, upon which hung a big, black, wooden crucifix. Dangling from the waist, often accompanied by a bunch of keys, was a large set of dark, wooden, rosary beads that clacked and jingled when they moved, the sound of which served as an excellent warning that a nun was in the vicinity.

'My name is Sister Cecilia.'

She had a big, pale, bespectacled face, covered in fine, downy hair, and she was the teacher in charge of the kindergarten. Almost immediately I noticed that there was a tension that hung in the air at this place, which was soon to be explained. For not only did the sisters dispense helpful gems like, 'Don't cross your legs, you never saw the Virgin Mary cross hers' (I had never seen the Virgin Mary breathing in and out but it was fairly vital to the smooth running of a person's day); or 'Beware of chocolate . . . it's a stimulant,' and offer strictures that patent-leather shoes were not to be worn because they reflected your nether regions, they also administered painful and random slaps to the head, meted out for such misdemeanours as whispering in class. During my first couple of weeks an incident occurred that was to set the tone for my time at this school.

After much hype and many homilies as to how careful we were going to have to be, the kindergarten was delivered of a set of new desks. They were all there in place one morning when we arrived in the classroom. Their tubular, metal legs were still wrapped in brown paper, wound around them in strips. When the class was assembled, Sister Cecilia warned us sternly that under no circumstances were we to undo this wrapping: 'Woe betide any girl found fiddling.' Within a day or two one of the legs on my desk, the left-hand front one to be precise, was beginning to unravel! I can recall the shocked and sudden intakes of breath as my friends noticed the thin twist of paper coming away from and revealing the pale-blue metal leg beneath. Then as if in a bid for freedom, another leg revealed itself and then another; I looked on appalled and helpless, day after day, until finally all four, having popped their wrappings, were shedding them like snakeskin. Each time Sister Cecilia came near me I expected the customary stinging thwack to the side of my head but somehow I managed to escape it. Soon other people's desk legs began to undo. One girl stayed away from school for a whole week, terrified of the consequences, but another brave soul decided to inform Sister of what was happening to her desk and to tell her that she, the child, had had nothing to do with it. She was dragged from her place and thrashed on the legs. I can see the two of them now, the girl with her cardigan half pulled off, careering into the front row of desks and knocking a tiny chair flying, then chasing one another around in a circle, the girl up on her tiptoes, her hips thrust forward, trying to get away, silent tears racing down her cheeks, and Sister Cecilia's large, white hand in a blur of slapping, and the big, black cross, being swung and tossed violently about in mid-air, catching the girl on the face before crashing down again on to the starched white bosom. It was an event that none of us discussed. I wanted to tell my parents but I didn't, projecting my own feelings of powerlessness on to them and feeling a need to somehow protect them from this.

Eventually, one Sunday night, unable to sleep, in a state of terror at the thought of going to school on the Monday and despair at my own childish impotence, I confessed to my parents in an explosion of gulping tears the awful tale of the mutinous desk legs. They stood dumbfounded and then, unable to calm me, my father went off to telephone the Mother Superior, my mother thinking the whole thing a bit of a storm in a teacup. I waited, in my pyjamas by the kitchen fire, sick to my stomach.

When he returned my father still looked dumbfounded; but he was also smiling.

'There's no problem,' he said, his voice lifted in bemusement.

'But what did she say? What did she say?'

'She laughed . . . She said it doesn't matter, Bab . . .'

It doesn't matter! It was incredible to me that the fear and trepidation of the previous weeks could be solved by two smiling adults in a matter of minutes, over the phone; but it seems that it was, for when I went into school the next day, we were told to remove the wrapping from our desk legs. Thus was the desk-leg saga brought to a close.

However, I never went into that classroom, or, indeed, that school without fear of what was in store and there was plenty in store over the coming years, the elocution lessons my mother had spoken about with such reverence being one of my unhappiest experiences. These were to be taken by a lay teacher. In some ways I could cope with the inappropriate nature of the punishments handed out by the nuns because they were like a different species, holed up together in an alien bubble of a life. But I felt somehow let down by the lay teachers, of whom there were only a couple, when they displayed the same lack of compassion and understanding as the Sisters. None of the teaching staff seem to have any joy in them and to my young self they nearly all appeared angry and unhappy. The elocution teacher was no exception.

Our elocution classes were held in a prefabricated hut at the back of the school. The girl sitting next to me had 'ELECTRIC CHAIR! ELECTRIC CHAIR! ELECTRIC CHAIR!' emblazoned on the front of her elocution exercise book. My abiding memory is of standing at the front of the class reading from a book. Throughout the reading I had consistently pronounced words that had a long A, such as 'daft', in the same way as words with a short A, such as 'cat'. This was the way I spoke then and how I speak today; it was the way we all pronounced such words at home, my mother being Irish and the rest of us having Black Country accents. I knew what was expected of me, but I simply couldn't bring myself to say this long A.

After the reading the teacher wrote out on the blackboard a list of words that were supposed to be pronounced in this way and asked me to read them out. I didn't get past the first one, which was 'bath'. Something in me, even though I was frightened, still refused to say it the way she wanted and every time I said 'bath' with a short

A she walloped my hand with a ruler. I can't recall how long I stood there but there were several stinging slaps and I know that I never gave in. It felt like some kind of final frontier to my self-worth. I was defending who I was. If I gave her what she wanted, I would be confirming my mother's fears — that we were not good enough — and I simply couldn't do that.

This difficulty with Standard English, or Received Pronunciation as it was then called, followed me to drama school many years later and beyond. It was not that I refused to speak it for a role, but that it caused me a certain discomfort that I never disclosed. It slowly but gradually ceased to be a problem as I came, in later years, to be more accepting of myself and who I was. My mother, of course, was forever disappointed that I didn't come home speaking like the doctors' daughters of her imagination, and I was unable at the time to understand and therefore to express why I couldn't.

I'm not going to list every punishment that took place at this school, but there is one more that remains strikingly distinct in my memory. I was in what would now be year five, making me eight or nine years old. Our teacher was Sister Ignatius, a towering figure — 'Mum, she's as tall as the door!' — with a florid face and thick black, beetle brows. She had a huge, booming voice and a nasty temper. One day she had had reason to leave the classroom for a few minutes, leaving the form captain in charge. There was total silence as we got on with our work. Suddenly one of the girls said, 'Isn't it quiet without Sister?' The minute Sister Ignatius returned, the form captain, a humourless swot of a girl for whom the term 'teacher's pet' had probably been invented, saw fit to report this innocent remark. The nun then launched herself at the child who had had the audacity to speak in her absence, the first blow knocking her clean off her chair. She then set about beating her while the girl lay cowering on the floor, trying to protect herself. After a minute or so of flailing and thrashing, Sister Ignatius dragged the child to her feet and into a small room off the back of the classroom that was used as a furniture and stationery store. She slammed the door behind them and continued to beat her.

We sat frozen, in breath-held, mouth-dry silence. Not a look was exchanged between us as we listened to the sudden violent scrape of desk legs on the wooden floor and the raining down on to this poor girl of blow after blow. When the nun emerged, some minutes later, still purple faced and enraged, we were forbidden to speak to the girl. She was shut in the room for the rest of the day. We were told to send her to Coventry until instructed to do otherwise, and I still experience a sense of shame when I think of that girl standing alone at break times and dinner-times in the days that followed, all of us fearful of what would happen should we dare to talk to her.

How on earth we learnt anything under this tyranny is beyond me. Long division? Forget it! Long multiplication? The same. If you didn't get it the first time, for whatever reason, it was better, at least in my book, to copy someone else's rather than suffer the humiliation that might result if you got it wrong. In year six under Sister Augustine's slightly less terrifying tutelage, I would spend library hour, on a Friday afternoon, reading a book from cover to cover without taking in a single word of it. All of Arthur Ransome's apparently wonderful novels simply passed in and out of my head in a blur of meaningless verbiage. It just felt as if the whole set-up was a club that I simply would never belong to, even down to reading a book for pleasure.

But something surprisingly healing did emerge from my time at this school and, even more surprisingly, it was during Sister Ignatius's terrible reign. On the odd afternoon we would play the miming game whereby she would get us up individually, in front of the class, to do a mime and the other children would have to guess what it was. I can still recall the euphoria I felt on hearing that nun's laughter the first time I stood out front and I can still see the classroom on that day, flooded with afternoon sun: how colourful and beautiful it suddenly looked. I also experienced a sense of power. I had, however briefly, quelled this woman's anger and unhappiness and somehow made her safe.

'You should go on the stage!' she said in her big, cracked voice, still giggling. I knew then that in her laughter and in the laughing faces of my classmates lay my salvation and the building blocks for my self-esteem.

7

'I Thought You'd Failed' — Senior School

My mother's ambition — or perhaps fantasy is more accurate — was for me to pass from the prep school up into the senior school, but I knew in my heart that there wasn't a chance in hell and so did she. She had already been hauled in when I was in year three and told that there was every likelihood that she was wasting her hard-earned money, nine guineas a term. I simply wasn't keeping up. I was separated off from the rest of the class with three or four other slow learners in order to try to bring me up to scratch and it wasn't entirely working. Mum said virtually nothing as we walked to the bus stop afterwards but her disappointment was palpable in the tone of her voice and in the few words that she did say. 'Oh, Julie . . . Oh dear . . . Tsk, tsk, tsk.' I felt the same humiliation and helplessness as I had when I had wet the bed, in that I did not know what to do to put it right and to stop it happening again. However, I wasn't thrown out, so my parents must have decided that it was best to keep me there and for me to soldier on and stay the course.

As predicted I didn't get in to the senior school, but this could hardly be called a disappointment, more a fortunate outcome, because it meant that if I passed the eleven-plus examination — and the alternative was unthinkable — I would go to Holly Lodge Grammar School for Girls in Smethwick, where there wasn't a nun in sight, and my brothers were already going to Holly Lodge Grammar School for Boys. The two schools were separated by a joint driveway. As it was, I nearly didn't get in there either. A letter came from the education authority, stating that I had in fact failed the exam. My chest tightens now as I recall my mother breaking the news as if she were announcing that I had been found guilty of some heinous crime and would be hanged by the neck until dead. I didn't feel as if I had failed an exam; I felt as if I had failed my whole life and all I had to look forward to was years of shame at a secondary-modern school, to be followed by the second-class existence of someone who had failed their eleven-plus! I went around in a state of total dejection for days, wanting to hide away as I heard my mother, brave in her chagrin, broadcast the news of my failure to friends and family.

One kind friend of my mother's, whose own daughter had failed some years previously, said, 'Never mind, Julie, you have always got your church.' Trying to take comfort in this, all I could think of were the middle-aged women who fussed around the parish priest at St Gregory's, our parish church, which we all, my father apart, attended every Sunday. These women, who cleaned the vestry and took charge of the flowers in the church, were poor souls whom my mother referred to as 'too holy'; unattractive spinsters who were always on their knees, making cow eyes at the priest, with no hope of marrying, and who wore sensible shoes and no make-up.

But then a week or so later, a letter came from Holly Lodge Grammar. It seemed I hadn't failed at all; well, to be more exact, I was what the letter referred to as 'borderline' and it said that the school were willing to take me if I promised to work hard. I felt as a prisoner must do on death row after being given a reprieve; now I could say, 'No, I have passed! They made a mistake! I'm going to Holly Lodge!' When I went to visit the aforementioned friend of my mother's to impart the good news, I was labouring under the innocent delusion that she would be pleased for me. She had had her back to me at the time, standing at the kitchen sink, but she spun around and with venom in her voice she almost shouted, 'I thought you'd failed!'

Arriving at Holly Lodge was like getting into your own bed after weeks of sleeping on someone else's hard floor. It was familiar and comfortable; people spoke as I did; they lived in houses like mine, in the same area; their brothers knew mine; older girls from the years above came up to me in the corridor and said, 'Are you Kevin Walters' sister? I grew inches taller with pride. In short I knew that this was where I belonged.

They also taught PE, which hitherto I had been deprived of, even teaching myself to swim just the year before at Thimblemill Baths in Smethwick. The saga of my learning to swim went on for a couple of years. When I was about eight, Mrs Carlton, a woman whom my mother worked with who lived only a few streets away, offered to teach me and so every Sunday morning throughout the summer at the painfully early time of six-thirty I would set off, my rolled-up towel under my arm, to meet her at the baths with her two sons, who both looked to me like Olympic swimmers and were both younger than me. Seven o'clock, when the pool opened, was an ideal time; the baths would be a perfect, untroubled oblong of clear, blue water just waiting to have its surface tension ruffled by the first time swimmer. It would be free of corn plasters, toenails and other unidentifiable debris as there were very few folk who had the inclination to turn up at that time of the morning to plough its widths and lengths. All very different from the people soup that formed later in the day.

Mrs Carlton would support me under my waist, encouraging me at every turn while I simulated breaststroke, and after a while she would let go. I was terrified of being underwater and it always ended in the same way with me flailing around in total panic, coming up coughing and spluttering, and my teacher saying, 'Just do the stroke as you were doing when I was holding you,' but I couldn't. I felt that despite the huge, mumsy size of this woman, with acres of white, dimpled flesh flaring out from the edges of her costume and floating freely in the water, I could not trust that she would save me were I to get into trouble. And on top of this I had to suffer the humiliation of going home, Mrs Carlton disappointed because she had not achieved her goal, and everyone saying, 'Well? Have you learnt? What's the problem?' Despite this woman's kindly assurances that I was almost there and that I would do it before the summer was out, I knew that I wouldn't. It wasn't until two years later in the summer of 1960 that I finally learnt.

I had a dream; one night I dreamt that I could swim. I dreamt that I was in the shallow end at Thimblemill Baths and, standing about two feet away from the side, I jumped and held quickly on to the rail that ran along it. Then I simply repeated it, standing further and further away, until I realised that I was floating towards the side and that my feet were off the bottom. The very next morning as soon as I woke up, without stopping to eat or drink a thing, I raced down to the baths, clutching my ninepence to get in, with my blue nylon, still-ruched, bathing costume rolled up in a towel, and I did exactly what I had done in the dream. Then with an elation I had never felt before this and rarely since, I was swimming; within twenty minutes I was swimming widths and then lengths. It became a passion. I went every single day of that summer holiday, stinking constantly of chlorine, and there, amongst the throng of splashing girls and dive-bombing boys, and adults trying to swim sedately up and down in between them, I felt my first tickle of lust for a lovely-looking boy who popped up like a beach ball out of the water directly in front of me, said, 'I think you're luscious!' and then disappeared again. I went straight to the changing rooms to look at myself, to see what he had seen, and then straight home to look up the word 'luscious'.

Like my brothers before me, I loved sport and at Holly Lodge spent most dinner hours and time after school in the winter playing hockey, with Saturday mornings playing right wing or right half and eventually centre half for one or other of the school teams. Once or twice the PE mistress invited the local Sikh boys' team to practise with us. They were gentle and friendly boys but their dark, long-limbed grace made us girls feel like a herd of carthorses; indeed, at the end of the practice, the sound of thudding boots on turf as we raced back across the pitch to the showers put me very much in mind of the Grand National. The Sikhs would practise shooting goals by placing a wooden school chair in the centre of the goalmouth and hitting balls from the halfway line straight between the chair legs with deadly accuracy. They put us to shame with their speed and skill.

At the end of the hockey season the first-eleven girls would play a match with the first-eleven boys' football team from the boys' school across the way. Every year I would watch from the sidelines and every year I would be more and more turned on by the spectacle of big, hunky, sixth-form boys bullying off with and tackling our first-eleven girls in sometimes quite ferocious tussles that looked as if, at any moment, in a parallel universe at least, they would fling their sticks aside and rip their clothes off. When it came to my turn to play them, in the lower sixth, I could barely run for the lust of it.

But for some, the highlight of the hockey season was the game we played against the staff. The thought of wrapping my stick across the shins of a certain teacher with stale, sulphurous breath, who had accused me of cheating when I hadn't, was almost sublime, but when it came to it, I couldn't do it, because she was a different person on the pitch, sweet, smiling and vulnerable. In fact, this was true of all of them, with the possible exception of a swaggering male teacher, who was deeply unpopular and who had the unsavoury reputation of slithering up to girls during lessons and placing his great hoof on the corner of their desk, thus thrusting his baggy, old crotch at them in a horribly intrusive and vaguely lewd way. So there was great pleasure and entertainment value in seeing him tackled and defeated by our heroic forwards, and excitement at the possibility of his actually being maimed by a flying stick or a rogue ball. He resembled a toad, with his jowly, pasty face speckled with warts and his unctuous, smarmy persona; his too-close-for-comfort tutoring had to be punished. So of course a huge, roaring cheer of enjoyment came from the crowd when he was helped, limping between two teachers, from the pitch, having been given a mighty thwack across the ankle by our towering centre half.

In the third year, a new sport was introduced

by means of an exclusive club, which was to meet every Wednesday in the gym, after school. It was basketball and the teacher running it had hand-picked us mainly from the hockey team. After several weeks of learning the game and practising, we formed a team called the White Tornados and played games against other teams of a similar standard every week or so, but the main thing that kept our interest up was not so much the playing of basketball, but the witnessing of what we imagined to be an affair between this teacher and one of the older girls. They always seemed to be having animated and hushed conversations in the PE teacher's office, out of which the girl would emerge either bubbly and ecstatic or red-faced and tearful, and the teacher looking slightly sheepish.

Then one day in the showers after practice, one of the girls blurted out, 'I think they'm lezzers.' And that was it; we watched them after that like hawks: the looks between them, clocking a certain tone of voice here, a little touch of fingertips on elbow there, checking to see the signs of snogging on their lips, but the evidence was never found to be conclusive. Sometimes they would be seen in close conversation outside the staffroom door, the girl looking up at the teacher with a swoon in her eyes, the teacher looking edgy and self-conscious. It was a soap opera that lasted a tantalising couple of years until we found out from several sources, after months of detective work, the devastating news that the whole thing was merely a disappointing infatuation on the part of the girl. Shortly afterwards half the team left. I stayed on with the team even after I left school, but eventually became disenchanted as my height became more and more of a disadvantage; everyone else towered above me and, tired of jumping for the ball only to be thwacked on the head by a pair of Amazonian bosoms, I stopped going.

During the summer terms I spent my free time preparing for the Smethwick inter-schools athletics championships, which were held every year at the Hadley Stadium in Smethwick. I was a sprinter and usually competed in the 200 metres and the relay, the winning of either, but especially the 200 metres, being almost a matter of life and death. To contemplate coming second or third was not an option, and the mere thought filled me with a sickening anxiety; indeed, I frequently threw up after a race, whatever the outcome of it. When I came third in the 200 metres, the first time I had ever run it, I hid in the toilets, vomiting and crying at the same time, which is actually quite difficult to achieve, and then waited, shivering and crouching on the floor of the cubicle, until everyone else had gone home. Facing them seemed an impossibility. It felt as if when I didn't win, I didn't know how to be, I didn't exist. I was ashamed and went home in dread of telling my mother. She wasn't an 'Oh well, it's the taking part that counts' sort of person.

When while still at primary school, my brother Kevin came home and told her with pride that he had come third in a maths test, she shot back instantly with, 'Who came first?' and when he told her, she said, 'Oh, he's clever!' reserving all her praise for some other child. Worse still, when my other brother Tommy got a first-class honours degree from Birmingham University, she just said, 'Ah well, they're turning them away from the Harwell nuclear plant with firsts.' So when I stood in the scullery while my mum was making a batch of her legendary rock cakes — the cricket season was, after all, upon us — and I told her of the disaster that had occurred that afternoon, I was shocked at her gentle and unperturbed response. 'Well, it's all right, it doesn't matter. Forget about it,' she said without looking at me. I presumed that she must have sensed my distress and that in her eyes I didn't need to be put right, as I was already having the correct reaction. I believe that, had I been pleased with the result, it would have been another story.

I never lost that race again and became Worcestershire 200-metres champion in 1966. As a result of this, an athletics scout from Smethwick Harriers came and took me under his wing, stating that I might have a modicum of talent. However, I had torn a muscle in my hip at these same county championships, whilst running the second leg of the 4 by 100 metres relay race, so instead of continuing with the sprinting, which would have damaged the muscle further, we embarked on a course of training that involved walking. This was not your normal walking, as used for getting around on an everyday sort of basis; no, this was a mode of walking that no mentally fit human being would employ to go anywhere for fear of attracting the wrong kind of attention. It involved a strong, pumping arm action, which was fair enough, but it also involved arching the back and making the arse stick out in a rather rude, baboon-like fashion. Then with legs straight, overextending the knee and always having to keep one foot on the ground at any one time, it resulted in a Max Wall type of somewhat vulgar mincing, at speed, with the hips and bottom swaying exaggeratedly from side to side.

This was competitive walking, and most athletics meetings had several walking races as part of the day's events. You don't see it so often today, but back then it was quite usual to see people waddling along at the side of the road, in training, much the same as joggers are a common sight now. I endured the humiliation of this by going training only either early in the morning or at dusk, and even then I couldn't escape the smirks and sometimes outright laughter, occasionally accompanied by rude pointing, of people in the street, let alone the jeers and heckles often alluding to the possibility that I might have shat myself.

There is only so much a sixteen-year-old can take and it all came to an abrupt end some weeks later when, at an athletics meeting, I was to enter a walking event for the first time, possibly a two- or three-mile race. I set off at a cracking pace, leaving the others way behind almost immediately. When I was nearly at the point of lapping them for the first time, after only a lap and a half and thinking, these people are hopeless, I started to tire, and gradually throughout the subsequent laps they began to overtake me, slowly but surely, one by one. I couldn't possibly keep up the pace I had started out with. When the last one passed me, I felt my face blush with shame and the old panic begin to balloon in my chest. I had no choice: I simply couldn't be the last person over that finishing line, and in this instance not only would I be the last person to finish, but I would also be the last by at least a lap.

So in panic mode and beginning to feel nauseous, I concocted a plan and, minutes later, I started to stagger and wobbled off the track on to the grass. After reeling around for a few seconds, I collapsed and lay there, doubled up, clutching my stomach and groaning. I waited. First there were shouts and then the thud of feet on turf as a couple of St John Ambulance men came running towards me. I was about to 'bravely attempt' to get up on to my feet when a stretcher was thrown to the ground, right in my eyeline. The day was going to end well after all! This was more than I could have hoped for, being carried off on a stretcher by two burly ambulance men, every pair of eyes in the stadium upon me, the centre of a drama, of my very own making; the young girl who all but had the race in the bag, only to have it snatched from her grasp by a mystery illness. The girl who had soldiered on, in agonising pain, until she could take no more: she is nothing less than a heroine!

Then Bernard, the coach, arrived, rudely

interrupting the kindly paramedics, one of whom was holding my hand and telling me I was going to be fine.

'No, it's all right, fellas, you won't be needing that.'

Sure he wasn't talking about the stretcher!

'She's just run out of breath. I told you, didn't I, to pace yourself? What were you playing at?'

'My stomach . . . I can't get up!'

'Don't be so silly, of course you can. It's just a bit of stitch.'

And with that he sent my knights in shining armour away. I watched them amble off, the glorious stretcher swaying empty between them.

'Come on! On your feet. You'll get cold down there.'

I wanted to rise up and lamp him one on the chin. Then others started to arrive and gawp, gathering around me in a little, curious circle.

'Is she all right?'

'Yes! Course she is! She just went off like shit off a shovel and then found she'd got no puff! I wouldn't mind but I've been training her for weeks.'

Oh, the humiliation! Now, I was no longer the tragic heroine, but the idiot who had whizzed off at a ridiculous speed, got a stitch and had to stop; it was almost worth telling them the truth! Of course I never did, but Bernard knew, and I knew that he knew, and he knew that I knew that he knew. I never went back.

I was to start my time at Holly Lodge, or 'The Lodge' as we called it, in Form 3C. This was the bottom class of four streams and it was here that

118

I made my friends, some of whom I am still in touch with today. On the first day we filed into our new classroom, which was in a semi-basement that half looked out on to the playing field at that side of the school, and our teacher, a tall, grim-faced young woman who wore Edna Everage glasses, taught History and seemed to be in a permanent state of resentment, took the register. After each name was called the appropriate girl replied by shouting out, 'Here!' When my turn came, just as I was about to answer, I felt a slight prick in my left buttock and my 'Here' popped out in a little falsetto yelp, causing the teacher to pause momentarily with a baleful look over the top of her glasses. I turned to see what was going on, to be met with a huge smile from the girl behind. She had stuck her regulation geometry set compasses point into my bum cheek. Her smile was quickly wiped away by the sound of her own name being called out like a threat but we had bonded in that moment. Not that I want you to think, dear reader, that the piercing of one of my body parts with a sharp implement is mandatory for the forming of any friendships on my part, but this girl had huge charisma and attracted around her a little clique of which I was very proud to be a member.

It was at her twelfth birthday party, during a game of Postman's Knock, that I had my first kiss from a boy who lived across the road from her. I would see him every time I went to her house and had taken to going there on the way home from school. He was a couple of years older, with cornflower-blue eyes, and was made more attractive by the fact that his father was in prison for robbing gas meters. It was exciting knowing what my mother's reaction would be if she were to discover this liaison, which, needless to say, in due course she did. My brother Kevin spotted me with him one day when he had walked me home and that was it; not only did he tell the boy to clear off, but he then got my mother involved, telling her that I was mixing with a rough lad from a certain part of Smethwick. Much as my mother was fond of my friend, I was duly forbidden to 'go hanging about there'. It was an area she referred to as the 'bottom end of Smethwick'. I tried to reason with her, explaining that there was no 'bottom end', it was all 'bottom', but she wouldn't have it and so I continued to go in secret.

I felt instantly at ease with the girls in my class and was able to let go of most of the self-consciousness that I had suffered at the prep with regard to the way I spoke, where I lived (I never invited anyone home, during the time I was there), what my parents did for a living, where we went on holiday (the summer before my last year at the prep, we went to Margate, another bone-numbingly long journey, and, whilst there, made a day trip to Calais). When I went back to the prep school after the summer holidays, girls were discussing their two or three weeks in Italy, Scotland and Cornwall. So when I was asked where we had been, I said, heart racing, that we had toured the south coast, well, we had visited Folkestone, as well as Margate, and been to France. Inevitably one of these girls, who had spent the previous summer in Provence, then asked where in France had we gone. I was at a loss, not having been anywhere else, and so had to admit it was Calais.

'What, the port? You don't mean where you get off the ferry?'

'Erm . . . ' Someone behind me let out a little squeak of laughter. 'Yes.'

'What? You got off the ferry and didn't go any further?'

I tried to laugh it off. 'Yes.'

'But Calais is horrible. People race off the ferry to get out of it.'

'Well . . . '

I was paralysed by my dissembling and stood there, my face boiling, my heart now deafening in my ears. The little group dispersed, suddenly distracted by the clanging of the bell for lessons to begin. As I went to my desk and lifted its lid, the girl at the next desk said, 'I went on a day trip to Calais once. I loved it.' I wanted to cry.

While I was there I was always ashamed of virtually anything that might give a clue to my background, right down to the material that my school uniform was made of, my mother always going for the cheaper option. My panama hat, which we were required to wear at the prep during the summer term, was unlike anyone else's, theirs being neat, pale and pork-pie shaped, and mine being large, yellowish and battered-looking with a misshapen, unruly brim, the sort of thing that wouldn't have looked out of place on a scarecrow or on Guy Fawkes, on top of the bonfire. It caused endless embarrassment, not

121

least when I walked up our street upon arriving home from school, running the gauntlet of the neighbourhood kids, all giggling and making country yokel noises, and Dermot sitting smirking on his wall. I didn't have the courage to remove it until at least year three, fearing that somehow the nuns would find out. And all this owing to the fact that Mum had found a bargain in a closing-down sale at a shop in town.

But at Holly Lodge, I slowly began to discover a pride, both in my family and in my home. I recognised my peers and found my place amongst them pretty quickly. I was the cheeky clown, calling out in class with comments to make the other girls, and sometimes the teachers, laugh. I would impersonate the headmistress, my grandmother, or a nutty woman who lived up the road, various pop stars and singers: anything to get those laughs. I recognised a power in it; it enabled me to be seen. It was inclusive; it both put things in perspective and cut them down to size. It stopped the world from being overwhelming and it was a lethal weapon.

The school had a drama society, but because of my daily performances in class I had little use for it. Also I wasn't generally keen on the girls who belonged to it, thinking them uppity and cliquey. Only once did I appear in one of the school's yearly drama productions, put on in conjunction with the boys' school, and that was as Moth in *A Midsummer Night's Dream* in my first year. I found it thrilling: not only the opportunity to perform, but also a chance to go and rehearse in the out-of-bounds boys' school, where it was to be performed and where I proceeded to fall head over heels in love with the sixth-form boy playing Lysander, a stocky youth with thick, curly blond hair and very pink cheeks. It was an infatuation from afar as he seemed like a man and I felt like a child, and I doubt that he had any inkling of it. I conducted myself in rehearsals much the same as I did in lessons: playing the fool, making everyone laugh and constantly interrupting the male teacher, whom I also had a bit of a crush on.

Finally, one day, this teacher dragged me in gorgeous masterly fashion to one side and said, 'Do you know why I cast you as Moth?'

'No,' I said, looking up flirtatiously.

'Oh, then let me tell you; it's because like a moth you are a bloody nuisance!'

The thrill I felt, standing backstage on that first night, listening to the excited chatter of an expectant audience, my face plastered in Leichner's greasepaint, dressed in my costume of lilac muslin wings that were attached by elastic to my thumbs, and a tunic, made from pink and lilac muslin and satin by my mum on the old Singer sewing machine, is basically the same stomach-churning, mouth-drying, heart-banging thrill that I feel nowadays waiting in the wings to go on, on a first night. And wherever it may be, that warm dark space at the back of a flat (a piece of scenery), smelling of wood, scenery paint and dust baked by stage lights, half lit by the spill from the stage, filled with whispered apprehension and expectancy, will always remind me of that night long ago, on the creaking, cramped side-stage of the school hall at Holly Lodge boys'. However, I never went for any more parts, preferring the instant fix I got from calling out and clowning in class.

Despite its rather genteel-sounding name, Holly Lodge Grammar was by no means a school for young ladies. In fact, Smethwick Hall, the secondary modern, where I would have gone had my 'borderline' pass not been looked upon kindly, was considered by some to be a better school, where the behaviour of the pupils, in particular, and the standard of the work in many instances was superior. It was said that there were several parents each year who, even though their girls had passed the eleven-plus, had elected to send them to Smethwick Hall, thinking that they would most likely mix with a nicer class of girl and fare better generally. This was apparently not true of Holly Lodge boys' school, which seemed to enjoy a higher reputation.

Although we had a uniform — school beret, navy-blue mac, blazer and skirt (gymslip in the first year), white blouse, navy-blue and gold tie, and black, flat, sensible shoes, accompanied by a satchel or briefcase — when I arrived that first day, bright and stiff in my new clothes, I found that the uniforms of many of the older girls, especially those in the lower streams higher up the school, were distorted out of all recognition. Berets, if worn at all, were folded in half and pinned on to the very back of the head with a couple of hairgrips. Hair would then be backcombed and lacquered up and over the top, often to gravity-defying heights, so that the thing was barely visible, while it was kept in place by hairspray that had more in common with glue than anything used today. Ties were discarded or left loosely hanging around the mid-bosom region; blouse collars were worn up with the tips turned down; skirts, which were meant to be mid-knee in length, were rolled over at the waist and hoicked, St Trinian-like, up to mid-thigh and, until tights came in, often revealing stocking tops and suspenders. Satchels, long abandoned, were replaced by 'gondola' baskets, shaped like boats, which were meant to be used only for domestic science. In the first two or three years I was there, shoes, not exactly fitting the sensible label, tended to be flat but with pointed toes and steel caps on the heels, so that the noise as girls walked along the stone corridors, in large numbers, from lesson to lesson, dragging their feet, was like something out of heavy industry, and any slipping or skidding, as happened frequently, would cause sparks to fly.

Out of school, en masse, some of these girls could be quite an alarming sight, trailing along Smethwick High Street on the way home, striking sparks, arms linked, four abreast, making passers-by jump into the road to get out of their way. Discipline varied hugely from class to class. Certain teachers hadn't got the power of personality required to get our attention and their classes were nothing short of mayhem, with everyone talking at the top of their voices, wandering around willy-nilly, completely ignoring the teacher's pleas to sit down and be quiet. On one occasion we barricaded the door with desks so that the teacher couldn't get in; on another we barricaded ourselves in a corner behind piled-up desks so that the teacher could barely see us. I can remember a teacher giving up and leaving in tears on more than one occasion.

My insecurity, although greatly reduced after leaving my junior school, still manifested itself at odd times in odd ways. For instance, I would never customise my uniform; in fact, my uniform made me feel safe, and I never looked forward to non-uniform days, always feeling awkward and embarrassed in whatever I wore, either the clothes feeling too childish for me or me feeling too childish for the clothes. Doing something different with your blazer or your skirt meant putting your head above the parapet; it meant you were open to comment, open to judgement. I never felt good enough about myself to do that. Choosing to personalise your uniform was a sign of wanting to be grown up and part of me just didn't want that; I wanted to be little and cute and funny, and to be loved for it. 'Love the baba . . . love the baby.' Even graduating from socks to tights was a cause for anxiety. So I put it off and put it off, becoming the last in my year to do it, first wearing thick ones that were more childish-looking lest anyone should say: who do you think you are? Because I didn't know.

This anxiety about clothes and my appearance reached a crescendo at around the age of fourteen or fifteen when one of the coolest girls in the class was taking a group of girls to see

Thank Your Lucky Stars for her birthday and I was invited to go along. This was a weekly Saturday-night pop show, filmed for ITV on Sunday nights in front of a live audience in Birmingham's Alpha studio. It boasted the first network television appearance of the Beatles and had made a star out of a local sixteen-year-old girl from the Black Country called Janice Nicholls who, when sitting on a panel to judge the latest releases, started a national catchphrase with, 'I'll give it foive,' in her thick Wednesbury accent, meaning, I'll give it five marks out of five.

A couple of weeks before we were due to go, I began to get into a state about what I should wear. Nothing was good enough. I scoured shops with money I had begged from my father and nothing was right; but what was right? I had no idea. So, just as in the walking race, I concocted a plan. I would just be off school, ill, and therefore unable to go. So two days before the event, I took to my bed, claiming that I felt sick. Then at lunchtime I had some soup and proceeded to make myself vomit it up. When my mother returned from work and brought me up something to eat, I did the same thing.

I continued to do this until the day after the girl's birthday but by this time I really did feel poorly and the doctor was summoned. He said it was obviously a tummy bug and prescribed some kind of antibiotic. For two whole weeks I lay prostrate on the sitting-room sofa, every turn of my head making me retch, unable to keep anything down except for the odd mouthful of water, weakening by the day. I was astounded and secretly thrilled that I had the power to make all of this happen and I was lapping up my mother's care and concern until the doctor returned for the third time and, worried that I had shown little if any improvement, started to talk of a possible hospitalisation.

Now I really was scared. The next day with monumental effort I arose from my sick bed and for the first time in two weeks I looked in the mirror, something I was quite capable of spending hours doing and which I did on most days, fiddling with my hair, picking at my skin, daubing on eye make-up. But on this day, as I stood weakly swaying in front of the mirror that hung above the fireplace in the sitting room, I saw why their conversation had taken on its frightened tone and why they had spoken with urgency about a stay in hospital. It was the face of someone else. I moved in closer, unable to take in the transformation. My hair was flat with grease and matted for the want of a good wash and brush; my skin had gone sheet-white with a yellowish-green tinge at the edges; the hollows beneath my cheek-bones were so deep that it almost looked as if I had a five o'clock shadow; my lips, shrivelled and cracked, had lost all definition and were virtually the same colour as my skin, and my eyes were enormous. This last effect I would quite liked to have kept. I stared into eyes that were strange yet familiar, like those of a relative, and I watched as big, shiny tears welled up and toppled over my bottom lashes, landing hot on to my bony chest. I touched the glass and whispered, 'I'm so sorry.'

And so began my recovery. When I finally returned to school, people gawped as I passed them in the corridor and didn't want to tackle me at hockey practice lest, as one friend put it, I should 'snap'. Although I had taken some pleasure in the attention I had received and my new-found power to make myself ill just whenever I wished, I was frightened by the fact that I could simply make myself believe I was sick and then become so, and by the subsequent way in which my body then took over. What if I couldn't have come back? This thought crossed my mind and made me shudder on many an occasion during the weeks that followed.

Throughout my entire time at Holly Lodge I felt younger than my peers. With the onset of puberty a lot of the girls in my class suddenly appeared a good few years older than me. Some looked as if they could be about thirty with a couple of kids, whilst others looked as if they were about nine. I was of the nine-year-old variety. A lot of them were sexually active and, if not, had a good working knowledge of how you went about things. I had no experience apart from a bit of kissing and fumbling. My sex education started when playing with my friends in Lightwoods Park aged about eight. One of them drew my attention to two dogs, one mounting the other, and said, 'That's what your mum and dad do.' I took issue with this, thinking it to be a personal insult to my parents, stating that it couldn't possibly be so because my mother was a Catholic. Even if it was true I didn't really want this piece of information and did my best to rid my head of the image of my mother on all fours and my dad behind her, slavering and looking slightly hairy.

Then once at secondary school, I laboured under the delusion, born of a rumour spread throughout my year, that if a girl had splayed feet, it meant that she had lost her virginity. This didn't quite make sense when I looked at the girl a couple of years above, who was from a very religious family, wore very long skirts, sported two plaits down to her bottom and was nicknamed 'Miss Smethwick 1918', but I still believed it and it didn't occur to me that my mother's feet, for instance, pointed straight out in front and what about those unfortunate girls with pigeon toes? I supposed them to be the ones I had heard about, who experienced a great deal of pain on losing their virginity, which was evidently to do with the wrenching apart of their toes and the resultant strain on their ankles. I was also told by some informed soul that you could get pregnant by sitting in a married man's bathwater, so I always gave the bath a good rinse if my father had been in before me.

My mother never broached the subject of sex education until I was sixteen, when she asked without looking at me, in a little girl's voice, 'Do you know about periods, Julie?'

'Well, I should hope so, Mum, I've been having them for two years.'

She knew this of course but obviously had not known how to tackle the issue. My periods starting late didn't help in the maturity stakes. The actual moment took place at age fourteen when I was staying with relatives of a friend and didn't feel I could ask the elderly childless couple for assistance, so I ended up stealing a pillow case from the airing cupboard and shoving it between my legs. I went home on the bus in some discomfort and got off it walking like John Wayne. When I look back, it seems that there was also something engineered about my immaturity with my peers. If I played a childish role, I was no threat and therefore more lovable, and I felt safe in it, but despite setting myself apart in this way I managed to maintain a prominent position in the group, primarily by being good at sport but mainly by entertaining them and playing the jester.

There was also insecurity around food. For the mid-morning break, which we referred to as 'lunch', people brought in sandwiches, crisps and fruit. I never did this. I spent the whole of the fifteen- or twenty-minute break begging titbits off the other girls. Seeing no shame in this, I went from one to the other.

'Please, please, can I have a crisp? Can I have a sandwich? Oh, go on! Can I have another one?'

They quite rightly got miffed: 'For Christ's sake, why don't you bring your own?'

It amazes me now how I put up with the humiliation involved, day after day, and it went on for two or three years. I had always blamed this odd behaviour firstly on the fact that my mother would never fund a daily packet of crisps and secondly on the fact that I felt I would be shown up in some way by whatever food I brought in. However, seeing as some girls brought in plain bread and butter, and others bread and dripping, I don't think that this can really be the case. Rather than any kind of shame or embarrassment being the cause of my daily cadging, I think it had more to do with the fact that if I had nothing, nothing could be taken from me. As I was the younger sister of two brothers, anything, and especially sweets or snacks, was open season. Even now I feel enraged when anyone takes food off my plate.

Although every school report said things like 'Julia could do better; is not working to her full potential; does not concentrate', as the years went by at Holly Lodge, my confidence grew and my schoolwork gradually improved. I became good at French, English and Geography, and in the fifth year a select group of us went up into the second stream, 5L. I got four GCEs, English Literature, English Language, French and Geography, while failing everything else. In the case of History, where I did no revision at all, I achieved an unmarkable grade nine. I had sat in front of the exam paper, staring at it, unable to answer a single question, so, not wishing to sit there for an hour and a half conspicuously doing nothing, I wrote about a pair of new shoes I had bought the week before, a holiday in Weymouth from a few years back and what I expected to have for my tea.

The GCEs were the peak of my academic achievement at Holly Lodge, for once I was in the sixth form things began to quickly slide. Many of my friends had left as in those days, particularly in working-class families, the imperative was to go out and get a job. My father never really expressed an opinion on this, just wanting me to be happy, but my mother, despite her penny-pinching fear of debt and poverty, always pushed the idea that education, particularly for the boys, was paramount. At the start of the new academic year various girls from different forms were now working alongside each other for the first time and so the whole dynamic changed and new friendships were formed. It was to be the setting for a very shameful episode.

I had become friends with an entirely new group, which took me away from some of my old friends. This little clique was led by an exceedingly bright and charismatic girl who possessed a wicked sense of humour. Whilst somewhat scared of her, like the others in our little group I was both captivated and in awe of her. After a few weeks she started to take against a certain girl, making snide comments and funny asides about her, often followed by crude little cartoons of her victim, which highlighted her bodily imperfections in a most exact and comic way and sometimes ended up on the sixth-form notice-board. Although underneath I felt distinctly uncomfortable and guilty about being part of this bullying, I did nothing to discourage it; in fact, it was the opposite. I, along with the others, supported it with giggles and laughter, joining in with vicious gossip about the poor girl that made our leader hoot with delight and made us, in turn, glow with pride. We had done good! And whilst someone else was the scapegoat, she would not direct her acid wit towards us. It was too late anyway; we were already ensnared and had now become her devoted acolytes.

But then it began to escalate; a chair leg was unscrewed in the school hall just before assembly, hoping that, when this poor girl sat on it, it would collapse in front of everyone. I sat a couple of rows back, holding my breath, hoping against hope that she would miss assembly, or choose a different chair, and praying that, if she were to sit in it, the chair would stay intact; it did. I breathed a huge sigh of relief but joined our leader in expressing disappointment.

Then another horrid plan was hatched: this time to rub butter on the pedals of her bicycle and put pepper in her beret. I stood with the others, unable to bear the thought of it, yet heartily agreeing to it, feigning glee and excitement; wanting nothing to do with it, yet lacking the courage to walk away. This girl had been a good friend of mine and I felt heartsore at the undeserved grief that I knew we were causing her, watching over the weeks as her bubbly personality seemed to melt away and her rounded frame became skeletal, as if she were trying to disappear. When it came to carrying out the plan, fearful of being caught and wanting to distance myself as much as possible from the dastardly act, I said that I would keep watch from the library window upstairs. I didn't; I just sat at a table staring blindly at some reference book or other, wishing I was somewhere else. I feel huge shame today at my cowardice and regret when I think of her sitting in the sixth-form classroom later that afternoon, her face burning from the pepper, her eyes smarting and bloodshot.

A couple of evenings after this, I was at home, lying on the sofa in the sitting room, watching television, when someone knocked at the front door. On answering it I found our victim's mother standing there. She looked small and pale with a headscarf tied tightly round her head. She asked whether she could come in. I was very scared, knowing of course why she had come and worried that my mother, who was only in the kitchen, might walk in at any moment. She made a little speech in a voice I thought was both angry and close to tears. She said that her daughter was desperately upset and didn't deserve this treatment; it wasn't fair and why were we doing it? I stood there dumbly, unable to answer any of her questions. When eventually she left, I showed her to the front door but just as she was about to walk off, she turned around and said, 'She's got a heart of gold.' And I knew it was true. I went straight to my bedroom, flung myself on the bed and cried myself to sleep, waking the next morning still in my uniform. I told the others the next day that the girl's mother had turned up at my door. They were shocked and said little, I suspect fearing that there could be repercussions of some sort, and the whole sorry episode drew to a close.

The incident was duly filed away, in 'the never to be looked at again' file, at the back of my head, but like anything that isn't aired it began to smell. Several years ago I could ignore it no longer and decided to write to the girl we had bullied. I wanted her to know my side of it and how I had felt, and I wanted to acknowledge my infantile cruelty, but more than anything, I suppose, I wanted forgiveness. I apologised for the pain she must have suffered and for my weakness and cowardice, at not sticking up for her or at least walking away. She, of course, was generous in her forgiveness and made light of it all. It is a tribute to her strength of character that she withstood the onslaught of our childish bitchery and I'm reminded of this every time I read of yet another child being kept off school or, worse still, committing suicide as a result of bullying.

The work in the lower sixth was a lot more challenging than ever before and so, it seemed, was getting up in the morning. Generally, having overslept and missed the school bus, I would amble in, in the late morning or at dinnertime, until I got so far behind that I couldn't make head nor tail of Geography A level, and Molière's *L'Avare* might just as well have been written in Mandarin. Eventually at the end of the lower-sixth year, Mr Taylor, our deputy head, took me to one side and gave me a letter addressed to my parents. Mr Taylor — who unfortunately didn't take us for A level and with whom a great number of girls, myself included, had been romantically infatuated — was a brilliantly inspired Geography teacher who got thirty hormonally challenged and totally uninterested girls through Geography GCE by the sheer force of his unique personality. You couldn't help but remember his lessons; he was witty, funny and eccentric and often attracted the attention of a chattering girl by hitting her on the back of the head with a piece of chalk, thrown from some distance and with deadly accuracy. Today, of course, he would probably be up for assault.

'Julia . . . ' Teachers always called me Julia. 'We don't want you to come back next year. You will never get your A levels now; it's a complete waste of everyone's time, as you are too far behind. You simply haven't put in the work. And we don't like your subversive influence.'

I looked up into the intense blue eyes behind the horn-rimmed specs whilst scrabbling for the meaning of 'subversive'. Did it refer to my truancy, which had got so bad that I was hardly ever there? Or could it have referred to the time when I had gone into an empty classroom, egged on by my friend, and thrown a metal tubular chair at a thin wooden partition, on the other side of which was our tight-bunned and straight-faced form teacher who, in her terrible Edward Heath French accent, was in the process of teaching the upper sixth French group? It was reported that the resulting clatter had almost caused her to collapse with fright.

I went home that afternoon, posted the letter to my parents, unread, into a dustbin outside a shop and told my mother that I had reached a momentous decision: I would take up nursing. There was no need for me to stay on at school; I would prefer to get a job for a year and save some money (the word 'save' was always a good one with my mother). Surprisingly, without any discussion, she agreed. I went straight upstairs and looked up 'subversive'.

8

The Little Nurse — Work

My first full-time job was in an insurance office in Birmingham. Prior to this, aged about fifteen, I had been employed on a Saturday and during the school holidays at C&A Modes in the centre of Birmingham, where, along with my friend Chris, I worked backstage, as it were, unpacking the crates and parcels of blouses, dresses and skirts and other assorted items of clothing, then counting each one, after mentally tearing holes in its sartorial tattiness, logging it and hanging it up.

We then found much more interesting employment at a sweet shop in Smethwick. It offered two advantages: there was no boss present, and every Wednesday night and all day Sunday we were left to our own devices. The shop sold every kind of sweet and, owing to the fact that there was no till roll and no real record of what was delivered and subsequently sold, we gorged ourselves freely on crisps, ice lollies, raspberry ripples, Bassett's sherbet fountain (a personal favourite), fruit gums and Caramac chocolate ad nauseam, literally. We gave away packets of cigarettes to boys we fancied and spent hours on the telephone, playing daft tricks on members of the public, claiming that we were from a market research company and asking them lewd questions about their sex lives and body parts, or telling them we were from the telephone exchange and then asking them to make a high-pitched squeal down the phone, as a means of 'testing the line, madam'. Needless to say, it was not a job that lasted long, once the rather absentee proprietor cottoned on to what was happening.

The insurance office, on the other hand, was a proper job. The office was divided into sections, each one consisting of a couple of rows of desks, with four desks to each row. Being the most junior, I was on the end of the second row and was in charge of finding the files that corresponded to the post that came in each morning. I soon tired of the tedious nature of the work and would spend as much time as possible staring wistfully out of the window at the traffic on its way in and out of town, longing to be in one of the cars speeding along and, more importantly, away from what I began to see as a kind of prison. Post began to pile up when I couldn't find particular files and eventually I resorted to putting it down the toilets. This practice was brought to a close when I came in one morning to find that the Ladies' toilets were closed due to some sort of flooding; there was water coming out from under the door and a plumber was going in and out with pliers and buckets. Luckily the blockage was cleared, the offending substance being too wet and mushy to be identified, but I wasn't the only junior with a red face that morning.

I sat next to a girl, a slightly more senior junior, called Linda and immediately created the same role that I played in school. We were always gossiping and I would spend most of the day trying to make her laugh. The names of various clients, as we went through the files, sent us both into purple-faced, hissing hysteria, often causing Linda to get under her desk so as not to be seen by Miss Kelly, our spinsterly section leader, whose head was continually whipping round in our direction to shush us. Sometimes I would scour the filing cabinets, not for files in connection with the morning post, but purely for names to make my new friend laugh. Cornelius Clark was an explosive favourite; John Smellie and Katarina Balls were others that can still get me going today. Every so often this behaviour would be punctuated by a serious bollocking from Miss Kelly after which we would knuckle down to work for a couple of days, only to slowly but surely return to our old ways. Linda was fifteen and had already been at the place for about six months.

'How old am ya?' she asked on my first day there.

'Seventeen,' I replied.

'Am yer engaged?'

'No.'

'Jesus! Yer ent engaged?' Her voice rose into a falsetto.

'No, I haven't got a boyfriend.'

'Blimey! If I ent engaged by the time I'm seventeen, I'll kill me bloomin' self.'

About ten years later, on a visit home, I saw a

woman I'm pretty sure was her, pushing a baby in a stroller along Smethwick High Street with two other children in tow. She had a badly bruised eye and a swollen and cut lip.

At the age of eighteen, in May 1968, I enrolled in the Queen Elizabeth Hospital School of Nursing in Edgbaston, Birmingham. My mother was never prouder, before or since. It is what she would have wanted for herself, had she had the opportunity. Frustratingly for her, her parents sent her younger sister, Agnes, to England to train as a nurse, but she never took it up, becoming a secretary instead.

My first ward, after six weeks in the preliminary nursing school, was an ophthalmic ward in the bowels of the hospital, dealing mainly with cataract operations. The ward Sister, a Sister Hartwell, was a relatively elderly and rather eccentric Irishwoman, who had lived in the nursing home across the road from the hospital since she was seventeen. This was a detail that I found both depressing and claustrophobic as at this point she was apparently sixty-seven. She never called me by my name; it was always 'Come here, Little Nurse' or 'Where's the little nurse?' booming embarrassingly from one end of the corridor to the other. Her huge blue eyes peered piercingly at you through thick dark lashes, over half-moon glasses perched midway down a largish, Roman nose. It was a slightly alarming stare for she could do it at any moment, and often for no fathomable reason. You might be engaged in some nursing activity or other and suddenly she would be at your side, a little closer than was comfortable, staring directly at the side of your face. She was equally eccentric when dealing with the patients; in fact the drug round, which occurred four times a day, was something to be endured by nurse and patient alike.

In order to administer drugs, in the form of drops, to the eye, it was first of all necessary to dilate the tear duct, which was done with a fairly small, pointed, sharp-looking implement. For the purposes of carrying this out, Sister whose eyesight wasn't all that it should be, would get up on to the bed, shouting down at the patient to relax and keep still. Then on her knees, wobbling about on the mattress and hovering over the victim, millimetres from their face with the said implement, she would, whilst peering myopically through her half-glasses, attempt to dilate the tear duct. If she didn't succeed the first time, she would loudly berate the terrified patient, blaming their inability to keep still for her inaccuracy, at which point they usually didn't have a chance in hell of keeping their eyes open out of sheer terror.

When I was on duty I generally accompanied her on the drug rounds and dreaded this procedure, because it often resulted in her shouting in exasperation, 'Little Nurse! Get up here now, you, and finish this off! You should be doing this, not me! You have the eyes for it. Come on!' On one occasion, red-faced with embarrassment, I started to move towards the patient with this dilating tool and just as I was about to pull the patient's lower lid down to insert it, she slapped me on the arse with such force I nearly blinded the poor woman I was trying to treat and I even let out a little screech of fright, for which I had to apologise to the patient.

'What are you playing at? Get up there on the bed. Let the dog see the rabbit. You can't do this standing by the bed, you're too small, Little Nurse.'

When I lost my fear of her, I became very fond of this Sister. Apart from being scarily hilarious on a day-to-day basis, she was immensely kind to the staff and I know she was fond of me. Although I worked on several different wards during my nursing life, my experience on this one was unlike any other.

I never really settled into nursing, feeling that I couldn't possibly be up to the task as well as ultimately knowing that I was there to please my mother and to fulfil her ambition rather than my own. I was terrified of being given any responsibility, constantly doubting my own judgement and ability. Mind you, this wasn't without cause. Within the first few weeks on the wards, I whipped out what I thought were my Spencer Wells forceps, which were kept in my top pocket and were used to clamp off tubing. In this instance the tubing concerned linked a bag of blood that was being used in a blood transfusion to the patient. Snapping them on to the tube, I found that it was not the forceps at all but my surgical scissors. I was sent back to the nurses' home to change, looking as if I had just performed major abdominal surgery with a blunt kitchen knife and no skill whatsoever.

Another unfortunate incident occurred, involving a faulty bedpan washer. Bedpans were placed in these contraptions, the heavy, round, nautical-looking door would be closed and then for several minutes the thing would spray the pans with hot water with the force of a fire hose. However, on this occasion, no sooner had I placed the bedpan inside and closed the door than it somehow fell open again almost immediately, but sadly not before the water had started to spray. Luckily, because the machine was faulty, the water was breathtakingly cold and it hit me full in the face and chest, sending me reeling backwards against the sluice room wall, where I remained in shock until the cycle had finished, my beautiful, pristine nurse's cap, which was made of paper, wilted and flattened into a sodden mulch. Whilst I stood there, rigid and winded, being battered by the spray, the staff nurse, having seen the incident through the porthole window in the door, came in and stood looking at me with an amused smirk on her face. When the water finally stopped, she said hand on hip, 'What is this? *Carry on Nursing?*' And then wearily, 'Go and get changed.' And so ensued another embarrassing walk back to the nurses' home in disarray, having to endure titters and 'witty' comments. Halfway back I suddenly remembered my cap and tried to take it off, only to find it ripping away in soggy handfuls.

I never got into any serious trouble, but came close to it once when I was working on a men's surgical ward. I was on the night shift and on this particular ward the consultant in charge insisted on every patient giving a mid-stream specimen of urine. This process involved first cleaning the area with cotton-wool balls dipped into a mild disinfectant, which was poured into a small foil galley pot. Then the patient would begin to urinate, catching some pee mid-stream in another little pot.

One night after most of the men had gone to sleep an old man appeared like an apparition at the end of the ward. It seemed that he should have been admitted earlier on in the day and, for some reason that neither I nor the senior nurse could glean, he had turned up at eleven o'clock. I showed him to his bed and, drawing the curtains around it, went to make a cup of tea for him, leaving him to get into his pyjamas. When I returned he was in bed and it was only then that I remembered the required specimen, the requisites for which were on his bedside locker.

'Oh, Mr Jackson, I'm going to need a specimen of urine from you before you go to sleep,' I whispered.

He smiled at me benignly and nodded, 'Yes.'

I waited, he smiled.

'Yes, I need you to do a specimen,' I said a little louder.

'WHAT?' This was extremely loud and rasping, and several people near by started to stir. I tried to keep my own voice down.

'Yes, now we are going to have to be very quiet, Mr Jackson, because everyone is asleep.'

'Fat bloody chance!' came a weary voice from the next bed.

'WHAT? YES . . . GOODNIGHT.' And with that he slid down under the covers and turned on his side, pulling them up over his head.

'No, no, no, Mr Jackson.' Now my own voice was rising in volume. 'You can't go to sleep yet.'

'No, neither can we!' came a voice from the bed opposite.

I pulled the covers back, at which Mr Jackson shot up and looked at me as if I was an intruder in his own bedroom.

'WHAT'S GOIN' ON? WHAT ARE YOU DOIN'?'

By now everyone was awake, and requests for cups of tea or exasperated moans of 'Oh Jesus!' and 'For Christ's sake!' were coming from all directions. After much negotiation and by this time virtually shouting at the top of my voice, I managed to get him out of bed, although he looked totally confused as to the reason why. I showed him the little pack on his bedside locker and told him that we needed to go down to the ward toilets. He seemed to pick up the word 'toilet' and spun around.

'THERE'S NO NEED TO SHOUT! PEOPLE MIGHT HEAR!'

'Shame *you* can't,' came the weary voice from next door again.

Eventually I part coaxed and part manhandled him down the ward and into the toilets. Once inside I showed him again the pack containing the little foil container of disinfectant and explained. 'Mr Jackson, I want you to clean yourself with this.' I handed him the cotton-wool balls. He stared down at them and then up at me. I dipped them into the disinfectant and pointed at his flies. At this he sprang back, cowering, his mouth agape with horror, protecting his nethers like a footballer defending himself from a free kick.

'WHAT'S YOUR GAME? I'M OLD ENOUGH TO BE YOUR GRANDFATHER!'

'No, no, Mr Jackson, I just want a specimen.'

And I showed him the little specimen jar. He then seemed to understand and I went through the instructions, with him nodding and loudly affirming his understanding at every stage. Then with fingers crossed I left him to it. Half an hour or so later I went to check in the toilets, to find that the pot containing the disinfectant was empty but so was the specimen jar, and the old man had gone. When I went back to his bed to discover what had happened, he was again snuggled down under the covers and this time clearly asleep, so I waited until morning.

'Good morning, Mr Jackson, what did you do with your specimen?'

'YES, YES, YES . . . ' he said dismissively. 'I DRANK THE MEDICINE.'

I stood there for several seconds, unable to take in what he had said. 'Oh my God,' I murmured ever so quietly when I realised that he had in fact drunk the disinfectant and simply had a pee straight into the toilet.

'AND WHAT'S MORE IT GAVE ME A BELLYACHE!'

'Oh my God!' I said again and went to make my confession to the senior nurse. I was hauled up in front of the assistant matron, who explained how irresponsible it was to leave an old deaf man etc., etc., etc.

I suppose I messed up quite a bit during my eighteen months of training, but none of my cock-ups came anywhere near that of a poor girl in my set. She was on a ward mainly filled with elderly women and one evening after bed-baths she got the brilliant idea that, instead of going round each old dear and cleaning her false teeth, she would collect all the dentures in a big bowl and wash them all together. She only realised her gaffe when it was too late and just had to guess whose belonged to whom. Patients were complaining of sore gums for weeks after, and night after night she apparently went round when they were all asleep, whipping dentures off the beside lockers and swapping them around with other people's, still trying to match the right teeth to the right mouth.

One of the most exciting places to work, I found, was the Casualty department of the General Hospital, which was situated in the centre of Birmingham and, along with the Children's, was the other major hospital that we trained at, all three being part of the United Birmingham Hospitals group. On a busy Saturday night on two or three occasions, I was sent down from my quiet men's medical ward to swell the numbers of this overstretched department. On one such occasion a very odd-looking man came in, in the small hours of the morning, walking with a strange, swinging scuttle. The conversation went like this.

'Can I help you?'

'No, dear, I wish to see a doctor.' His face was pale and sweating.

'I'm afraid the doctor's busy at the moment. Can I help?'

'No, no, I need to see the doctor. I don't want to see you, dear. It's got to be the doctor.'

Having showed him to a cubicle, I went to find the nurse in charge. Finally the doctor went in to see him, taking me with him. When we got behind the curtains, the man was standing in the corner.

'No, no, dear, I want to see the doctor, I don't want you present.' So the doctor signalled for me to leave.

Some time later, I saw the man being wheeled on a trolley, presumably to a ward, lying on his stomach with what looked like some sort of cage over the top of him covered in a blanket. It turned out that he had the handle of a wire-mesh, deep-fat fryer stuck up his bottom. When asked by the doctor how it happened to be there, the man replied, 'I 'ad an itch.' It was inserted so far up and with such force that it had pierced his colon and he had to go to theatre to have it removed.

I encountered death many times whilst nursing, but never got used to the shock of finding a bed empty when arriving on duty and discovering that someone you had got to know, whose face you'd washed, whose bed you'd made, whose bottom and feet you'd rubbed to prevent bedsores and whose family you had met and chatted with, was now dead. The first time this happened, I had come on duty for the afternoon shift, which was from two till ten, and the ward was frantically busy. Usually at the beginning of a shift the senior nurse going off duty would give notes on all the patients, so that those coming on duty would be up to speed. But on this particular day they were still carrying out their various duties; nurses were rushing up and down, curtains were pulled round beds; patients were still having their pressure areas tended to, and it was clear that help was needed. At the top of the ward, next to Sister's office, was Mr Claydon's bed. He was a long-stay patient and had been unconscious for at least a couple of weeks. Seeing that the curtains were closed around his bed, I decided that this was where I would start. I went in and immediately began chatting. We were told that unconscious patients could more than likely hear what you said, as hearing was the last sense to go in a coma. In fact, hospital gossip had it that a nurse who had talked about how fat a female patient was whilst the patient was unconscious was slapped across the face by the woman when she came round, the woman having heard everything that was said, even though she had been unconscious at the time.

Mr Claydon was lying in a normal position on his back and next to him on the table was a bowl of tepid water. Someone was obviously intending giving him a bed-bath. Thinking the water a little too cool, I set off with the bowl to the sluice room to get some more hot. On the way, the ward Sister asked what I was doing. When I said I was getting some nice hot water for Mr

Claydon, she said, 'Oh, it doesn't need to be hot, he's not exactly going to complain, is he?' I was speechless: to treat an unconscious and therefore vulnerable patient like this, even when run off your feet, was unconscionable.

I ignored her cruel assessment and carried on into the sluice room. When I returned to Mr Claydon's bed, he was in much the same position and I began the preparations for his bath, getting his toilet bag and towel from his beside locker, whilst plucking at a large bunch of black grapes in his fruit bowl and talking away as I did so.

'I expect your wife will be in soon, so we'll get you nice and fresh for her.' And so forth.

Then I pulled the sheet down and proceeded to wash him, whilst telling him what the weather was like and how busy the ward was. At one point the staff nurse popped her head through the curtains and said, 'Oh! Are you doing this? Good . . . good . . . ' Then shortly afterwards she popped her head through again and said, 'You do know he's dead, don't you?'

I felt sick and immediately, almost as a reflex action, spat out the grape I had been eating, which landed splat in the middle of her apron bib. It stayed there, all chewed and purple, for a second or two and then dropped to the floor, leaving a magenta smear in its wake. We both stared at it.

'Oh no! I've been eating his grapes!' And again I felt nauseous.

'Well, they're no different now to what they were half an hour ago when he was still alive.

You've been stuffing them down you all week. His wife must be wondering how come he gets through so many, considering he's been in a coma for two weeks. Now, do you know how to lay him out?'

'Erm . . . No.'

'Well, just carry on and wash him and then I'll be back to show you what to do.'

No sooner had she left than I began to turn him on to his side, so that I could wash his back and as I did so he let out a long, low, sinister moan, rather bovine in tone. I was so shocked that I jumped back away from him and, in doing so, banged into his locker, sending his false teeth, which were in a jar on top of it, flying to the floor and skidding out under the curtain into the ward beyond.

'He's not dead!' I shouted to no one in particular. 'There's been a mistake!'

With that the same staff nurse came back through the curtains, brandishing the teeth in one hand and, putting the top set together with the bottom ones to make them work like a mouth, said in a ventriloquist's voice, 'Oh, yes I am! I was just having a moan about you eating all my bloody grapes!'

She then went on to explain that the moan that I had heard was simply air passing through his vocal cords as he was being moved.

Death on a ward was a potentially disturbing and lowering experience for the other patients, and some ward Sisters were more sensitive in this regard than others. Later in my training I worked on a women's medical ward, which was mainly populated by the elderly, so that death on this ward, while not an everyday occurrence, was nevertheless more frequent than on other wards, and so they had the unobtrusive, laying-out procedure down to a pretty fine art. When, for instance, a corpse was being taken from its bed down to the mortuary, it was transported on a special trolley. This looked for all the world like a normal gurney, but the thin mattress on the top could be lifted up and underneath was a secret compartment, into which the body would be put, so that when being wheeled along it just looked like an empty trolley. We were instructed from the start that if anyone were to die on our watch, we were not to make a 'song and dance about it'; in fact we were to play it down, so that the other patients were unaware of what was going on. And so it was that one lunchtime when the lunches or, as we called them, the dinners were being prepared for serving, I was sent on ahead of the main course, with the soup trolley. The first patient I came to was an ancient woman by the name of Mrs Kent. I drew the trolley up to the end of her bed and dragged her bedtable to a comfortable position. She was sitting up in bed, her head resting on the pillows, staring down at her hands.

'Mrs Kent? Mrs Kent, your dinner's here. Are you going to eat some soup for me?'

I touched her arm and instantly knew from the bluish discolouration around her lips, and the inordinate stillness surrounding her, that there was a good chance she might have popped her clogs. I immediately set into motion my instructions for 'finding a patient to be deceased', and after surreptitiously feeling for her pulse and finding that there wasn't one, I decided that the best course of action was to pretend that everything was normal and to carry on with the soups. I then ladled her soup into a bowl and put it in front of her.

'Mrs Kent, here's your soup; eat it up now, while it's hot.'

I took her hand, wrapped her already icy fingers around the soup-spoon and placed it in the soup. I then hoicked her up the bed — she weighed very little — into a more normal eating-in-bed position. Now she looked as though she was poised on the brink of sampling her soup and was merely examining it first, which was fair enough as only the week before someone had found a cotton-wool ball in theirs. I then continued on up the ward, handing out soup to the other patients. When I reached the far end and was just beginning to come down the other side with my trolley, a couple of the old ladies called out to draw my attention to the fact that Mrs Kent had bent over and toppled face first into her soup.

'That soup's hot, nurse! She must have fallen asleep!'

I rushed back to her, leaving my trolley to clang into someone's bed and soup to slop out of the tureen in all directions. Then remembering my instructions to keep the whole thing low-key, I instantly slowed down and, smiling at all and sundry, spoke calmly to the corpse that was Mrs Kent.

'Now what's going on here, Florrie? You really must use your spoon, it's very bad manners to suck your soup up like that. You're going to get it everywhere.'

With a little laugh I lifted her face out of the bowl. Her nose and mouth were covered in a thick coating of pea soup. This I quickly remedied with a paper napkin, while the hand into which I had forced the soup-spoon was now raised up, still holding the spoon but as if she were going to attack someone with it. I tried to make the hand, which was now level with her ear, come back down again, but it seemed to be somehow locked and I couldn't budge it. By this time other patients were beginning to take notice.

'What's up with Florrie? Is she playing up?'

'Yes, I think she needs the bedpan.'

And with that I drew the curtain around the bed and went and told Sister, who instructed me to lay Mrs Kent out with as little fuss as possible. When I returned to the bed Mrs Kent was still in the same position, arm raised, brandishing the soupspoon, with somewhat horrifically a tiny dollop of the thick pea soup hanging from one of her nostrils. After cleaning this away I proceeded to remove the spoon from her hand, but the fingers were clasped around the handle, claw-like, rigid and tight. However, with monumental effort and a lot of cracking of finger joints, I managed to free the spoon. I could then begin to carry out the procedure of laying out, which involved the washing as before, labelling the body and tying the two big toes together, then placing the corpse in a shroud, which I couldn't quite close owing to the fact that her arm was still in the attacking position and refused to lie down. Eventually Mrs Kent was wheeled off in the secret gurney and no one said a word.

Sister suddenly collared me and said, 'Did you get her teeth?'

' . . . Her teeth?'

'Yes, you'll need to take her teeth out and put them with her belongings. Go on and catch the porter, he won't have got far.'

I chased after him, catching him just as he was in the lift and about to press the button, to take himself and Mrs Kent down to the basement. I jumped in and the lift doors closed.

The porter, as was true of a small section of the ancillary staff, was somewhat strange looking, like something out of Central Casting: Herman Munster's better-looking cousin or a member of the Addams family on work experience. He had a rather large head and a livid-looking scar across the side of his forehead. Presumably something that most of us need in order to function as normal, sociable human beings had quite recently been removed, for he never spoke as far as I knew, never made eye contact and moved with a creepy, gliding slowness. I didn't relish being alone in the lift with him, never mind alone in the lift with him alongside a corpse going down to the mortuary, in the bowels of the hospital.

'I've been sent to get her teeth.'

He opened the top of the gurney and pulled

back the shroud without saying a word. Mrs Kent greeted me with her raised arm but when I tried to open her mouth in order to retrieve the teeth, it proved impossible; it simply would not open. It was set solid in a kind of snarl and the teeth, which were tantalisingly visible, were a lurid green colour, owing to a coating of pea soup. Not particularly wanting to be in the mortuary any longer than was necessary, I was determined to get the teeth out before we got there, so I hopped up on to the gurney. Just as I was wrestling with Mrs Kent's jaw, the lift clanked and juddered to a halt at the second floor, the door opened and a cocky medical student, whom I recognised from the wards, stood there, staring.

'What on earth are you doing?' he said with a snigger.

'I'm just having a last snog before they put her in the fridge.'

'God, if anyone sees you . . . '

'I'm trying to take her teeth out, for Christ's sake!'

'Why? Does she owe you money?'

And with a click of the jaw, out they came.

Later that day, I returned to the mortuary and, carrying a small polythene bag containing all Mrs Kent's belongings, I entered the visitors' room. There are few things more poignant than the little bag of belongings that are handed over to relatives when a patient dies. In this case, a wedding ring, a pair of glasses, a little bottle of 4711 eau de cologne, a hairbrush, a toilet bag and those teeth. Her daughter, a woman of about fifty, was standing there in a shabby coat, looking lost and red-eyed. When I handed her the bag she looked inside.

'Oh, her teeth,' she said, sounding as if she was about to cry. 'She never let anyone see her without those.'

Not long before I made my decision to leave nursing, I worked on the Coronary Care Unit at the Queen Elizabeth, which for me was an entirely stressful and enervating experience. Virtually every patient was wired up to a machine that measured his or her heart rate. These things were attached to the patient by means of a set of electrodes that were stuck to their chest. When I was left alone on night duty, the senior nurse having gone for her dinner, I would pace about, constantly checking the patients and their machines for any sign of potential heart failure.

I knew exactly what to do should someone's heart stop for some reason as I had played a significant part in saving a patient's life, when on another ward a man had keeled over. I gave him mouth-to-mouth and cardiac massage, together with another nurse, until the crash team arrived and his heart did, in fact, start again as a direct result of our efforts. It was a tremendous feeling, giving me huge confidence and an illusion of omnipotence for at least a couple of days, but I still found the responsibility of this unit, alone at night, albeit only for an hour, overwhelming. My nerves and anxiety weren't helped by the fact that the electrodes were constantly coming unstuck from the patients' chests and each time it happened it would set off the same alarm that would be activated should their heart have stopped. It was a constant, high-pitched beep and the electronic graph, which normally blipped up and down with the heart's activity, would flatline.

Whilst waiting for the senior nurse to return from dinner, I realised that I had to be careful about what I might have in my hand at the time of one of these things going off, as I had already bent a small plastic ruler, snapped a pencil and, on another occasion, an old-fashioned, glass thermometer, cutting my hand in the process. During my first week on this ward, one of the alarms, attached to a huge Irish labourer, was activated. Quick as a flash, a diminutive medical student, who had been going round practising taking blood from the patients, vaulted the cot-side and, landing on top of the man, proceeded to carry out cardiac massage by bashing his breastbone with some force; I was once told that if you broke the sternum you had done a good job. Within seconds the Irishman rose up in the bed and, thinking he was the victim of an assault, punched the student in the face, knocking him clean out.

I wasn't much enamoured with the operating theatre either. I was too short to watch my first operation, the repair of a hernia, and was given a stool to stand on. I was dreading the scalpel making the first cut into the unmarked, pristine and healthy flesh of the patient, but once this was over I was fine and found it fascinating, not least the conversations between the surgeon and the anaesthetist, chatting away about where they had been at the weekend, gossiping and telling jokes. On one occasion the theatre Sister was hit in the centre of her forehead by a splash of blood and the surgeon said, 'Oh, changed your religion?' And all this whilst sorting through the bleeding innards of an unconscious human being.

The most interesting operation I saw was on the brain of an Iranian woman with Parkinson's disease, which involved drilling holes in her skull. The drill, of the hand variety, bore a close resemblance to one my dad had in the shed and made a similar and unforgettable sound as it cracked slowly through the bone, just as my dad's did when it went through plywood. Once the brain had been reached, it was the surgeon's task to locate the overactive cell that was causing the patient's tremor, then try to zap its nucleus, which he did by watching the brain on a monitor in another room entirely. It was like *The Golden Shot* quiz programme: 'Up a bit . . . Now left and down a wee bit.'

I was shocked to find on surgical wards that a neat scar depended entirely on how well the surgeon could sew and there was a huge difference in their sewing capabilities. For a time I worked on a ward that did a lot of colostomies, carried out by two different surgeons; one was extremely tidy and the other one, nicknamed by some 'The Butcher', made what can only be called a pig's ear of the job, with a great piece of colon lolling lumpily about on the abdomen, where the other one's efforts were neatly finished off. The same was true of appendectomies: the neat one's scars were small and straight while 'The Butcher's' efforts were wonky and sometimes a bit gathered in places. And for the poor patients, it was just a case of who got the luck of the draw.

Surgeons, generally speaking, tended to be more of an extrovert nature than physicians, flirting more with the nurses. Their dress erred on the side of flamboyance, with brightly coloured bow ties and waistcoats, in contrast with the more conservative suits of the physicians. Surgeons were the show men, the stars of the hospital, and one or two were known for their short fuses, screaming and shouting during operations, throwing scalpels, kidney dishes and worse when things weren't going exactly to plan.

Once I was summoned to a theatre that was short staffed and asked to help clean up after a major operation. I was just wondering what that operation might have been when I plunged my hand into a sink filled with bloody water, in order to pull out the plug, and found something soft and cold lying on the bottom. On taking it out, I found it to be a man's severed leg, from a below-the-knee amputation. I yelped and flung it away from me across the room, at which the nurse helping me said, 'Oh, not you as well! That thing has been tossed about like a bloody caber all afternoon.'

My experience on the Coronary Care Unit and in the theatres, I believe, went a long way to convincing me that perhaps I wasn't in the right profession and it was probably not going to get a lot better. There was a side of nursing, however, that I loved. It was the basic nurturing: the feeding and the washing of patients, making their beds, eating their grapes, chatting and making friends. I ended up writing to several ex-patients for some time after I had given up the profession altogether. I fell in love with them frequently; other people fell in love with doctors, but not me: I fell in love with the patients. There was something about having a man captive in a bed and seeing to his every need.

Well, nearly his every need. We were told in no uncertain terms in preliminary nursing school that we should whip out our biro, which was to be kept in the top pocket at all times, and give the offending member a short, sharp rap with it, but knowing my propensity for unknowingly pulling out the wrong thing, this was a little worrying, as whacking an erect penis with my Spencer Wells forceps, which were kept in the same pocket, could be very nasty. I never had cause to take this drastic action; only once or twice did my hand hover over my biro and both times when I looked at my pocket, it was in fact hovering over my torch.

My favourite ward was a men's medical. Thirty men, all on bed-rest! Unlike the Coronary Care Unit, I used to long for the odd shift, usually evening, when I would be left in charge. As soon as the staff nurse had gone, I would stand at the end of the ward, hands on hips, and shout, 'OK, you horrible lot, get your goodies out! Who's got chocolates and who's got a nice grape? Come on, the wife must have brought you in something nice.' I would then do my version of tap-dancing around the ward, picking up the odd chocolate here and grape there, whilst cracking a few jokes and telling one or two stories. On this particular ward at the end of the shift, I would go round and kiss them all goodnight. On the cheek, of course.

Another ward I had adored at the Queen Elizabeth was a men's surgical, dealing mainly with peripheral vascular disease, which seemed to be caused almost entirely by smoking. The men on the ward were all of a particular type, almost without exception: small, thin, wiry and funny. It took a few days for me to realise that the reason I was so at home on this ward, and got on so well with the men, is that they reminded me of my own father: the physique, the humour and, of course, the heavy smoking. One man, whose veins had been destroyed by smoking, had had an arm amputated some years earlier and was back in to have the other one removed. Just before he went down to theatre, he asked the staff nurse to light him a last cigarette, such was his addiction.

One of the symptoms of this condition was called intermittent claudication, which meant that after walking a certain distance the patient would experience pain in the calf muscle, presumably because enough blood couldn't get through to it via the ravaged veins. One weekend whilst I was working on this ward, I went home and heard my parents talking in the scullery.

'Well, you've probably pulled a muscle, that's all.' The clinking of plates and cups and the smell of soapsuds indicated that my mother was washing up.

'No, I don't get it straight off. If it was a pulled muscle, it'd hurt all the time I was walking, but, like, I was walking down to the post office and after about thirty yards I suddenly got the pain and I had to stop, and I, like, rubbed my leg and it went off and just as I got to the post office it was coming on again.'

'Well, that's strange, I don't know what that would be.'

But I did, I knew exactly what it was.

'Dad, get it checked out.'

'No, it's all right, it's just old age.'

'No, Dad, you're sixty not eighty. Go and see the doctor.'

'Nah, don't you worry about me.'

But as ever I did.

However, ultimately, nothing was going to keep me in nursing. When Sister Ignatius had said to me, all those years ago, 'You should go on the stage,' she wasn't telling me anything I didn't already know. I had always known, from as far back as I can remember, that what I really wanted to do was act. I stared at my name indelibly printed on my laundry bag and I thought of Sister Hartwell, still living in the nurses' home after fifty years, and knew I had to do something. But what?

I looked up drama in the telephone directory and found something called the British Drama League. I rang them and told a very posh-sounding woman that I wanted to become an actress. What should I do?

She said, 'Well, really you should go to university.'

'But I've only got four O levels.'

'Oh, then you can't.'

And that was the end of that.

It was during my last few months of nursing that I had met and fallen in love with my first proper boyfriend, whom I shall call DT, on midsummer's eve 1969. It was a sublime period in which I staggered about the wards, this time of the Children's hospital, completely knackered after nights of unbridled shagging, even falling asleep during the morning note session on one occasion, after which I was taken aside by a concerned ward Sister and given a lecture on the restorative power of sleep. I had discovered sex, in a big way, but it hadn't all been smooth going; it took me at least several days to lose my virginity because I was so tense: clamped shut, I suppose. At one point I seriously questioned whether I had a vagina at all and began to reason that perhaps this was how the vagina actually took shape: from the continual hammering at the door by the penis. However, after those three days, there was no stopping me.

Meeting DT was a revelation on every level. He came from a wealthy middle-class family, living in a big detached house in a well-to-do part of Birmingham. Entering his house for the first time was like entering an unknown foreign country. There was a big, spacious sitting room with a grand piano in one corner and french windows that opened out on to a large and, to my eyes, rather wild-looking garden, which was a far cry from the little rectangles of earth planted with a military parade of bedding plants, all standing to attention in pristine, weedless rows, that seemed to be the fashion round our way. No, this garden had a liberated, unselfconscious feel to it, more akin to parkland than any garden I'd ever known. It had a pond and a willow tree, and from the branch of a large oak hung a tyre suspended on a length of rope for people to swing on: for fun! It was a garden built for the pleasure of being outside, for people to truly use, rather than some kind of badge of neatness and respectability.

The kitchen had the wonderful, hitherto alien aroma of freshly ground coffee and garlic. It boasted a dishwasher, which in those days was referred to as a washing-up machine. I don't think I came across another until they were actually called dishwashers, about ten years later. Next to the kitchen was the breakfast room: a room whose sole purpose was to sit and eat breakfast in! The dining room being another room entirely!

Upstairs, Mr and Mrs T had an en-suite bathroom, another luxury I didn't come across for another ten or twelve years, and then only in a hotel. They read the *Daily Telegraph*, cooked and ate spaghetti bolognese and macaroni cheese, and spoke without a trace of a Birmingham accent. At dinner there was more than one knife to the right and more than one fork to the left, and they drank wine. The only wine I had come across at this point in my life was port, drunk out of tiny glasses decorated with a scratched ring of little gold and black roses. There always seemed to be half a bottle of it on the sideboard, along with a bottle of Advocaat, a bottle of Martini Bianco and some Johnny Walker Red Label, all of which were only ever opened at Christmas. They called dinner, lunch; tea, supper; while dinner itself was a more formal meal that you ate at eight o'clock in the evening.

The September of the year that we met, DT went up to Manchester Polytechnic, now Manchester Metropolitan University, to study Sociology. I was heartsore and any will I had left to continue nursing completely disappeared almost immediately. Every day that I had off was spent getting to Manchester at the earliest opportunity, staying until the last possible moment and coming home miserable. On one such visit I confided to DT that I wanted to become an actress, whereupon he told me that there was a Drama course right there at the poly and why didn't I apply? I duly did and an audition was set up for the following January. Now all that there was left to do, was give in my notice to the school of nursing and *tell my mother* of my plans.

Before I did anything I went home to talk to my brother Tommy, because, apart from Sister Ignatius, he was the only person who had ever said that I should become an actress. He was always full of praise, laughing at my imperson-ations of various relatives and the day-to-day characters that peopled our lives, and he crowed about my little acting debut at the church hall, claiming that I was the best, a moment in my life that I had held close to my heart. Once again, he was encouraging and said that I should go for it, especially while I had DT's emotional support. I went to see my other brother, Kevin, and his wife Jill, both of whom reiterated Tommy's sentiments, Kevin offering to come over and be there when I told my mother, a task I dreaded.

On the appointed evening, I took my father aside to brief him of my impending change of career and, as I thought he would, he said if that's what I wanted, I must do it. Then he added shockingly that the principal of the school of nursing had rung only the day before to tell my parents that I had given in my notice and to find out whether they knew. My dad, God love him, told her that yes, of course they knew and that he was all for it. He added ominously, 'Thank God it was me and not your mother that answered the phone.' He had kept it to himself.

Finally with my brothers and my dad standing in between my mother and me, I broke the news.

'Mum? I'm going to leave nursing.'

'What? What are you talking about?'

'I'm giving up nursing. I want to be an actress.'

'Don't be ridiculous! Has she gone mad?'

'Well, if it's what she wants . . . ' My dad as ever was trying to mediate, while drips from my mother's underslip, drying on the pulley above, dropped down on to his head.

'What are you talking about, Tom? Don't talk so bloody daft! She'll ruin her life.'

'She doesn't have to stay in nursing if it's not what she wants. There's no point.'

This was from Kevin, slightly aggressive and with a touch of the old teenage insolence. He and Mum had rarely seen eye to eye, especially through his adolescence. I can picture them on one occasion, chasing one another back and forth through the house, kicking each other up the bottom.

'Oh, Gad, what have we reared? You'll be in the gutter before you're twenty!'

I thought she might lunge at me and then Dad said, 'Well, the more you are against it the more she's going to want to do it.'

And Tommy joined the fray: 'Dad's right, and there's no point in her staying in a job that makes her miserable. She should go for it now, while she's young.'

'Oh Gad, I might have expected that from you!'

Tommy had had a couple of stabs career-wise before embarking on his degree in Theology at Birmingham University, one at teacher training college and the other when he entered the Jesuits, staying only a matter of weeks. My mother had wept bitterly on the day that he left home to join, thinking that she would never see him again, and then she had gone totally mad, calling him every name under the sun, when she'd heard that he'd packed it all in and was coming home.

'Acting!' This was said with the downturned mouth that she used to convey utter contempt. 'You've been watching too much television! May the great God look to me! *Acting*!'

And that was it, it was all over bar the shouting. I then announced that as soon as I had worked my notice at the hospital I would be moving up to Manchester, where I would get a job for a year before hopefully getting into college to study acting. The course I had applied for was also a teaching course, which went a long way to assuaging my mother's anxiety, but it also left her disappointed, in that she could no longer live out her own ambition to be a nurse through me.

9

'So You Want To Be an Actress?' — Manchester

I moved to Manchester in November 1969, after a nursing career that spanned all of eighteen months, to live with DT, and I stayed at first with an old friend from school, whom I had been put into contact with by a mutual friend in my nursing set. After a week or two, we found a bedsit in Maple Avenue, Chorlton-cum-Hardy. It was in the attic of a Victorian house, with a tiny separate kitchen tucked into the eaves where anyone standing at the stove had to bend double in order to cook. Downstairs, on the first floor, we had the use of a bathroom that we shared with the rest of the house, which I think comprised two more flats, one on each floor.

I remember one evening, a matter of just days after we had moved in, I arrived home, thrilled at having found a job, to see that a small envelope had been posted under our door. At first, on opening it, I thought it was empty but then I saw down in the corner a small square of folded paper. When I opened it out, it contained a little clump of dark pubic hair and on the paper was written in neat, small handwriting the words, 'Found in the bathroom. Yours, I believe.' It was unsigned. I was mortified. It was obviously meant for me as DT had gorgeous, bright-red hair. Someone must have used the bathroom immediately after me and ... Oh, it was too awful to contemplate. After this incident I didn't use the bathroom for about three months, choosing to wash standing at the sink in the freezing kitchen rather than ever exit that bathroom again where I might bump unknowingly into the anonymous writer of the note. Leaving and entering the house also proved to be potentially shaming experiences. On coming in I would mount the stairs two and three at a time, to arrive sweating and panting at the top.

My parents, even my father, thought that I was still living with the friend from school and that DT was living elsewhere. It would have been too much, on top of abandoning my respectable career in nursing, to tell them the truth. When recently I played the role of Mary Whitehouse, who hailed from just down the road in Wolverhampton — the self-styled moral campaigner who was very much in the news at that particular time because of her monumental battle with the BBC and its lack of censorship — it brought my rebellious, angry, anti-establishment, nineteen-year-old self into sharp focus. My mother might not have been religious but she was of the same generation as Mary Whitehouse, although she thought her a 'bit of an old fuddy-duddy', when it came to sex before marriage she virtually shared the same views as this woman. Mrs Whitehouse was more or less universally loathed and ridiculed by our generation, representing everything that we balked at and rejected. 'Living in sin' felt like one in the eye for her and her ilk; we were, after all, the 'Make Love, Not War' generation with a whole new philosophy and a strong and vivid identity. Of course, playing her at the age of fifty-seven, I saw her differently and, having a daughter of my own, I understood her fears for her children in the face of such a whirlwind of a cultural and sexual revolution. Although she went too far in many instances, without her we wouldn't now have the much needed nine o'clock watershed.

After I'd been up in Manchester for just over a year my parents finally came to visit me. I had started my first year at college and there was a frantic hiding of all things DT, but what I failed to do was put away my birth pills, which my mother's hawk eyes spotted straight away. She never said anything, or even remotely hinted at it; it was my brother Tommy who told me years later how she'd seen them on the bathroom shelf and was somewhat miffed at me, thinking I'd pulled the wool over her eyes.

Once I settled into living with DT, I began to realise that there was something wrong with my sleep. I would frequently shoot up in bed in the middle of the night, often screaming, my heart banging, my face and the top half of my body covered in sweat. Although this would wake DT, I would not always remember it. As the years went on it became increasingly worse. Every single night I would have a disturbance of one sort or another. On a good night, it would be a brief and sudden panic that would cause me to wake. This would be followed by a second or two of confusion, whereby I would try to work out the meaning of some jumbled, dreamlike logic that suggested an imminent disaster of some kind, and usually I would sort out that it was a dream and then go back to sleep fairly quickly. However, on a bad night, this waking could happen every hour and, weirdly, the hourly interval would be just that, exactly an hour.

These night terrors were not like a normal nightmare. First, they would take place at the beginning of the sleep period and I began to time them; sometimes it would be just a half-hour after I went to sleep, sometimes one or two hours, but it was always exactly the half-hour or hour, give or take a minute or two, never forty minutes or one hour twenty, and it was never at the end of a sleep cycle, which apparently is when the classic nightmare takes place.

There was no story to them; it was more like a terrifying image presenting itself to my psyche, like a snapshot being flashed up, and I would wake, quaking with terror for my life. The image, or sometimes just a single thought or feeling, would often involve dark water and drowning: the house, for instance, sinking down into deep water. I would suddenly see the water rising up the bedroom windows and I would wake with the certain knowledge that I was the only one who knew and who could do anything about it. I would then often get up, pacing around, trying to work out what was going on, staring hard out of the window, and then beginning to not know why I was doing so, as the night terror and its awful image slipped from the grasp of my memory into a muddled and puzzling conundrum. The remnants of this conundrum would sometimes filter into the next day, leaving me with the troubling sensation that something vital had been left undone.

When I was away from home I started to dread going to sleep, much the same as I had as a child and feared wetting the bed. This wasn't helped by my propensity to sleepwalk. Once whilst staying in a hotel on location, I walked out of the hotel room stark naked and was only awoken by the sharp click of the heavy door as it closed irreversibly behind me. I stood in the corridor, shaking and soaked in sweat, desperately trying to work out where the hell I was. Luckily a female hotel guest was returning to her room and she got me a towel to wrap around myself, allowing me to sit in her room while she called the receptionist to come and let me into my own. One night when my daughter was critically ill as a child, and I was sleeping at the hospital on a put-me-up next to her bed, I woke to find myself running down the corridor towards the nurses' station, shouting at the top of my voice, 'Please, somebody, please! My daughter! Please, come and help me!' I ran with the nurses back to the bed but before we even got there I began to realise that I had somehow forgotten why I had called them in the first place and that this was probably a dream. She, of course, was sleeping peacefully. At that point I just broke down.

This particular incident was unusual as my terrors went, in that it actually related to something that was obviously stressful in my everyday existence. Normally I could see little correlation between my nightly insanity and what was occurring in my life on a day-to-day basis. I would have the terrors irrespective of whether I was worried about something or whether I was totally relaxed on holiday, although there was the odd sequence of work-related terrors.

A common one for me was dreaming that the camera crew were in the bedroom. I would actually open my eyes and see them, and then I would start getting panicked because I would realise that I had no clothes on and that I didn't understand what the scene was that I was meant to do, and why wasn't anyone speaking or at least telling me what we were supposed to be doing? In another instance, whilst living in my friend's Camden flat, I tried to get out of the bedroom window, waking up as my foot touched cold, damp concrete. It was a basement flat so I was in no real physical danger. I fact I never seemed to sleepwalk dangerously.

Frequently, I would wake up thinking that there was someone in the bed next to me whom either I couldn't identify or whom I knew only vaguely, and so I would end up nudging my poor, long-suffering husband awake, asking, 'Who are you?' How my marriage has survived the nightly turmoil that these disturbances caused is nothing short of a miracle. When we first got together, Grant would cuddle and soothe me back to sleep.

'Shhh, shhhh, it's all right, you're just dreaming, it's all right, you're safe, go back to sleep.'

After about ten years it became, 'You're bloody dreaming!' accompanied by a swift turning over, taking most of the duvet with him. Sometimes we would have lengthy conversations that often turned into arguments, all whilst I was still asleep.

'You're dreaming!'

'I am not dreaming!'

'You *are* dreaming!'

'Don't tell me I'm dreaming. I know when I'm asleep!'

And so on. However, I was eventually to find salvation in the form of acupuncture. After reporting my condition to several doctors, I had tried sleeping potions of every kind and although they made me sleep soundly, I would still sleepwalk, scream and do all the night-terror stuff, but without waking or remembering any of it, which was terrifying in itself. So it was at the ripe old age of forty-eight, after thirty years of badly disrupted sleep, where I could count on the fingers of one hand how many times I had slept through the night, I had an acupuncture treatment. On that very night I slept through without waking and the next morning I cried and I cried. It was so wonderfully restorative and I grieved for what I had so missed. This only lasted the one night but I went back every week so that gradually it became the norm and the screaming habdabs became the odd exception. Then just as I started to get a good night's sleep, the menopause started, but that's another story.

In the year prior to college, I did a series of temporary jobs, working for Carrera's, the cigarette company, counting cigarettes; as a sales assistant in a shoe shop; plus a myriad of others, under the auspices of Manpower Services, the worst of which was quite possibly a factory on the outskirts of Manchester. Here, I spent my days screwing tops on to large cans of oil and trying to take my mind off the all-pervading stench of the place, which I can still smell today and which, I'm afraid, is indescribable. Everywhere was covered in a thick layer of filthy grease, making the floor lethal, and after working there for only about a month, my shoes were coated in it and had to be thrown away. However, the worst aspect of this job was not the mind-numbing tedium, or the ever-present, sick-making smell, or the ubiquitous grease; it concerned certain of the employees.

Amongst the workforce were a number of mentally handicapped people and one such girl worked on the same floor as me. She was blonde, sweet, innocent and slow, obviously much younger than her actual years, always happy, smiling and willing, and rather pretty. Every day of her life while I was there, she was subjected to humiliating teasing at the hands of a group of four or five men. This usually took the form of lewd sexual jibes, which for the most part seemed to go over her head, but sometimes I saw her emerge from behind a partition adjusting her clothing, with raucous laughter coming from the men on the other side. At first

I felt impotent, because of my status as a temp, but I became very upset on behalf of this vulnerable girl, obsessing about the awful, bullying behaviour to the point where I couldn't concentrate on my 'screwing' and I began to lose sleep at night. In the end I took it upon myself to approach the foreman and told him what I had witnessed.

'No, it's only a bit of fun. She loves it. She's been working here years. No, no, don't worry your pretty little head!'

I don't know how I stopped my hand from forming a fist and punching his big pockmarked nose right into his ugly, pockmarked face.

'No,' I said, 'I want *you* to worry *yours*.'

When I checked in with Manpower on the Friday of that week, they said that I would be going somewhere else to work on the Monday. It seems the factory no longer needed my services.

Whilst in a practical sense I missed the comforts of home and the institutional nature of life in the nurses' home — where the domestic side of everyday living, like laundry, cleaning and cooking, were completely taken care of — I found my new life of cohabitation both challenging and exciting. There in the tiny kitchen at Maple Avenue, from a fairly narrow culinary repertoire, DT gave me my first real cookery lessons. How to boil potatoes and how to make spaghetti bolognese, two 'skills' that have formed the basis of the cook I am today!

It was here that the exploding haggis incident occurred. I had just left the kitchen for a second when a bang like a football rupturing brought me running back in to find the innards of a haggis, which had been boiling on the stove, dripping from the ceiling, the thing having burst in the pan. The downstairs neighbour stood on the landing looking a touch scared. This was after the pubic hair business and, unsure whether this neighbour was the anonymous author of the note, I was struck dumb, so the two of us just stood there, him wondering what on earth had happened and me picturing him gingerly picking my pubes out of the bath.

Another disaster took place when I decided to surprise DT with something a little different and purchased for the hefty sum of sixpence a pig's head. I popped it in the Baby Belling oven with a few rashers of streaky bacon artistically placed on top of the head, two between the ears and a couple down each side, which had the effect of making it look like hair and, without realising it, a prototype for Miss Piggy. I couldn't wait for DT to arrive home from college; the smell from the kitchen was mouth-watering. However, when he finally did get home and the time came to reveal my culinary surprise, I opened the oven door only to find a sight worthy of a Hammer horror film. The head had indeed roasted to a gorgeous golden brown and the rashers had crisped into a set of curls, but out through the eyes, nose and mouth was oozing the creature's brain, which I didn't even know was in there, and it was a sludgy, burnt, greyish colour. We had fish and chips that night.

One Saturday, having gained a little confidence, I invited a couple of friends around for

Me as a baby, and toddling along a promenade.

Where I grew up – 69 Bishopton Road, with the park at the end of the road.

With my knickers hanging down in the garden of Bishopton Road, a sign of things to come.

My maternal grandmother and grandfather in County Mayo.

Mum and Aunt Agnes, sisters newly arrived from Ireland.

Mum as a young woman in 1934, and obviously having a good time (below, far left) at a picnic in 1936.

A photograph taken by
Dad of Mum standing
alone in a field.

Dad in his courting days.

Just married.

As a child, my family's holidays were invariably taken in England, Ireland or Wales in resorts like Tenby, Blackpool (below, Mum is cleverly balancing the tower on the back of her head) and Margate.

With Mum and Dad, Kevin and Tommy in Blackpool – a rare portrait of all the family together at the same time.

Brother Tommy doing his Buddy Holly impersonation on Blackpool beach.

The notorious daytrip down the new M1 to Trafalgar Square with Aunt Agnes and my grandmother, who is (of course) looking away from the camera.

Now I am looking away from the camera as we walk along the promenade at Blackpool, Dad smoking the inevitable cigarette.

Me aged six.

The family in the back garden at
69 Bishopton Road, including
my grandmother.

With Nelly's kittens.

The ill-fated Guinea, a
Bachelor Boy among pets.

Holly Lodge Grammar School for Girls, Smethwick, where I went in 1963. My school report sometimes refers to me as Julia as well as Julie. Either way, it was suggested I wasted too much time in lessons.

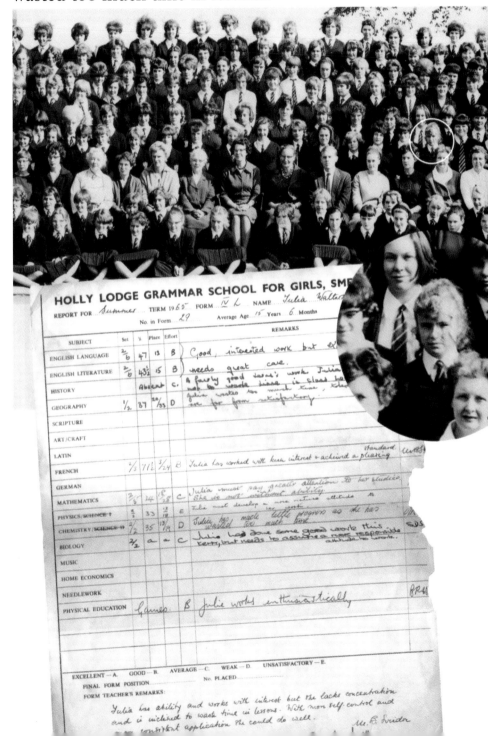

My first starring role – in a school production of *Midsummer Night's Dream* as Moth (seated second from right). My teacher said I was perfect casting, as moths are such a nuisance.

On the day of my father's funeral, with my brothers at Bishopton Road.

As a nurse – I am in the back row, second from the right.

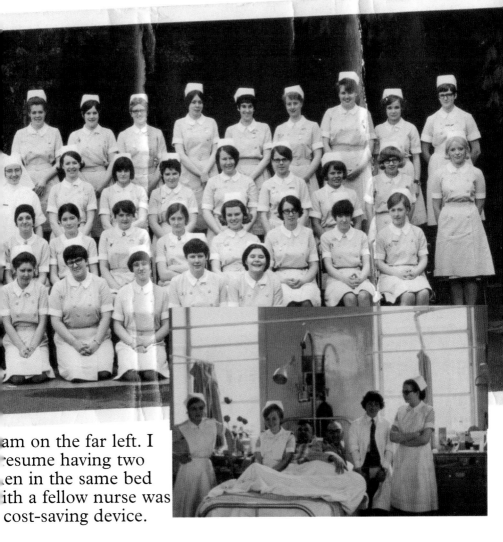

am on the far left. I esume having two en in the same bed ith a fellow nurse was cost-saving device.

My very first *Spotlight* directory picture.

The Stable Theatre Club where I would literally sit at the feet of Peter Flannery and learn.

A student production of
'*Tis Pity She's a Whore*.

With 'DT', my first
serious boyfriend.

Playing a stunt girl in
Flaming Bodies at the ICA
Theatre, the nearest I
have got so far to playing
a Bond girl.

At Tippi Hedren's ranch with publicist and friend Ros Toland, and a leopard.

With my friend Ros March on an Amsterdam waterbus. God help the poor person who had the audacity to snap us.

With Victoria in the early days.

Together in her brilliant play *Talent*.

With Stuart
Orme, director
of *Wood and
Walters*, in
1981.

A scene from
Victoria's
television play
*Happy Since I
Met You.*

In attendance as Mrs Overall
at the coronation of Victoria,
also known as a BAFTA
tribute.

With Pete Postlethwaite and
Babs the dog in a photobooth.

In *Scully*, playing Scully's grandmother – one of my first
'old lady' parts – at The Everyman Theatre, Liverpool,
with Pete.

Cut! A scene from *Educating Rita* with Michael Caine.

On the grass between scenes with *Educating Rita's* director, Lewis Gilbert.

The movie's success led to me promoting it all over America, though why I am wearing a Department of Sanitation tee-shirt in New York, heaven knows. I also enjoyed the poolside of the Beverly Hills Hotel, a trip in Burt Reynolds' helicopter (as you do) and the chance to meet some distant Japanese relatives in Los Angeles.

In the Anthony
Price dress I wore
to the premiere of
Educating Rita.

With Brian Cox in *Frankie and Johnny in the Clair de Lune*, which had a successful run at the Comedy Theatre in 1988.

With Phil Collins in *Buster*. I was pregnant during the filming and never felt happier.

In *Personal Services*, in a typical scene with Shirley Stelfox and Anthony Collin.

With David Leland, who wrote the screenplay.

The Golden Globes, 1984, for *Educating Rita*.

With the BAFTA award for *My Beautiful Son*.

With some of the cast at the premier of *Billy Elliot* – the film's director, Stephen Daldry, is on the left, and I have my arm around Jamie Bell's shoulder.

As Mrs Weasley in *Harry Potter and the Chamber of Secrets*.

Calendar Girls with Helen Mirren.

The gorgeous Petula in *dinnerladies*; one of Victoria's greatest comic creations, with brilliant make-up thanks to Christina Baker.

Talking Heads by Alan Bennett consisted of brilliantly written monologues telling tales of ordinary, uneventful and desperate lives. Here I am playing Lesley, a frisky small-part actress who lands a role in a video, set on board a yacht, which is to be targeted at a German audience.

Mrs Overall, the cleaner, in *Acorn Antiques*, a sketch based on a badly made soap opera. She is my favourite character of all.

As Serafina in Peter Hall's production of Tennessee Williams' *The Rose Tattoo*. My mother had died a year earlier and playing this part allowed me to mourn her further.

As Mary Whitehouse in the BBC drama *Filth* in 2008.

With Mum in 1985.

With Grant in Budapest.

The birth of Maisie, the happiest day of my life.

lunch. The lunch was to consist of a quiche, a fairly unusual dish in those days and very trendy, plus some salad, followed by apple crumble and custard. I was totally thrilled with the result as I got the two dishes out of the oven. They looked cookery-book perfect, golden and delicious, but when we came to eat the quiche, no one could get their knife through the pastry. What made it worse is that no one said a word; they just soldiered silently on, trying to force their knives to cut into it, one friend placing his knifetip down vertically and banging on the end of the handle with the palm of his hand, hammer-and-chisel style.

'Look, look, since we haven't got a pneumatic drill, it might be best to just scrape the filling out and eat that, and if anyone's got a roof that needs mending please feel free to take the — what I laughingly call — pastry case home with you.'

I have never made pastry since. I've always seen cooking as some sort of measure of my womanhood, a kind of performance that I must rise to, and so apart from preparing meals for my own family, it has been an unspeakable trial. The thought of giving a dinner party to people I don't really know is anathema to me. Only in the last few years have I been able to enjoy cooking to a degree and see it for what it actually is, and for that I thank Queen Delia.

In January 1970, I had my audition for a place at Manchester Polytechnic School of Theatre. I had bought a couple of books of audition speeches as I had been asked to prepare three

181

pieces, one of which had to be Shakespeare. I chose Lady Macbeth, *Macbeth* being the only Shakespeare I knew, having studied it at O level. The other two I barely remember, except that one was from a play I had never heard of, with a speech by a character contemplating suicide, and the other was a play by Clemence Dane, whom I had also never heard of. I was interviewed on the day by Edward Argent, the principal of the school, who was wearing a black velvet jacket. I recall thinking that this was a good sign as I was wearing my new black velvet trouser suit with the bell bottoms, the tunic-style top being cinched in at the waist by a thin, black-leather belt belonging to DT, and my new knee-length, black leather boots.

'So you want to be an actress?' He was a round, teddy-bearish man, with dark, twinkling eyes, thick dark hair and a full beard, threaded through with grey.

'No. I am an actress,' I said. 'Whether I am employed as such is another matter, but that's what I am; I am an actress.' I believed that absolutely and felt that if he were to turn me down, it would be his loss.

'So, do you think you'll be able to learn anything here then?'

'Oh yes, I'll be learning about the actress that I am and how to use what I have.'

He then asked me to stand up and perform my pieces. Never since have I performed anything, first time, with such confidence. First of all I did my Lady M, the 'screw your courage to the sticking place' speech, feeling totally in

182

tune with every single line. I was pleased with it, sensing that I had made the right impression, and then, buoyed up by this, I went on to my second piece, the suicide speech. Again I soared through it, convinced that I was completely at one with the character, that I was inside her skin.

Edward Argent didn't say anything straight away, just creaked slightly in his chair. 'Mmm, that was interesting and very, very good.' I felt as if I might just float up into the air buoyed up by my very own ego, but then, 'Tell me, why did you choose to play a man's part?'

'Oh . . . ' I laughed; what the hell was he talking about? A man's part? My brain instantly melted into a fuzz of anxiety. And then I realised that because I'd bought a book of audition speeches, I didn't really know the plays that the speeches were taken from and therefore, of course, I didn't really know the characters either. Clearly there was more to this than my just acting words off the page, regardless of context.

I laughed again. 'Oh, I just thought it would be . . . you know . . . I thought . . . Oh . . . Oh . . . Oh, what the hell, I had no idea it was a man, I just liked it and I wanted to play that speech and express those feelings.'

Now he laughed.

'I like your honesty, good for you. Now what else have you got for me?'

'I bet you can't wait!' I laughed nervously. 'It's by Clemence Dane and before you ask, no, I don't know anything about him and I haven't read the play either, but I think he must be pretty good, judging from this speech anyway.'

'Oh yes . . . Incidentally, Clemence Dane is a woman. Fire away!'

About three weeks later, I received a letter accepting me on the course, to start the following September, but this depended on my gaining one more GCE, as five were required in those days in order to teach. I instantly embarked on a course one evening a week at a college in Stockport, to study GCE Anatomy and Physiology. This was about as useful to my future as an actress as a lawnmower would have been, but as it was now February, and having missed the first term and almost half of the second term, with the exams coming up in June, I thought it best to choose a subject that I already had some knowledge of. Because of my nursing course, this seemed to be the best choice and, indeed, I managed to pass it with a grade two, my best grade to date.

In the summer of 1970, DT and I decided to hitch-hike down to Arcachon on the south-west coast of France, camping as we went. He had borrowed an old tent belonging to his father. The tent was stowed in an ancient, stained, green-canvas tote bag and had been in there since it was last used, some twenty-odd years before, probably for his father's National Service. Our first stop, after finding it very difficult to secure lifts in France, was at a campsite in the Bois de Boulogne on the outskirts of Paris. We arrived in the evening, just as people were preparing their evening meals. I looked around at the state-of-the-art tents (the French take camping and caravanning very seriously), and theirs were all, without exception, brightly coloured, modern jobs, blue, green, red and yellow, with bendy poles that screwed together. Some had separate bedrooms and covered extensions to sit out under. People were cooking elaborate meals on full gas ranges, while others were barbecuing or drinking wine at elegantly laid-out tables, complete with vivid tablecloths and proper cutlery. There was that smell of coffee and garlic wafting in the air, which made me excited about setting up camp and cooking our very first meal out in the open. Then DT got the tent out.

It wouldn't come out at first and required me to hold on to the bottom of the bag while DT tugged it free. When he finally did so, it came out so suddenly that he went careering backwards and fell on his arse on top of a child's beach ball, causing it to burst with quite a bang and the child, almost simultaneously, burst into tears. I went immediately to the rescue with my school French, which up until this point I had been fairly proud of.

'Oh, je me remercie! Pardonnez nous! Nous acheterons un bal nouveau.'

I noticed the man opposite, who had hitherto been engrossed in his barbecue, begin to titter and mutter something into the tent. This brought his wife out, who stood and joined in, both openly staring and enjoying the scene. Then the child's father came over, and I was off again.

'Oh, je me remercie! Mon ami est un imbécile! Pardonnez nous, s'il vous plaît!'

'Oh, it's all right, love, he's got another one.

We thought you were the local theatre group, come to put on a bit of slapstick for us!' And he laughed a big, fat-bellied, Barnsley laugh. Scooping up the bawling child, he made to leave, but as he passed the spilt contents of the tote bag, he dropped down on to his haunches and, turning over the wooden tent pegs and picking up the not insubstantial wooden mallet that was needed to knock them into the ground, he said, 'Good God! Where did you get this from? The Imperial War Museum?' Another big-bellied laugh. 'Eh, Maureen, come over here and have a look at this! Jesus! It's like *Camping Through the Ages*. When was this last used? The Crimea?'

Secretly I was a bit miffed, but putting a brave face on it I joined in with the good humour, and DT and I started to erect the cause of the hilarity. It was made from extremely thick and heavy green canvas and, as we unfolded it, we noticed several mysterious brown stains and a couple of small holes, just to add to its allure, whilst every crease and fold was full of long-dead flies, spiders and cobwebs.

'Oh! Brought your insect collection with you, have you?'

More laughter, and by now we had attracted a small audience. Putting the tent up then became an activity for the entire camp. The man opposite brought over his mallet and was knocking in the wooden tent pegs, while the Barnsley couple were trying to lay flat the filthy and extremely thin groundsheet, while laughing and marvelling at the age of the thing; it was not sewn in like today's models, but simply attached to the main

186

tent by a series of toggles and hooks. Finally it was up. We got out our primus stove and I heated up some frankfurters and beans, but every so often a little group would gather and watch us as if we were an exhibit. Going to fetch water in the green canvas bucket with the white rope handle had people fairly rushing from their tents to point and 'ooh' and laugh.

We had done well on the first leg of our journey to Dover, securing lifts easily, but when we got to Calais we waited hours for a lift that took us no distance at all, and had to wait some time again until a kindly French lorry driver stopped and took us all the way to Paris. He suggested that DT's very long hair might be the cause of people's reluctance to pick us up and if it was cut short we might have more luck. So it was a pretty clean-cut DT who stood on the roadside thumbing a lift to Poitiers the next day and there was a rubbish bin full of red curls on the edge of the Bois de Boulogne.

It was an idyllic holiday. Camping in amongst the cypress trees in the sand-blown site at Arcachon, the hot sun bringing out their clean, astringent scent, and sitting at the pavement cafés, sipping huge cups of milky coffee while we observed the passing folk, giving them histories and characters and relationships, passing judgement and laughing is set like crystal in my mind. Even taking into account the antiquated tent and the difficulty with rides — not to mention the Spanish lorry driver who offered us a lift from Arcachon to Calais on the way home and proceeded to molest me as I sat on the engine in the middle, between him and DT, something I tolerated in silence because the lift was so valuable but which I avenged with a quick, sharp knee to the balls in the car park at the ferry terminal while DT was in the lavatory — it set a joyous benchmark for every holiday that has followed since.

From the moment I started at Manchester Polytechnic School of Theatre, I felt as if I belonged. It was as if I had been struggling uphill in the wrong gear all my life. Now, everything made sense, everything connected and fitted together. However, I did have a little trouble staying awake in the History of Theatre classes, and I tended to dread and try to get out of the make-up classes, which I found a trial because I might have to remove the thick layers of mascara and black kohl eye make-up that I daubed on every morning after removing the previous day's lot. This was always done in the privacy of the locked bathroom or, in the post-pubic days of Maple Avenue, in the kitchen, with DT under strict instructions to keep out. I hadn't allowed a single person, except possibly my parents, and then very briefly, to see me devoid of eye make-up for about three years: in fact, from the moment I first started to wear it, when I realised the effect it had on my eyes, making them darker and larger. Without it I thought myself ugly in the extreme. I had, and of course have, tiny eyes; nowadays this rarely crosses my mind but back then we had just come out of the sixties and eyes simply had to be huge. Girls wanted to look like Twiggy, waiflike, flat-chested, stick-limbed, eyes wide with innocence, or more likely starvation, as not many young women had Twiggy's natural skinniness. So my eye make-up started at my browbone and very nearly finished at my cheek, much in the style of Fenella Fielding, except without the wig. Every time we had a class I would suffer acute embarrassment if I just had to remove a little; I never removed the mascara and I only ever partially removed the kohl. One Sunday morning, in my second year, I was luxuriating in the bath, having washed my face free of probably several days' worth of eye make-up, when the boyfriend of the girl from upstairs and his mates, having heard from DT that I was having a bath, started banging on the door and demanding to see what I looked like without my make-up.

'Come on, let's see you without your war paint!'

I can remember feeling quite sick at the thought of them witnessing the exposing ugliness of my bare face. I lay silently in the bath without moving a muscle, a flannel over my eyes, until they went away, long after the water had gone cold, and I blushed whenever I bumped into them afterwards.

This belief that I became acceptable and attractive to others only when I had emphasised my eyes with a black pencil line went on, but in a less and less extreme way as the years went by, until my thirties and it only stopped completely when I met my husband. It was largely cured, though, by having to be made up for filming. When I first started out, I would go into the make-up bus with a tiny line around my eyes and a very light scraping of mascara, thinking that the make-up artist would never notice, only to have it wiped off almost instantly and dismissed as a bit of 'slap' left on from the night before. So, of course, I would try a little less and then a little less still, until it just wasn't worth it any more, and what a relief it was to finally accept the way I looked.

There are so many legendary tales about famous actors presenting themselves to be made up when already in full slap and I didn't want to belong to this absurdly deluded band. There was one such story going the rounds about a famous opera singer who was playing a character who wore a wig and, during the course of the story, the wig was to be ripped off to comically reveal that he was really bald. The singer himself was actually bald and wore a full wig at all times to conceal the fact. It was such a sensitive issue that the wig maker for the opera was instructed never to allude to the fact that this man was wearing a wig and to treat him as if it was indeed his real hair. This meant that instead of using his own natural baldness, a bald cap had to be made to fit over his own personal wig and another wig, the one to be ripped off in the course of the action, had to be made to fit over that.

In the second year of make-up classes we turned to the making of Greek masks, which were composed of plaster of Paris. We were sent home with some of the necessary materials to practise making and applying it. Usually people made casts of their arms and legs, but I decided that DT's penis might be a more interesting appendage to practise on and he, probably thinking it might perk up our sex life, but with a whiff of fear about him, agreed to it.

The first step in the procedure, in order to facilitate the easy removal of the plaster when dry, was to apply Vaseline and, as you might imagine, this also produced an effect that made the member more conducive to the application of the plaster. Once this was on, all we had to do was wait for it to dry. It looked marvellous and we were both thrilled, but probably for entirely different reasons. Some half an hour later, when it was nail-tapping dry, I gingerly began to try to slide it off, but this brought a huge scream from DT. I couldn't understand it; I had slathered him with Vaseline, but on closer inspection it seemed that some of the hairs on his testicles were deeply embedded in the plaster of Paris.

I tried to get the kitchen scissors that I had been using in between the plaster and the bollocks, but they were too big — the scissors, that is, not the bollocks — although the bollocks were of a decent size, of course . . . And now I'm getting into very hot water. I then tried to employ a pair of nail clippers, but they were too cumbersome and the thought of them clipping his scrotum sent DT into a total panic.

'We'll have to go to hospital. They'll have to cut it off!'

'Isn't that a bit drastic?'

'What? . . . No! I mean cut the plaster off! This isn't funny!'

He was now shouting and trying to pace

around the room with his trousers round his ankles, holding the plaster cast in place so that it wouldn't pull on his pubes any more than it already was doing. The thought of taking him to the hospital on the bus, trying to conceal this huge white erection protruding rudely from his trousers, was too much. As I watched him shuffle awkwardly back and forth, I had a terrible urge to laugh. The winding round of the plaster of Paris had made his member look almost twice its natural size and, as it was already sizeable, with his long curly hair and beard he resembled one of those little Greek statues that you can buy in tacky tourist shops, of tiny men with disproportionately large phalluses, which are supposed to be fertility symbols.

'Don't panic! Someone will have some nail scissors.'

'Oh, Jesus.'

This howl of despair as he sank down in the armchair instantly turned into one of agony, the appendage having pulled at his testicles as it caught on the edge of the chair cushion.

'I'll go downstairs and see if they've got some nail scissors.'

DT didn't say anything, he just looked at me as if to say, 'Why did I ever listen to you?'

I went off to knock on the downstairs neighbour's door. She was a trainee solicitor who lived by herself and I was never sure, with her neat and anal look, that she wasn't the phantom pube collector.

'Hello, I was just wondering if I could borrow a pair of nail scissors?'

'Oh yes, of course.' Great; with a small pair of scissors I should be able to get inside the cast and snip off the pubes. 'Here you are.' She produced a pair of clippers neatly placed on a folded paper handkerchief, a detail that was enough to convince me that she had to be the 'phantom'.

'Oh . . . no, actually I needed scissors, not clippers, sorry . . . '

'Oh, well, I've got scissors but . . . what's it for?'

'Oh, don't worry . . . Well, it's for trimming my boyfriend's beard.' She disappeared again and came back seconds later with a pair of long pointed hair scissors in a see-through plastic sheath. Oh well, slimmer than the kitchen scissors and better than nothing.

'These are my best hair scissors and they can be used only for hair; anything else will blunt them.'

'Oh, don't worry, it will definitely just be the hair. Well, that's what I'm hoping, anyway!' She looked concerned. 'No, no, no, I'm only joking, I'll take great care of them. Thanks very much.'

When I re-entered the flat, brandishing what could be the answer to our prayers, DT's hands, which had been holding his head, shot down to his groin.

'You've got to be joking!'

'Well, let's just . . . give it a go.'

'Oh God.'

It was fine; I managed to slip the scissors down between cast and scrotum, and snip the first pubes free, after which it was plain sailing. It was a perfect cast, coming away completely intact, except that the inside now sprouted several ginger pubic hairs, which simply wouldn't detach.

'I suppose it's like having your name inside.'

'Yes.'

DT wasn't laughing, but I think he was pretty chuffed with it, as it took pride of place on the mantelpiece for some months, prompting admiring glances from female visitors as well as several male ones, come to think of it. When I went to place the scissors back in their sheath, I noticed one or two of his pubes were still attached to the blades. I removed them, but couldn't resist leaving one. I then waited to see whether it would reappear under the door in a little envelope, but of course it never did.

In the summer holidays after my first year at college, I was working as a ward orderly at the General Hospital in Birmingham. I loved the job and had far greater success in it than I ever had in my original nursing role. This was largely because less was expected of me as an orderly and my nursing experience bumped me up above the others in terms of competence. So I shone, also because my confidence had been hugely boosted by my year at the polytechnic. My mother thought that I was staying in the nurses' home at the General, whereas I was in fact renting a room with DT in Varna Road, a notorious street in the Birmingham red-light district called Bordsley Green.

One Sunday morning, Sunday, 23 July 1971 to be exact, I had come on duty, and was

194

immediately summoned to the matron's office.

'Sit down, Miss Walters.'

A thin, weary and distracted-looking woman sat at the other side of the desk, fiddling with a ballpoint pen. I could think of no reason why I should have been summoned. Had someone made a complaint? Was I being made redundant? And then, just as I was thinking that maybe I had been found out in my lie to my parents about living in the nurses' home:

'Your father passed away last night. Your mother has been trying to contact you; she seemed to be under the impression that you were living here.'

I sat staring at her, aware that I still had the same half-smile on my face that I was wearing when I entered the room, only now it was immovable, a moment of innocent bewilderment frozen on my face, from the other part of my life. My parents . . . My parents . . . My parents think . . . No, no, no, my mother . . . ? I couldn't make the syntax of what she had said fit into any discernible or sensible order.

'I presume you were expecting this?' She was flicking the biro between thumb and forefinger so that it blurred like the propeller of a plane.

'My d — ' I'd got it! Dad was dead; I'd got it now. A gunshot through the centre of my chest and I was still smiling the stupid smile. 'Oh yes, yes, we were . . . expecting it.'

No we weren't, no we weren't! I stood up, and the smile started to shift with a series of muscular twitches in my cheeks.

'Well, you'd better get off home to your

195

mother, she'll be needing you.'

Where had I heard this before? I wanted to say something to her, but my throat had closed, so I turned and left. Outside, in the long echoing Victorian corridor, where the endless cacophony of the hospital could swallow up every human sound imaginable, I let out a little trapped yelp of sorrow; the smile was gone and the tears came. My Auntie Clare, my mum's sister-in-law, picked me up from the hospital and, driving the wrong way round the one-way system in Birmingham city centre, dropped me, surprisingly without incident, at the flat of my brother Kevin. As soon as we looked at each other in the hallway, his face became a mask of silent pain to which he gave vent in the privacy of his bedroom. We raced home, to 69 Bishopton Road, in Kevin's Mini van, the two of us in a fog of feeling that neither could express, and then suddenly my brother went flying headlong into the back of the car in front. The driver got out, shocked and furious, and began to shout and swear at my brother.

I immediately jumped from the car and screamed at the man: 'You leave my brother alone, our dad's just died, we've got to get home!'

He didn't say another word, even apologising for an accident for which he was in no way responsible.

I was anxious about seeing my mother. How was I to make sense of her without my father? I was almost expecting to see a piece of her physically missing. She was sitting in one of the easy chairs in the kitchen, bunches of newspaper crackling beneath its thin foam cushion. She looked up as I came in, her face bright red and tearstained, helpless with grief.

'We were five and now we're only four.'

She looked smaller and strangely childlike. Several neighbours were standing round including the one who had comforted me when she thought I had failed the eleven-plus but was pissed off when I announced that I had in fact passed it. Now she took me to one side and said in a confidential tone, 'You'll have to keep an eye on your mum, you know, she's suffering. I mean, I'm sure she'll be all right . . . She never was erotic.'

'Pardon?'

'Your mum, she was never an erotic woman. She's always been very stable.'

After my small release in the hospital corridor, I didn't cry again until the funeral a week or so later. I had felt oddly numb, possibly because my mother was so upset and I felt I needed to be strong, but sitting in St Gregory's church, waiting for the funeral service to start, I spotted two little blonde girls walking up the centre aisle. They must have been about four and six. I could see them only from the back, I didn't know who they were, and yet my heart broke.

In the days that followed we started to sort out some of my father's belongings. On going through his filing cabinet, I found a lock of my hair from years ago when it was blonde and a diary from when I was fourteen. It was full of random, mundane facts like: 'Went to school' and 'Hockey practice' and 'Spot on chin' in a childish scrawl, and then I found ten Park Drive tipped. I took them out into the yard and stamped on them over and over, snot and tears flying this way and that as I screamed down at them, 'You bastards! You bloody, fucking bastards!'

My mum rushed to the back door with a rolling pin in her hand and flour on her chin.

'Julie! What on earth are you doing?'

Now I was down on my haunches, the battered fag packet in my hand.

'I'm just so angry about these bloody things.'

'Well, there's no point talking like that now, your father's gone.'

I threw them down and stamped one last time. I then crouched down again and, with my chin resting on my knees, I said in a small voice to myself, 'Thank God I'm a grown-up, thank God he died now and not when I was a child.'

A few weeks later the woman who had referred to my mother as 'erotic' came up to me in the street, and said, in the same confidential tone that she'd used on the day of the funeral, 'How is she?'

'Oh, she's doing all right.'

'Good. She needs to eat more, you know.' This woman, incidentally, was enormous. 'I saw her yesterday, she's starting to look emancipated.'

My mum did do all right. In fact you could say that, in some ways, she eventually flowered after my father's death. She started going out more, attending a night school to learn French, and asking me on one occasion whether I'd like to put my feet up and have a *coup d'état*, thinking she was offering me a cup of tea. She began to take the foreign holidays she had yearned for all her life, my father having had no interest. One of the first of these was a trip to Lourdes that was organised by the church. She came back with conjunctivitis and was most put out when we suggested that she might have contracted it from the holy waters, citing very forcibly the air-conditioning on the coach as the obvious cause. She seemed to worry less and when after some time I asked her whether she would ever consider marrying again — after all, she was only fifty-six when Dad died — she said, 'Good Gad, no. Why should I spend my old age running round clearing up after some old man?'

She died in 1989. I stood in a field and screamed at a pale sky until my voice went ragged, 'Where are you? *Where* . . . ?'

I had driven back from my brother's house in Birmingham a couple of days after the funeral, berating my new Mini for having so little power, only to discover that I had driven the entire journey home with the handbrake on. I stood in that field at the back of our house in Sussex, a house that she had never been to. We had just moved in and she had said that she would wait until the days got longer and lighter to visit us. I stood in that field until the pale sky went black, hoping for a sign, a sign that this incredible energy that was my mother was still in the world, unable to comprehend how her huge presence and extraordinary drive, without which I would now probably be languishing in a job for which I had no heart, were no longer here.

The love between us was prickly and fierce, combative and competitive, but I never doubted its power. The mourning of her was hard and painful, and some of it was carried out in public. In the West End stage production of *Frankie and Johnny in the Clair de Lune* later that year, the character of Frankie, whom I played opposite Brian Cox's Johnny, has a very moving speech about her mother towards the end of the piece, and every night I cried for the loss of my own mother as I spoke the lines. And again the following year, I was allowed to mourn her further, in Peter Hall's production of Tennessee Williams' *The Rose Tattoo*, through the character of Serafina, who continually cries for a sign from her dead husband.

The mourning continues to this day, but now it is softened by a bit of understanding of what it is to be a mum and, of course, it has mellowed with age. I no longer look for signs as once I did; there is no need. They are everywhere.

10

Foreign Adventure

Later in the summer of 1971, DT and I took off overland in a Mini to Istanbul with another couple from London, whom we had met working at the hospital. Both were students at Birmingham University and the chap, whom we codenamed Rupert, was the owner of the said Mini. I'm not saying that he was a car owner 'who loved too much' but heavy breathing could often be heard coming from under the bonnet as he drooled over the engine beneath. It was always best to knock before entering his garage and pages of his *What Car?* magazine were frequently found to be mysteriously stuck together. He was one of those car anoraks who spent all his free time sniffing around underneath the vehicle, twiddling and tweaking, and although DT was meant to share the driving with him, Rupert could never quite bring himself to let him take the precious wheel. People often refer to their cars as 'she', but somehow when Rupert did it had a greater resonance. Interestingly, he called his girlfriend, who did all the navigating, by her surname, firing orders at her as we went along.

'Henman? Passports!' or 'Henman? Chewing gum!' or 'Henman? Consult map, please!'

Almost as an omen, and after Rupert had spent days fiddling and ferreting under the bonnet in preparation for the trip, one of the wheels began to wobble free as we drove off down the Balham High Road, just minutes into the first leg of our big adventure.

We went through France, Germany, Austria, Italy, Hungary, Bulgaria, Rumania, Greece and finally Turkey, with Rupert driving as if a homicidal maniac were in hot pursuit. DT and I were squashed into the back seat with assorted belongings crammed in around us. Convinced that it would prevent the engine from overheating, Rupert insisted that we had the heater on inside the car, which became unbelievably stifling almost as soon as we crossed the Channel. I'm not entirely sure when we discovered that we might have made a mistake embarking on that trip, but it was probably on the Balham High Road.

In Rumania we travelled through the High Carpathians, where bears are meant to roam and where huge mountains on either side of the road almost touched in places, leaving just a tiny blue crack of sky above us. We set up camp in a borrowed tent that was slightly superior to the one we had used in France, and at night we listened to the sounds of wolves howling. In the little towns, the local people crowded around the car, stroking it, with Rupert darting about to check that they hadn't left any mark. They were saying its name, incredulously, over and over again, almost chanting with wonder, 'Owstin Meenee!'

It was like an incantation, with Rupert joining in each time it was said, and nodding in confirmation.

'Yeah, yeah, yeah, Austin Mini, yeah, that's right, mate, yeah, yeah, don't touch the windscreen wipers, mate. Yeah, yeah.'

One man, who had stroked virtually every inch of the car as if it were a flying saucer newly arrived from outer space, spoke a little English.

'You are from London?'

Rupert was straight in there, polishing with his cuff where the man had put his hand.

'Yeah, that's right, mate, well, I am, me and Henman are. These two are your bloody Northerners.'

'I know Londoner.'

'Oh yeah?'

'Yes, Derek Brown . . . Do you know Derek?'

'Never heard of him, mate.'

The people simply couldn't believe that we had travelled all that distance, from London, England, and by this time neither could we. When we passed through the border between Hungary and Rumania, Rupert surpassed himself with his tactful cockney charm. As the Hungarian border guards were walking around the car, one of them signalled for him to open the boot. Rupert swaggered around to the back to flip it open and, as they rooted through, he pointed at the contents and said with a smirk, 'Yeah, bombs! Yeah, there's bombs in there, mate! Yeah, that's it, bombs!'

If DT and I could have slid down our seats and disappeared, we would have, but as the cramped conditions in the back of the car prevented it, we were forced to cringe, sitting up in full view of anyone who cared to look. Clearly thinking that these men couldn't speak English, Rupert made an exploding sound, blowing his cheeks out and throwing his hands into the air, as a rather excellent visual aid, just so that they got the full picture. Whereupon the guard, in perfect English, of course, said, 'Take everything out, please.'

We were there for hours as they emptied the contents of every single container out on to the ground: soap powder, washing-up liquid, shampoo, orange squash, etc., all of which we would have to replace. By now DT and I were furtively discussing where we could jump ship.

However, we stayed the course and arrived in Istanbul, needing to stretch our legs but relatively unscathed. On our first day there we were walking down the main street when we heard a familiar cry. It was another couple whom we vaguely knew from Manchester Poly, walking along on the other side of the road. Rupert immediately introduced himself but we made our excuses, dived down a side alley and got away. We spotted them some two hours later, the four of them sitting at a pavement café, Rupert holding court, the guy slouched in his chair with a white sunhat pulled down over his face and the two women nodding but with a glazed look in their eyes.

On our return journey, the plan was to take a ferry from Igoumenitsa in Greece to Otranto in Italy. When we arrived on the dockside our boat was there waiting for us. Smaller than we had imagined, it was called *The Rumba*. This name turned out to be more appropriate than we could ever have anticipated. We sat there in the boiling, airless Mini, wondering where on earth the cars were meant to go, when a hole appeared in the side of the ship and all became clear. Once the car was sardined in on the little deck below, we scrambled up to the top deck so as to secure a place to sunbathe. It was a perfect Mediterranean day, with a cloudless blue sky and a sea that barely moved, and people were stripping down to their swimwear and stretching out on towels on the hot wooden deck. After the cramped, sweaty conditions of the car, I have to say it felt like the *QE2*.

Everything was perfect until we pulled in at our only port of call, which was Corfu Harbour. A few passengers embarked and then as we pulled out a wind came, seemingly from nowhere, to tickle the untroubled surface of the sea. To begin with this was a welcome relief from the relentless sun but, as we left the harbour behind, it began to pick up speed and white horses were starting to pop up everywhere around us. The water became choppy and turbulent, and people were putting their clothes back on. Within minutes it became very difficult to stand or walk about the deck as *The Rumba* lurched from port to starboard and then from bow to stern, shoving its windswept, laughing passengers into drunken little scurries to grab hold of whatever solid thing they could. This, I thought, was the Mediterranean Sea; this could not be a storm of any note; and surely it wouldn't last that long?

Four hours later, when we should have been halfway through our journey, we had barely moved, *The Rumba* now being lifted up almost vertically, first on to one end and then the other, by huge dark waves and 80-mph winds. The deck was virtually deserted, everyone having taken refuge in the cramped little bar below, where apparently the floor was already covered with vomit that slid from side to side and aft to fore with every lurch of the boat. The only people left up on deck were a couple of young blokes, hardly able to stand, hanging on to the ship's rail for grim death and retching over the side, blizzards of vomit flying on the wind; and me, lying on the deck, no longer in my bikini, but wrapped, shivering, in my sleeping bag, wretched and weak from continuous nausea.

Soon the blokes disappeared too, having staggered off to join everyone else, and I was alone, not daring to shift in case the vomiting should start again. DT had gone off to find somewhere for us to shelter, so when I felt a hand upon my shoulder, I thought it was him, come to get me and take me below.

'Oh, missy! Blue sleeping bag — green face!'

It was one of the Greek sailors.

'Come, I take you to lie down.'

'Oh . . . oh . . . I don't think I can move. I feel so sick.'

He had a kind, weather-beaten face, with a black hole in his mouth where a front tooth was missing, and I was too weak to argue.

206

'Come.'

And with that he scooped me up in his arms and carried me down some stairs into a small cabin that smelt of oil and TCP, which immediately made me gag.

'Come, you sleep here, the captain's cabin.'

He lowered me gently on to a bunk, made me drink half a tumbler of water, pulled a coarse blanket up over me and stuck a piece of cotton wool in each of my ears. The blanket stank of a combination of diesel and a sharp, citrus aftershave, but I managed in my exhaustion to fall heavily into a deep sleep.

I had no idea how long I'd been asleep when an icy hand pushing back the hair from my forehead woke me up. I opened my eyes and it was pitch black; there was a smell of garlic, French cigarettes and that citrus aftershave. A face that I could barely make out, but I knew didn't belong to my sailor friend or DT, was almost level with mine. As my eyes adjusted to the dark, I could see the outline of a big, round face with a full beard.

'I come sleep with you. This . . . my bed. I sleep now.'

And with that he began to get into the narrow bunk. I still felt very sick and my head was pounding as he squashed himself in beside me and began to kiss my face.

'No, please . . . I am sick . . . please.'

'It is OK. You are like daughter.'

I quickly turned my back on him, praying that this wouldn't make matters worse.

'I am very sick.'

When freezing fingers fumbled under my sweater and around my waist, I felt panic begin to rise, bringing with it a fresh wave of nausea. I shifted on to my back, trying to shove his hands away.

'Is OK. I sleep with you . . . like daughter.'

Poor bloody daughter! I bet she doesn't look forward to you coming home from the sea! The hands slid downwards.

'Please, no . . . Stop it!'

Then it came to me, a trick I'd learnt at school. I took in a very deep breath, swallowing a good portion of the air, forcing it down into my stomach and then let out a long, loud, resounding burp. It stopped him in his tracks. Then I sat up, my head reeling with dizziness, and, partly leaning in his direction, I did it again.

'Oh, I'm . . . going to be sick . . . sick . . . Please, sick . . . sick . . . '

He jumped from the bed and switched on the light. My assailant was a huge man wearing nothing but a Guernsey-type pullover and a very grubby-looking pair of powder-blue Y-fronts stuck into the crack of his not insubstantial bottom. With his back to me, he was rummaging through a heap of clutter on top of a small cabinet.

'Wait, wait! I have . . . '

He turned to me, offering up a shiny, pink, conical-shaped paper party hat with a broken elastic chinstrap dangling from it. Then just as I was thinking that I couldn't possibly have anything more to bring up, the water that the sailor had made me drink when he put me to

208

bed came shooting up like a fire hydrant. As I grabbed the party hat in what turned out to be a futile gesture, the water spurted out of my mouth, forming a perfect arc over the top of it, to land, hot and splashing, on the bare feet of the man. He instantly jumped back, muttering something in Greek and, grabbing his shoes and trousers, he left, saying simply, 'I go now.'

Yeah, you do that. And too weak to get up myself, I flopped back down in the bed and slept until morning.

Thirteen hours later, making it a journey of seventeen hours, we arrived in Otranto. The same bloke who had tried to molest me came and woke me up to disembark.

'We here now. We in Italy. We in Otranto.'

He was wearing a big smile as if we had both been on a long and jolly journey to a favourite holiday destination and now, wasn't it heaven, we had finally arrived. I got weakly to my feet, whereupon he gave me a huge hug and kissed me on the forehead.

'You like my daughter.'

It took me days to recover, but needless to say I did and I have never really suffered from motion sickness in quite the same way since. Up until this point, a rowing boat on a fairly placid pond would send me staggering for the sick bag, but I guess where there's adversity . . .

11

Learning to Teach

During my last two years at the poly, I moved into a bedsit at the top of a tall Victorian house in Demesne Road, Whalley Range. DT had gone off to Bristol to do an MA and the two of us had decided that we would get married the following summer. Despite the fact that our street was in fact pronounced De Main Road, all the bus drivers shouted 'Dmeznee!' as the bus approached the stop. Once, when I took a cab from town driven by a West Indian man, he drove to the nearest busy road.

'Oh, I thought you wanted the main road.'

Whalley Range was an area that had definitely seen better days. It was not a place to be out in, alone, after dark, as I soon discovered. I had been in my new bedsit only a short time when, as I was walking home, lugging three bags of shopping, a car drew up slowly alongside me. In my innocence I went over to see what the driver wanted, thinking he was lost or something.

'Are you all right?' I asked. He stared at me and I wondered for a minute whether I knew him from somewhere.

'I don't know. Am I?'

'I beg your pardon?'

Then something caught my eye, a flash of

white in his lap, and there, caught in the cold light of the street lamp, was a very small, soft willy, about the size of a child's forefinger, nestling in the folds of his open flies. I looked back up at his face, expecting an expression that said, 'Please take pity on me, I am so small.' Instead I got one that said, 'Yeah, baby! What do you think of that? Get in the car and let me do you some damage!'

'Do you think I'm a prostitute?' I was furious.

'I think you might be a dirty bitch.'

'Do you honestly think I'd be touting for trade, carrying three bags of groceries? What did you expect? A shag, with a couple of pounds of potatoes thrown in? And as for *that* — ' I looked down at the teeny willy again, 'I should put it under your pillow and smoke it in the morning if I were you!'

And I scuttled off, gathering speed as I went, in case he should turn nasty, but thrilled that I'd managed to think of the derogatory punchline.

All of us in the house in 'Dmeznee Road' were from the polytechnic and the place was presided over by Dolores, a kind of caretaker who lived in a tiny, cramped room beneath the stairs in the basement. She held keys to the bedsits, kept a stash of shillings for when people's meters ran out, cleaned the common areas and took in parcels, etc. She was Irish, probably around her mid to late fifties, a thin, reedy woman with ashen skin, and eyes made most alarmingly pale by the black, smudgy pencil line she drew around them; a woman, in fact, after my own heart. She had long, dyed, blue-black hair, which

211

after a week or two of regrowth would sport snow-white roots; these she would often neglect for months, so that the contrast of the two colours gave her a badger-like appearance. She wore her hair pinned up and you could plot her movements through the house by following the trails of hairpins that fell from her beehive wherever she went. Failing that, you could track her by the smell of stale cigarettes, as she was never without a Rothmans Kingsize hanging, seemingly unsupported, from her bottom lip.

Dolores was lonely and would often hover about at the bottom of the basement stairs, purporting to dust but actually waiting to catch people as they came in from college, whereupon she would pounce with tales of woe, often connected with the men who passed with some regularity in and out of her life, each one leaving her disappointed, each one a 'loser' and a 'no hoper', and 'all of them users'. On the odd occasion the echoes of a drunken row with one of her beaux would float up the stairwell, usually ending with his being turfed out into the street at some ungodly hour with a bone-shaking slam of the front door.

We all tried to avoid having to go down to her room, knowing that it could mean being trapped there for at least an hour or so. She had an amazing skill for keeping people metaphorically pinned to the wall, unable to utter more than the odd word, while she unleashed torrents of verbiage at them before they had time to think of an escape route.

One Saturday night I was cooking a meal for a

212

friend, not a particularly comfortable experience for me at the best of times, when the electricity ran out, so I was forced to go down and cadge some shillings off her to feed into the meter. When she opened the door, she had the look a hunter might have on spotting a prize prey.

'Hello! Are you not out this Saturday night?' She'd already clasped hold of my arm to prevent any escape.

'No. How are you?'

As soon as I said this, I knew it was a mistake.

'I have cancer.' Oh my God and it's a big one.

'Oh . . . oh . . . I . . . I'm so . . . I'm so sorry.'

'Yes, I had this pain in my chest for weeks and I finally went along to the doctor and . . . '

I didn't speak for another sixty-five minutes. Halfway through her monologue, around the part where she was describing what they had found on her first set of X-rays, I remembered that I'd left the sweet and sour pork that I'd been cooking bubbling away on top of the gas stove. I had to listen while she told me, verbatim, what the doctor had said of her prognosis, what the actual operation and her subsequent recovery would entail, plus the details of her Uncle Pat's tumour, its removal and his eventual demise, before I managed to free my arm and get a word in edgeways about the imminent fire that was about to break out in the attic at the top of the house.

As I rushed up the stairs two or three at a time, clutching several shillings that I had promised to pay back on the following Monday, a dreadful smell of burning aluminium and melting plastic met me, full on. The sweet and sour pork was no longer recognisable and what you might call extreme caramelisation had taken place. From then on I kept my own stash of shillings. On hearing the radio playing in her room on the Monday, when I went down to pay Dolores back, I slipped the money under the door in a previously prepared envelope and raced back up the stairs. Halfway up I heard her door squeak open.

'Oh, Julie, thank you, pet. I coughed up blood this morning.'

I could just see her face between the curving banisters of the stairwell, a Hammer horror shot of Bela Lugosi's sister. Her skin was waxy and even paler than usual, corpse-white with what looked like the beginnings of a mystery black eye.

'Oh dear, did you?' Careful! Don't ask questions!

'Yes, awful big gobfuls, mixed up with green gunk.' What did I tell you?

'Oh . . . '

'I could barely breathe.' Yes, she is off.

'Oh . . . '

'And the pain was intolerable, intolerable!' There were just six steps left to my door; I could see it, the heavenly gateway to a Dolores-free zone.

'Well, I've — '

'I had to take myself off to see the quack again.' She lets out a loud rattling cough.

'Oh, that's — '

'I don't know why I bother. He's no use to

214

man or beast.' Another long, bubbling cough. 'All he can say is I ought to give up smoking! I ask you!'

Thank God there was nothing on the stove.

Dolores was a close relative of the theatrical landlady, a legendary figure in the acting world. I imagine there are very few of them left today, with the almost complete demise of the repertory system, but back then they were plentiful, as were the stories surrounding them. When I was staying in digs in Sheffield back in 1980, my landlady was a colourful, warm, if slightly brassy woman with what could be described as a bit of a twinkle in her eye. One night I returned to the digs rather late after the show and, entering by the back door, I snapped on the kitchen light to find the landlady on the kitchen table, going at it hammer and tongs, her big flowery skirt up around her chin, with the young stage manager, who had just moved in and who looked about twelve. Momentarily paralysed by shock, I stood there smiling and speechless. When I had gathered myself together I managed to murmur, 'Oh . . . hello . . . '

I then snapped the light back off and tried to squeeze past them as if they were merely having breakfast. This meant a lot of chair scraping, with the landlady having to shift and move her knee out of the way and me trying to avert my gaze whilst muttering, 'Sorry . . . oh sorry . . . If I can just . . . '

Then the woman looked over the top of the stage manager's shoulder and with breath that, had it been said in close proximity to a naked flame, would have turned blue, said, 'Oh goodnight, Miss Walters. Sleep well.'

The next day I tried to creep out of the house without bumping into her to save us both from embarrassment, but just as I was leaving she rushed down the stairs and said, 'Oh, Miss Walters, I'm sorry about last night. You must think I'm a terrible flirt.'

On another occasion I was staying in a scarily neat and tidy house on the outskirts of Manchester, where an empty coffee cup would be whipped from your hand before it had even reached the coaster upon which you had been instructed in no uncertain terms to place it. One morning having finished my breakfast, in the bright, lemon-fresh kitchen, I repaired to the lavatory next door with my *Guardian* crossword, leaving the other lodgers still sitting around the table with their cups of tea. All of a sudden there was a sharp rap on the door and within full hearing of all and sundry, the landlady called out, 'Oh, oh, Miss Walters? Do remember, no solids in the downstairs toilet. Thank you.'

In the first term of our second year at college, we were scheduled to do teaching practice. I was placed in a primary school in north Manchester and given several different age groups to teach. At this point both my brothers and my sister-in-law were teachers and, although they all taught different subjects, it gave me a peek into their lives. I loved teaching and saw how close in many ways it was to acting. It was necessary to give a kind of performance and to keep children interested in what you had to say. The six weeks' practice culminated in a nativity play, which I had helped to get together, along with one of the class teachers, Mrs Forbes, a nice woman I immediately took to.

On the afternoon of the first performance I was in charge of the sound cues and sat to the side of the little stage with a small cassette player at the ready, in full view of the audience. With a sign from Mrs Forbes who was standing at the other side of the stage, also in full view of the audience, I pressed the play button. Mrs Forbes's sign, although she was a matter of feet from me, was achieved by stretching her arm straight up towards the ceiling and waving it slowly from side to side as if she were on a crowded beach and needed to be seen, which consequently drew all eyes towards me.

My first cue was a beautiful rendition of 'In the Bleak Midwinter', which in turn was the cue for Mary and Joseph to enter, which they did, trudging wearily across the stage. Then after another huge wave from Mrs Forbes on the far side, with the audience's heads swivelling Wimbledon-like from her to me, I faded the music out and the narration began. This was read by one of the eleven-year-olds, describing how Mary and Joseph had walked for miles, Mary heavy with child, and how they had battled through the wind and the snow. This was my next cue, but instead of the sound of a howling gale, out from the little cassette, loud and clear, came instead the sound of pouring rain, accompanied by great claps of thunder. Mary

217

and Joseph stopped in their tracks and looked helplessly towards Mrs Forbes, who was now standing opposite, doing big winding actions with her hand, interspersed with dragging her forefinger across her throat.

Now in panic mode, I tried to fast-forward the tape and, squeaking and squealing, Disney-like, it whizzed on to what I hoped was the next cue, but when I pressed the play button, blaring out into the hall came a police siren. People were beginning to whisper and giggle, at which Mrs Forbes's winding action now went up a notch, into a rotating blur of overdrive. I then decided that perhaps rewind was the best course of action and whizzed the tape backwards, randomly stopping and inwardly begging the gods to make something sensible come out, but no, this time we were treated to gunshots and the galloping of horses.

However, Mary and Joseph, who had been glued to the spot since the thunderstorm had set in, decided to do a bit of improvising and on hearing the shots Joseph threw Mary to the ground, causing her to let out what sounded like a rather real scream. Covering her with his cowl, he proceeded to hold the unseen gunmen at bay and pick them off one at a time with his staff, which, miraculously, had turned into a rifle. Now Mrs Forbes was fairly whipping her hand across her throat, so much so that I feared she might do herself damage. I pressed stop, plunging us into a sudden and much appreciated silence. Everyone froze, Mrs Forbes, with her hand across her throat, looking as if she were striking an old-fashioned photographic pose, and nobody spoke. Joseph made one more half-hearted popping sound, directing a last shot at the enemy. Silence again. No one moved. Then from underneath the cowl Mary yelped, '*Ow!* You're on my hair!' And Joseph, raising his eyes to heaven, shifted.

Just as Mrs Forbes was about to come to the rescue, the narrator said, 'And Joseph killed every one of those muggers, and they went on their way towards Bethlehem.' And then as a little nudge to Mary, who was still under the cowl, and Joseph, who still had his eye out for stray 'muggers', '*They went on their way to Bethlehem!*'

My second and final teaching practice, in the third year, was a very different experience altogether. It was to take place at a girls' secondary school, which pleased me because of its close proximity to my bedsit. I was teaching all years except the sixth form and, almost without exception, the bottom streams. On my first day, I was just sitting down for lunch in the canteen with the girls when an altercation started at the next table, gradually attracting the attention of everyone around. A male teacher, a man in his mid-forties, was asking a girl to leave as she was in the wrong sitting and she was refusing to go. Suddenly, a towering girl, probably about six feet tall, appeared seemingly from nowhere and, squaring up to this poor bloke, said, 'You lay one finger on her and you got me to deal with!'

He tried to ignore her and carried on, in a

calm, quiet voice, trying to reason with the girl who wouldn't go. Eventually he made the mistake of touching her lightly on the arm, whereupon the Amazon launched a shocking attack, hurling punches and kicks, and lashing out at his face with great curled talons painted blood-red. Girls and staff alike were standing open-mouthed as the two of them became locked in a fierce struggle in which his shirt was ripped from button to armpit and her blouse was torn open, sending buttons flying, Incredible Hulk style, in all directions and revealing a bright-red bra beneath.

They fell to the floor, the girl viciously grabbing at the man's face and hair. Some people began to cheer and egg them on, while others got up on to the benches to get a better view. They were right next to a set of stone steps and, suddenly rolling over and over, they began to tumble down them. Every time she was on top as they rolled, she would grab his hair and bang his head with a sickening thud on the stone step. This finally stopped when they hit the bottom and for a few seconds they lay there without moving. Then the girl stood up and, with a half-hearted attempt at adjusting her clothing, she swaggered off, complaining about a broken nail as she went. The teacher got slowly and unsteadily to his feet and stood there for a moment, stunned and ashen-faced, his hands trembling, staring at the floor, his hair, which had been neatly combed flat, now standing up in messy, spiky clumps. There was a trickle of blood from his nose, which had dripped on to his shirt, his lip was cut and he had bitten his tongue. When at last I could speak, I turned to the teacher standing next to me and said, 'Please, tell me I won't be teaching her.'

Fortunately, I wasn't. The police were called in, which resulted in her exclusion, but I was given what they referred to as 'the Easter leavers'. These were girls who were not going to stay on and do their GCEs or CSEs, but would instead leave at Easter, some of them aged just fifteen. This meant that they had absolutely no incentive to learn and therefore no interest whatsoever in any form of schoolwork. I knew that if I was going to survive this, I had to get them on my side. So the night before my first lesson with them, I wrote my script.

The next day, I went in and told them how I was on teaching practice and my every move was being watched, so I needed their help. I asked them to each get out their Shakespeare textbook and have it open on the desk as if we might be discussing it, should the teacher that was monitoring me walk past and look through the window. It was a gamble on my part but one that paid off because they thought the whole subterfuge was a gas. I then assured them that we wouldn't in fact be studying Shakespeare because I knew very little about it and what I really liked in terms of Drama was modern stuff about real people's lives. That was it; from then on we were friends.

We talked, very casually, with girls sitting on top of their desks and lounging about with their feet up on chairs. This normally frowned-upon informality was a battle I was prepared to forgo in exchange for their participation and interest. One girl kept watch; every time a teacher came down the corridor our lookout would alert us, and the girls would jump down behind their desks, burying their heads in their Shakespeares. We discussed everything, from their feelings about being 'left to rot', as one girl so aptly put it, because they weren't academic, to abortion and racism, and we started off with the fight in the canteen.

'Did anyone see that fight in the canteen? Blimey! What was all that about?'

And they were off. Should teachers be allowed to manhandle pupils? Should men be allowed to teach in a single-sex school? Was there a racist element, with the girl involved being black and the teacher being white? How do black girls view white men in authority? What constitutes assault? How are teachers meant to keep control? Every time they got loud, I'd ask them to pipe down, reiterating the fact that I would be in trouble with the teacher if she heard the noise and as most of them were in constant trouble with the teachers, they were totally with me.

After a week or so I got them to act out some of the topics that we were discussing. Mother — daughter relationships is the topic that has stayed with me. A small black girl, looking much younger than her years, improvised a situation between a mother and a daughter, and brought in elements that had obviously come from her own life, living in a one-bedroom flat with

222

her mother who was a prostitute and drug addict. It was some of the most honest, raw and moving acting I have seen to date.

These girls weren't going to get their GCEs but they were highly intelligent, articulate and passionate once they engaged. I became hugely fond of them and felt that I had shared real intimacy with them in these classes, brought about by the power of Drama. They could express their fears and hopes through it and it promoted discussion and understanding of some of the bewildering elements of their lives. And I, personally, learnt that Drama was concerned with more than just being an actor and acting lines off a page. It was therapeutic, cathartic; it helped to develop emotional intelligence and the use of language and communication skills; it was educational for both performer and audience alike. I think, if taught moderately well, it is a vital part of a healthy education, and it is sadly and foolishly neglected today.

12

'Can We Still Go on the Honeymoon?' — Breaking Up

DT and I had decided that we would marry in Bristol, where he was studying for his MA, in the summer of 1973. Everyone was thrilled; my mother approved and he had bought me a gorgeous antique engagement ring, set with three vibrant turquoise stones. One night, just three weeks before the wedding day, on one of his weekend visits to Manchester, I shot up in bed in the middle of the night, filled with only one, very certain thought.

'Oh, DT . . . I'm so sorry!' I couldn't get out any more than that. I was paralysed by gulps and sobs.

'What? What is it, love?' He sat up and put his arm around me.

Eventually I managed, 'I can't get married. I'm just not ready. There's too much of life to do first. I just can't!'

And I knew it to be right because the relief was enormous, as if something had been surgically removed, something that I hadn't even registered as being a problem, but now that it was gone I was light as air.

But I loved DT and hurting him was painful.

'Look, DT, I just really, really can't do this. I

don't want us to split up . . . Let's just carry on as we are. I just don't want to get married.' And finally, he stopped asking why.

We lay there in silence and then, 'DT? Can we still go on the honeymoon?'

Well, we were going to Lisbon and I couldn't give *that* up, and neither could he.

I wasn't looking forward to telling my mother, thinking she would feel let down in some way and be critical of me, seeing my decision as irresponsible, but to my surprise she said, 'Well, thank God you found out that it wasn't right now and not after you'd got married.' And then, perfectly timed, 'So you weren't pregnant then?'

A couple of months later we did go off on our 'honeymoon', staying in a pension in Lisbon for only a couple of nights, then hitch-hiking north and stopping where we were dropped in a little fishing village just south of Oporto. With no accommodation booked, we had to go and enquire in various shops, restaurants and bars as to where we might stay. At the last minute, just as the sun was going down, in a tiny grocery store we were given the address of the local doctor who, it seemed, had a room that he occasionally let out to tourists. It was an attic room up in the eaves of the family house with a ceiling that sloped down to the floor on both sides. There was very little space because, besides the bed, it was used for storage and contained lots of boxes and cases, etc., but it was perfectly adequate.

We spent the days reading, lying on the beach sunbathing, watching the fishermen bringing in their catch and mending their huge nets spread out on the sand, and eating freshly caught sardines that were barbecued right there at the water's edge by the fishermen's wives. Our evenings were passed in the cafés and bars, and we only returned to our room late at night in order to sleep.

One night, after we had been there three or four days, I was awoken by a creaking sound and on opening my eyes was met by the creepy sight of a shadowy figure moving slowly about the room. I was paralysed with fright and didn't even nudge DT who was dead to the world; instead I buried my head under the covers. At long last the creaking of floorboards ceased and a peek from beneath the sheets reassured me that the figure had gone. I gradually slid into a fitful sleep. The next day I was convinced I had seen a ghost and endured much teasing from DT on the subject, but I knew what I had seen and felt very spooked. The following two nights I slept very lightly, making up for it by falling into a coma on the beach the next day. There was no repetition of the event on either of those nights, although two or three times I awoke, thinking I could hear something, but on each occasion there was nothing there and the shadowy figure did not materialise.

On our last night we got back to our room with the intention of making an early start in the morning. We were hitching back to Lisbon for another two or three days before returning home, so we decided to pack up our things before getting into bed. I had lost a flip-flop and was on all-fours looking for it under our bed when from somewhere close behind me came what sounded like a low, gravelly snarl. Instantly hitting my head on the bedstead, as if in a daft comedy sketch, I screeched and stood, backing away towards the door. At that moment, DT returned from downstairs, where he had been paying the doctor for our stay.

'Bloody hell, DT, there's something living in here.'

'What? What is it?'

'I just heard it clear as day. It was growling.'

'What? Where?'

'I don't know but I think it came from behind there!'

Opposite our bed, running along the bottom half of the sloping roof, was an old, thick, green curtain on a length of saggy curtain wire. I had looked behind it when we first moved in and there were just some cardboard boxes, a pile of towels, a basket of clothes-pegs and a heap of old clothing. DT moved towards it on tiptoe, pulling a cartoon expression of angst by stretching his mouth wide from corner to corner, baring his teeth and making big scared eyes. Just as he bent down in order to peep inside, there was, somewhat comic in its timing, a long-drawn-out, rippling fart. He jumped up and fell back on to the bed.

'Jesus Christ!'

We stared for a moment as a sulphurous odour filled the little room. I turned to DT.

'Well, don't look at me!'

'Oh my God, DT, I'm scared! What is it?'

'I don't know. Do you think it's human?'

We were now talking in Albert Hall-sized stage whispers.

'I don't know. I haven't smelt anything like that since Grandma sat on the sofa and ate a raw potato, so I suppose it might be. Oh God, I'm scared.'

DT gingerly started to get up off the bed, accompanied by a discordant, dull twanging from its springs.

'Shhhh!'

'Shhhhhh!'

Then, taking a deep breath in, and with one hand covering his nose and mouth against the acrid stench that still hung in the air, he slowly, with the very tips of his thumb and forefinger, his pinkie lifted, teacup-style, began to pull the curtain back. The room itself was not well lit and the space down behind the curtain was in virtual darkness. I crept forward and we both peered into the gloom until our eyes became accustomed to it. There seemed to be a dark, hunched shape on the ground and we could hear it breathing, deep and slumberous. I edged closer until I was able to see not only that it was indeed human but that I recognised the set of its profile.

On one or two occasions when we had popped back to the room during the day, we had passed an ancient woman on our way up the steps to our attic. She was coming down, clutching linen that she had stripped from the bed, and was dressed in the classic widow's garb of long black skirt and shawl. She was apparently the doctor's mother and never spoke a word to us in passing, and yet there she was, a set of rosary beads wrapped around her hand as she slept, sharing our room! She must have got up at dawn before we woke and gone to bed while we were out in the evening. I guess it was her room, but the doctor saw a chance to make a little extra cash and had shoved her behind the curtain. We went into hysterics, thinking about our lovemaking on the previous nights and wondering whether she had lain there, listening, and perhaps getting a bit of a kick from what she heard.

'She must get up really early in the morning, I suppose.'

'Well, we'll be chatting in the queue for the bathroom tomorrow, then.'

I slept soundly that night. At least I did after DT opened a small window in the roof.

DT and I split up for good the following year, going through a wistful little ceremony where we divided up our few domestic acquisitions. I can see them laid out on the floor of my bedsit, with DT and me looking sadly down at them. In the middle of the little heap were the two square camping tins that we had used in France and on our trip to Turkey; I handed them to him, unable to make eye contact. There was a motley set of cutlery, a cheap plastic pedal bin, a plastic plate rack and a washing-up bowl to match. We focused our pain on the washing-up bowl, which, if not exactly fought over, was definitely the subject of some discussion, although, on the other hand, not enough of a discussion to prevent us from being good friends thereafter.

13

Life at The Everyman — Liverpool

We did major productions at the Manchester Polytechnic. In the first year we put on a play that I'd never heard of, although that wasn't saying much, titled *The Dark of the Moon* by William Berney and Howard Richardson. It was a strange piece set in the Appalachian Mountains and based on a European folk song, 'The Ballad of Barbara Allen'. I suppose it was chosen because it had a huge cast of characters and although it wasn't a musical members of the cast were required to sing. I played the dark witch and can remember little about the experience, except that we put it on in the studio theatre, which in fact was a derelict church with holes in the roof through which rain fell and pigeons shat on a regular basis. A mop often had to be employed before a class or a rehearsal could take place, and buckets placed here and there were a regular feature, as was the sound of raindrops drip-drip-dripping into them.

The studio was situated next to the art college at All Saints and was to all intents and purposes where we were based. We also had the use of a derelict shop on the corner opposite for voice classes and rehearsals, this later becoming the student union, whilst movement classes were held in the art college gymnasium. The 'make-do' nature of the old church and the filthy old shop premises, with its curling linoleum tiles and peeling walls, which had literally not been touched since the day the shop moved out, together with the scattered layout of the facilities, gave the course a feeling of having been shoved in as an unwanted afterthought, which did little to promote a sense of belonging to the wider faculty of Art and Design and even less for the collective student sense of self-esteem. In fact, in our second year a demonstration was organised by the third years to protest about the low level of health and safety measures, but I don't recall many turning up or it making much of an impression. Although I attended the protest and agreed with it in principle, in reality I loved the School of Theatre as it was, with its makeshift, leaky, falling-down premises, and felt that something of importance was lost when, in 1973, the School of Theatre moved to the Capitol building in Didsbury, which was an old television studio with all the character and atmosphere of a civic toilet.

The second-year production, *Summer Folk* by Maxim Gorky, was staged in the University Theatre. The role I played was that of Varya, the female lead, and the moment I stepped out on to that stage for the technical rehearsal, I knew that I was home and that this was right. I felt for the first time in my life that I had a voice, and that this is how it would be heard, and this was how I would be seen and measured.

Our third-year production was *The Playboy of*

231

the Western World by J.M. Synge, in which I played Pegeen Mike. It was staged at the Library Theatre, which was the main repertory theatre situated underneath the huge, circular library in St Peter's Square. This venue made it feel real and professional. To be able to inhabit an Irish accent, for the play was set in the West of Ireland, and to be able to use it to express a complex character instead of my usual comic caricature of my mother or grandmother, was a deep thrill.

It was here at the Library Theatre, in a cold scene dock (the first place where scenery is stored), that I did one of my very first auditions for a job: the Sylvia Plath poem 'Daddy', my beloved Lady M. and a piece from *Juno and the Paycock*. I was auditioning for the 1974 autumn season, and the woman who took the audition, whose name I have completely obliterated from my memory, was in a fairly grim mood, with a 'just hurry up and get on with it' air about her. Although we were in the scene dock, it was cold and draughty for the time of year, which was May, and she was wrapped up in a vast winter coat and swathed around the neck and mouth with a big, woolly scarf, so that I could barely hear a word that she said. The speed with which she got me in and out was, to put it kindly, insensitive or, to put it another way, bloody rude. I didn't get in, unsurprisingly, and subsequently discovered that this woman had had all her teeth out on the morning of my audition. Nice of her to turn up, really.

Before sticking my head above the parapet

with regard to getting a job, however, I applied to Granada Television and was awarded a bursary for a one-year postgraduate course in acting and stage production at the Stables Theatre, next door to the studios. The course was jointly run by the polytechnic and the university combined, and about fourteen students enrolled in the autumn of 1973. We functioned like a complete company, with student actors, student directors, student stage designers and student administrators.

After getting off to a wobbly start by staging a mutiny over the choice of our first play, *The Hollow* by Agatha Christie (the lecturer's argument for it being that this was the kind of unexciting thing we could expect to be doing in rep), we went on to do *'Tis Pity She's a Whore*: guess who I played? Then a little-known piece, written in 1915 by Leonid Andreyev, titled *He Who Gets Slapped*, set in a tatty French circus, in which I played Madame Zenida, a liontamer. Our final production was *The Marriage of Figaro* in which I took the part of the maid. It was during the preparation for this that I started to audition for work. After my disastrous audition at the Library Theatre, I heard that the Everyman Theatre in Liverpool needed a couple of actors for the summer, so I applied, securing an audition for the following week.

The Everyman was one of the most unique, innovative and exciting repertory theatres of the day. Alan Dossor was the director, but at this point he was taking time off and Jonathan Pryce, the actor, was directing while he was away.

Therefore it was Jonathan who took my audition. One of my pieces was again *Juno and the Paycock*, which I had left till last, considering it my *coup de grâce*. I couldn't wait to do it, but when I told Jonathan with some excitement what my final piece was to be, he announced that he had played it only recently and knew it very well. This would not normally present too much of a problem but I had decided to beef the piece up a little, adding a gag here and a gag there, generally rewriting it to suit myself, even adding a little song at one point in it. It never struck me once, even after my experience of auditioning for Edward Argent, that (a) perhaps I should play the script as written or (b) that anyone would even notice or care. And such was my arrogance, I was only slightly put out that Jonathan already knew the piece and that was because it might spoil any element of surprise. Nevertheless, I still launched into it, thinking my version a great improvement on Sean O'Casey's. Luckily Jonathan found it funny, but looking back he was more likely to have been amused by my youthful conceit than my comic invention. He gave me the job and I started work on 14 June 1974.

From the minute I stepped down from the train at Lime Street station, I knew that I would love Liverpool. As I was struggling with a huge bag, a short, rotund woman who happened to be walking by at the time said, 'Come 'ead, love, let me carry that for ya. No, come on! That's heavy, you've got enough to carry!' And she carried my biggest and heaviest bag to the taxi rank for me. Then when I told the taxi driver that I wanted to go to the Everyman Theatre, he said, 'It's only up the road, you know, love?'

'I know but it's really steep and I've got too much to carry.'

He drove me there and refused any payment. 'No! Go on, girl. You gerron that stage and knock 'em dead.'

The Everyman in those days was housed in an old cinema called Hope Hall. It had very little in the way of dressing rooms: possibly one for the boys, downstairs stage left, and two for the girls, downstairs stage right, both extremely cramped; and it was also dusty and rat infested. I remember an electrician being called in to look at the electrics, which required him to go beneath the stage. He took one look and said, 'I'm not going under there. There's hundreds of pairs of eyes looking at me!'

The theatre was, and still is, situated at the top of Hope Street. The Catholic cathedral, looking as if it was about to launch itself into outer space, which the locals referred to as Paddy's Wigwam, stood at one end and the magnificent Protestant cathedral at the other. It had been arranged for me to stay in a bedsit at the top of a Georgian house in Canning Street, a five-minute walk from the theatre. Below me in another bedsit, and also working at the theatre, was Geoffrey Durham, who later became the magician, the Great Soprendo, and the husband of Victoria Wood.

He was a fantastic actor. One of my fondest acting memories is of Geoff making a splendid entrance in a superb production of Brecht's

Coriolanus at the Everyman. As we did not have enough actors, he was playing the whole of the Roman army. He walked on with a majestic presence but, unbeknownst to him, a wire coat-hanger had become attached to his bent elbow and was swinging from his sleeve like a handbag. I entered soon after, playing Coriolanus's wife, I'm ashamed to say, crying with laughter, my face twitching with the effort of keeping it straight.

However, acting never really did it for Geoff and the embryo of the magician that he eventually became was already forming in that bedsit below mine. I would often pop down when at a loose end and watch him do mind-boggling stuff with a piece of rope, or hair-raising stuff with his fire-eating equipment, once seeing his whole beard catch alight. I sat there for a minute thinking that it was all part of the act and it was only when he began to slap his own face rather viciously that I realised it wasn't.

Below Geoff, on the ground floor, lived an alcoholic recluse called Mikie. More often than not I would return late at night after a show and fall over Mikie's prostrate body lying on the floor in the complete darkness of the hall, where the bulb had blown in 1952 and had never been replaced. Mostly, even though I would end up inadvertently treading all over him as I got to my feet, he didn't wake up and by morning he was gone. On certain nights, when in a lighter stupor than normal, he would rear up, howling terrifyingly like a wounded ox, and on one such night he caught hold of my ankle as I scrambled for the stairs and would not let go. In a complete panic, I kicked out violently, not caring what my boot came into contact with, as long as I got away, which of course I did. A day or so later I saw Mikie in the street, diminutive and dishevelled as usual, and I expected his face to be black and blue from the encounter, but not at all; in fact he looked surprisingly chipper. Then as I got closer I noticed a bruise on his chin like part of the perfect imprint of a boot.

I had been taken on at the Everyman to replace a member of the cast of a pub show titled *Flash Harry*. This was performed by Van Load, the part of the company that went out to Liverpool schools, pubs, parks and sometimes the streets, though I think the last was abandoned when, during a performance of a show on the streets of Kirkby, the police had to escort the actors home after they were threatened by a group of twelve-year-olds wielding golf clubs.

The main company were leaving to go down to London because the show they were in was transferring to the West End. It was a musical about the Beatles, titled *John, Paul, George, Ringo and Bert*, whose book and music were both written by Willy Russell. Cast in it were Bernard Hill as John Lennon, Trevor Eve as Paul McCartney, Philip Joseph as George Harrison, Antony Sher as Ringo, George Costigan as Bert and a young Scottish folk-singer friend of Willy's with the voice of an angel by the name of Barbara Dickson as a kind of musical narrator. It turned out to be a huge hit, transferring to the

West End from the Liverpool Everyman Theatre in 1974 to rave reviews, and going on to similar success on Broadway.

Flash Harry, on the other hand, was a raucously funny show about a Liverpool flasher in which, amongst other things, I was to play his mother. My first spot in the show involved a monologue on the trials and tribulations of being the parent of a misunderstood flasher and I stood at the microphone, knitting a long woollen willy warmer as I spoke. I had to learn the Scouse accent, for which the legendary Winnie was drafted in to teach me. Winnie, the cleaner at the theatre, put many an actor through their paces when it came to learning the Liverpool lingo. A kind, witty and gentle woman was waiting for me in the middle bar downstairs, which was still littered with empty glasses from the night before, and stinking of stale beer and cigarettes.

'So you want educatin', do ya?'

And she took me through my speeches, writing them out phonetically.

The show was a bit of a free-for-all, hanging loosely around the central tale of the flasher and his escapades, and our contribution was pretty much left up to us. Geoff Durham, who was also in the show, did his own, brilliant version of the song, 'The Laughing Policeman'. So when I told Roger Phillips (now a famous local character and radio host in Liverpool, but then our director) that I did a passing impersonation of Shirley Bassey, a sparkly dress, covered in green sequins, with huge holes cut into it around the waist, was fished out of wardrobe, a wig was bought from Woolworth's and Birley Shassey was born. I absolutely loved doing it and felt that now I really had come home! The number I chose for the show was 'Hey, Big Spender' with my innuendo-filled version of 'Goldfinger' as an encore. Accompanied by Roger on the tinny old Everyman piano (with drawing pins stuck into the tips of the hammers inside to add a honky-tonk, harpsichord twang), I would wander down off the stage, sashaying around the tables and draping myself over dockers and the like, singing, 'I don't cock my pork for everyone man I see!' in some of the roughest pubs in the universe.

The audiences were — almost always — at least as funny as we were and every time we took a breath in, there was the possibility of a sharp one-liner being pinged at us from somewhere in the crowd. We rarely had any real trouble, which was quite something as the punters didn't pay to see the show; we were generally booked by the landlord, just turned up in their pub and got started. 'It's the long 'airs from the Everymans' is how I once heard us described.

The one really hairy occasion that I recall was when we were doing Alan Bleasdale's *Scully*. This we adapted ourselves from his novel about the life of the eponymous Scully, an anarchic, Liverpool lad with a dysfunctional family. It also happened to be a popular Saturday morning local radio slot with Alan reading the serialisation of his book. We were appearing one rainy Wednesday night in a particularly heavy pub in

Cantrell Farm, a suburb of Liverpool that for my mother would definitely have come under the banner of 'bottom end'. Peter Postlethwaite played Scully and was supported, amongst others, by Bill Nighy, then a handsome blond mixture of James Dean and the lead singer of the Bonzo Dog Doo Dah Band. He had a brilliant, soulful singing voice and the ability to whip out his mouth organ at any given opportunity to play blues and rock riffs; nearly every girl in Liverpool was in love with him. Also in the cast was Matthew Kelly, who had been in the year above me at drama school, then a six-foot-five-inch stripling who, with his full lips and long hair, looked like Mick Jagger's more handsome brother but with a warm, camp wit that audiences loved. There was also Kevin Lloyd, with his cheeky, dark, Bisto Kid looks, and myself as Scully's gran.

Some way into the show, we had all clocked a scruffy, peevish-looking drunk sitting at a table in the corner of the room. Suddenly he shot up from his seat, during one of Pete's monologues, and zigzagged his way to the front of the stage. At first we ignored him, as drunks often approached the stage; either they would get fed up with being shouted down by both actors and crowd and go back to their seats, or fellow members of the audience would coax or threaten them into retreating. However, this bloke was on a mission. He stood there, face flushed, spit flying hither and thither, finger jabbing the air, veins sticking out on his neck like cables, and berated Pete at the top of his voice. Eventually,

240

after an unintelligible string of rants, he lunged at Pete, sending the microphone and a couple of people's drinks on the front row flying. Two or three blokes pulled him off and the show came to a standstill. Sensing the lull in the proceedings, the man then grabbed his opportunity and, struggling free from these blokes, took the floor, swaying about like a drunk in a pantomime and looking down the barrel of his forefinger at Pete.

'I 'ave 'ad enough of you! No! I 'ave! I've been driven mad by ya! I had to put up with you on the radio every Saturday morning for fourteen months while I was in Walton Gaol. I swore to me mates and I promised meself that if I ever came across that friggen' Scully when I got out, I'd friggen' well kill him. And 'ere yer are in me own friggen' pub! I'll friggen' well rip yer friggen' 'ead off!'

And he lunged again, this time held back by a jeering, laughing crowd. Eventually Bill and the others calmed him down by setting him up with another pint and explaining that Pete was just an actor and was not Scully at all, and that Scully, the young lad, was just a character in a book. He looked incredulous and a bit miffed by this explanation, the chance to beat Scully's brains out having been snatched so cruelly away from him, but the promise of more beer as an alternative to being turfed out on to the street seemed to do the trick. The show was got through without further ado with him and Pete now such good friends that they were almost planning a holiday together.

241

Another instance of what you might call trouble was when, later on in the season during the run-up to Christmas, we did *Dick Whittington and his Pussy*. Matthew Kelly played Dick and I played his Pussy, in a manner of speaking. It was a show that we largely wrote ourselves and, as you might imagine, it was packed from start to finish with gags about genitalia. 'Would you like to see my Pussy?' or 'Have you seen my Dick?' Well, you get the picture.

After we'd been performing it to packed pubs for about two weeks, we got word from the landlord of our next venue that someone had reported us to the vice squad, so could we possibly tone the show down somewhat and also take out any swearing as the boys in blue would be paying us a visit that very night. We held an emergency meeting, in which we removed from the script the more salacious jokes and all the swearing. When we went to our gig and started the show, there wasn't a policeman in sight but just as we were beginning to relax and go back to the old script, we spotted them coming in at the back, supposedly incognito but actually unmistakable: huge, with very short hair (remember it was 1974), navy-blue overcoats, pale-blue shirts and great big feet in great big policeman's shoes. So back we went to the expurgated version. This did not please the audience, who stared silently and balefully at us, some turning their backs and talking amongst themselves. A show that was normally a riotous one and a quarter hours long, without the risqué jokes and the swearing ran for just a measly twenty minutes. But the coppers left happy enough, wondering what all the fuss was about.

My days with Van Load were invaluable, lessons in pure survival on stage. We simply had to entertain or go under, or, in some places, fear for our lives. I recall one occasion when, after the show, things got a little out of hand and as we were trying to pack things into the van, I looked up to see Matthew Kelly being carried off round the back of the car park by several very drunk blokes. Luckily there was little malice in it and a lot of drink. Alcohol played a large part in these pub shows. In fact, I don't know how we functioned. A great deal of beer, in my case bottled Guinness, was swilled and I don't think I ever did one of those shows properly sober. I can remember standing outside pubs as we were about to go in and taking in a particular establishment, knowing that it would probably be the last time that I would see it with any clarity. My slight, eight-stone frame probably absorbed a good three pints on most nights. First I had to keep up with the lads, and second the audience insisted on buying us drinks, so who was I to argue? I couldn't, even if I wanted to, contemplate the thought of even one drink before a show nowadays.

My first production on the main stage of the Everyman was Shakespeare's *The Taming of the Shrew*. It was directed by Jonathan Pryce with Kate Fahy as Kate and Del Henny as Petruchio, making a spectacular first entrance on a motorbike to Eric Clapton's 'Layla', the strains

243

of which caused the old theatre to vibrate like a boom box. Anarchy was never very far below the surface of an Everyman production and irreverence was *de rigueur*. One night whilst making his entrance, Nicholas Le Provost tripped over an awkwardly placed stage weight and, careering on to the stage, let rip with, 'Shit! . . . I' faith!'

I played the part of Bianca, Kate's sister, and hated every second of it. I thought the character a wimp and longed to play the Shrew. I loved the unfeminine, mouthy, angry nature of the part and felt that I understood her, whereas Bianca was the opposite. I had no time for her girly, spoilt, petulant nature and this was reflected in a series of night terrors that started in rehearsals and went on nightly, throughout the three-and-a-half-week run. I awoke to find myself ransacking the drawers of my dressing table, in search of the little pink cotton dress, decorated with white hearts, that I wore in the play. Not finding it there, I would turn my mattress on to the floor, thinking it might be underneath. Finally I would fall back down on to the mattress, feeling panicked, distressed and at a loss as to what to do. Then every night the same thing happened: the sliver of light between the top of the curtain and the window frame would catch my eye, and somehow it would draw me back down to reality so that I would realise I was dreaming. I never understood Bianca and I didn't want to be her; she represented at that time the kind of woman that my generation felt they had left behind. I was constantly trying to find some means of making her palatable to me, looking for a way to make her mine. I guess the search for the dress was an echo of that search for the character.

In November 1974 we started rehearsals for the new Everyman Christmas extravaganza, *The Cantrill Tales* by Chris Bond, and a new actor was to join our ranks. He walked into rehearsal on the first morning, wearing an old, faded, window cleaner's jacket and a pair of flared denim jeans, its large skirt-like flares, from knee to ankle, in pale-pink cotton giving the impression that he had been wading up to his knees in blancmange. I was in love! Or possibly, lust: it remained to be decided. Even with the slightly theatrical spotted neckerchief knotted cheekily around his neck, he would have looked more in keeping if he'd come to mend the boiler than to start rehearsals for a play, but his charisma was all too evident. He had extraordinary, mad, impish eyes either side of a big, battered nose and high wide cheekbones. Later in his career a critic described him as looking as if he had swallowed a pelvis.

It was Peter Postlethwaite, later losing the R and becoming a matey Pete; he moved into my little bedsit almost immediately and we slipped into a roller coaster of a relationship that lasted five years. He was the most daring, stunning and intelligent of actors, brought up a Catholic, with a rough, working-class edge that I understood and felt at home with. He took everything to the limit and I loved his startling unpredictability. His performance in Brecht's *Coriolanus* is one of the most terrifyingly riveting performances I have ever seen. His mother came one night and during this particular performance a couple of girls started to giggle. They were seated in the circle and the stage itself was built up over the stalls. Pete, on hearing this giggling going on throughout an important and impassioned speech of his, leapt from the stage on to the edge of the circle, causing a collective gasp from the audience. He then jumped down in amongst them, all while remaining in character, and aimed a good portion of his monologue directly — and weirdly appropriately — at these poor girls, as if they were part of the crowd in the play. They screamed as he approached them and then sat there in petrified silence, unable to move, as did the rest of the audience, probably fearing that they might be next in line. Afterwards, his mother said, 'Oh Peter! You'll go round the bend if you carry on like that!'

One Friday night after the show, in the packed little bistro underneath the theatre, I was up at the bar, getting a drink, and had got chatting to a guy and his friends who were often in there in the evenings and who had befriended a lot of the actors. I was about to go back to my table when the guy grabbed hold of my hand.

'How would you like to go on a magical mystery tour?'

He then handed me what looked like a tiny bit of lead from a propelling pencil, stuck between two pieces of Sellotape.

'Here y'are, Queen. Want to come on an adventure?'

'What is it?'

'A tiny piece of heaven . . . It's a tab of acid.'

'What do you do with it?'

'Just stick it in your mouth and swallow. It's totally harmless, just a bit of fun; while the others are getting pissed, you'll be having a party. Go on, what are you scared of?'

'I don't know. What will it do?'

'Jesus! You are a scaredy cat, aren't you? It'll just make everything bright and fun for a couple of hours.'

I unstuck the two pieces of Sellotape and, dropping the little black speck into the palm of my hand, I stared at it.

'Go on! You can come with us, we're only going for a few drinks, it's just a bit of Friday-night malarkey. I dare you to enjoy yourself!'

Before another thought could possibly have time to enter my head, I slapped my palm across my open mouth, propelling the thing to the back of my throat; one swallow and it was gone.

Some twenty minutes later, unaware of what I had done and unprepared for the consequences, I collected my coat and bag and joined the group as they bundled out of the theatre and into the street. We had walked no more than a few yards when I had to stop to do up my shoe. I had begun to suspect that this drug would have no effect on me but, as I bent my head, everywhere around me was flooded a bright crimson, staining the whole of my field of vision, like blood through water. When I stood upright again it disappeared, as if it was being sucked back up into my head; and so the trip began. We went into a darkly lit drinking den that I had never visited before, just a few doors along from the theatre, and I was plunged into something that looked like a Hogarth painting, its characters lolling around, toothless and scruffy, in what went from eighteenth-century to modern garb and back again with bewildering speed. I made my way to the lavatory and passed a woman who laughed directly into my face, a big, fag-stained laugh that stopped me dead in my tracks. I looked back at her and watched her laugh melt away, her face becoming plain and neutral, as if she were waiting for something, and then I got it.

'You are just a figment of my imagination, I have just made you up!'

She laughed again but with less gusto. 'Yeah, that's right, love.'

We then went on what was probably, for the others, a normal night out down the Dock Road and into town, in and out of pubs, but for me was a succession of bizarre and alarming freak shows; the whole world was an out-of-control circus. It was as if parts of people's make-up became exaggerated. One landlord, who was usually a jolly red-cheeked man, when viewed on acid became an impish Toby jug of a figure, his cheeks cartoon red, his eyes ablaze, his humour insanely heightened. At some point during the night — I had no sense of time by this point — I said goodbye to the others on the corner of Canning Street and headed back to my little bedsit where I began to wonder when the nightmare would end. I had become increasingly uncomfortable in the company of the people I was with, seeing in every glance and every half-heard sentence a sneer or a slight or something much more threatening, the nature of which I could not pin down. Once back in my room I tried to make tea in the little kitchen but became utterly distracted by a sweater that I had washed earlier and left scrunched up on the draining board; like a scene from a horror film, it appeared to be seething with worms, but I then realised that what I was experiencing was what I had heard the others refer to as a 'retinal circus', an hallucination, and that the worms were simply fibres sticking out of the wool.

I lay on my mattress on the floor, knowing somewhere that I was exhausted and desperate for sleep, but in my jangled state there was little chance of that. My whole body was vibrating with a ferocious, uncomfortable energy, my muscles jumping and restless, and I had the feeling that I could, and possibly needed to, run a couple of miles and then some.

My attention was suddenly grabbed by a poster of Marilyn Monroe that I had stuck up on the wall a few days previously; it was in colour and her face filled the frame, her big, scarlet lips kissing out at the camera, like the end of an elephant's trunk. Abruptly, with an unpleasant, wet snap, her tongue whipped out of her mouth. It was long, black and forked, like a snake's, slithering maniacally around her face, and just as abruptly it was sucked back in again. Although I knew that this wasn't real, it was nevertheless very disturbing. I jumped up and ripped the poster from the wall, screwing it up and throwing it into the corner of the room. I stood over it and watched, my heart crashing against my ribs, as it began to slowly unfurl, and I screamed as the tongue exploded through the crushed folds of paper to lash again around Marilyn's by now distorted face. I stamped on it repeatedly to no avail as the tongue still managed to emerge, unscathed and with vigour, from the now-flattened poster. Gingerly I picked it up, holding it by a corner between my thumb and forefinger, keeping it at arm's length, lest the tongue lash out and entangle me in its vicious toils like some exotic lizard, drawing me back into the moist hungry mouth. I dropped it in the waste-paper bin and placed a dinner plate on top.

I lay back down on the bed. Desperate to occupy my fizzing mind, I stared up at the ceiling and began creating my own cartoons upon it, anything I wanted appearing instantly in beautiful Technicolor: clouds and forests, water-falls, Tom and Jerry, Sylvester the cat, Sister Augustine as a seaside-postcard bathing belle: 'Have you seen my little Fanny?'

Then crashing into my mind came the thought that my small bedsit was in fact the universe in its entirety and that there was nothing else beyond it. Outside the door there were no other bedsits, there was no staircase, no front door with Canning Street on the other side, no Geoff, no Mikie: all these things were superb creations of my own imagination, necessary for my emotional and mental survival. Outside was a void, a vacuum, and what we saw from the window was an illusion. I lay there frozen by this thought. I could see myself in the tiny little box of a room, lit by a dull yellow light, floating free in space, and all around me was a lifeless, black nothingness.

I jumped up from the bed; please, God, this could not be true! I had to get out to disprove it and so, sweating and shaking, I tentatively opened the door. Everything looked as it always did, except for a strange crackling, pink glow from the electric light bulb, suspended, shadeless, in the gloom. I tiptoed down the stairs, every creak underfoot threatening to burst my eardrums, and at the bottom, half lit by the morning sun flooding through the small window above the door, lay Mikie in his usual heap, but now he was a big snoring, throbbing walrus, complete with whiskers, and not frightening at all.

I began to laugh, the sort of laughter I long for in my life, doubled over, painful, liberating and cathartic, and off I went into a beautiful, bright Liverpool morning, a sharp wind coming up off the Mersey and blowing away the thought that the world stopped at my door, blowing it away into the ether. About eight hours after it began, the trip finally started to come to an end by my being drawn, heavy and drained, into the Catholic cathedral, where, in the great, echoing calm, my throat tightened and I felt I might cry. It was still early morning; I sat shivering in one of the back pews, the sun streaming down in bright, laser-like rays upon the altar, occasionally going in and coming out like a stage light being tested in a rehearsal. Then an altar boy, a young man, entered like an actor on a stage and walked about the altar, the sun making a halo of his hair, his rubber soles squeaking on the polished floor. He was laying out, with great delicacy, the props that were necessary for the celebration of the mass. Just a few short hours later I was laying out my own props, backstage at the Everyman, dressed in a full elephant costume, plus substantial headdress for the Saturday matinée performance of Brian Patten's children's play, *The Pig and the Junkle*. I felt fuzzy and detached, whilst knowing with a cast-iron certainty that this would never happen again and noticing that every time I bent forward the world went ever so slightly pink.

I stayed at the Everyman Theatre for eighteen months, with a summer season in Aberystwyth in the middle, to which almost the entire company decamped and during which almost the entire company were banned from every pub in the vicinity. It was one day during that summer that Pete came home and produced a tiny black-and-white Jack Russell puppy from his pocket, like an unwanted child, claiming that, if he hadn't taken her off the farmer there and then, the farmer would have shot her. My heart sank; what could I do? So she was christened Babs.

I felt blessed that I had got into the Everyman. I had no idea at the time that theatre could be like that. Previously I had believed it to be the preserve of the middle classes, but here at the

Everyman the audiences were a complete mixture; it felt as if we were reaching out to the entire community and that we were on the front line of some kind of revolution. During those eighteen months, two productions stick out for me: *Funny Peculiar* by Mike Stott and *Breezeblock Park* by Willy Russell. These were new plays that had never been performed before and were directed by the redoubtable Alan Dossor, who ran the theatre at that time. He was a fearlessly inventive and clever director, handsome and moody, and I was terrified of him.

In *Funny Peculiar* I played a homely, ordinary housewife and mother of a young baby who is constantly pressurised by her husband to be more sexually liberated and is eventually driven almost to breaking point. There is a cracking scene, which comes directly after a scene of high slapstick comedy, in which Irene, my character, breaks down and tries to express her own pain and bewilderment. I had no idea how to tackle it; it was inarticulate, raw and outside the realms of my own life experience. Alan, immediately recognising my problem after the read-through, took me aside.

'Don't worry about that scene. We'll deal with it without the others present. Don't learn it.'

I was dreading it, this rehearsal with just the two of us; it felt as if I was going to have to recite a not yet invented times table for Sister Ignatius, with a wasp stuck under her wimple. In fact it was the best acting lesson I've ever had. The lines of the speech concerned were disjointed half-sentences and odd, disconnected, isolated words held together with a series of dots. We talked about Irene, who she was and what exactly the feeling was that propelled these words from her mouth. Again he said, 'I don't want you to learn it or to try to act it. I just want you to feel it.'

And once I got that feeling, it was deep and powerful, something that I have hankered after in numerous performances ever since. He led me respectfully and sensitively through the rehearsal and the lesson I learnt — that emotional honesty is what draws an audience to you; that it is not something that you demonstrate on the outside but something that first comes from your core; and that this is true of every single part — has stayed with me and it is something I have tried to adhere to throughout my career.

14

Funny Peculiar in London

The combination of my breakthrough with Alan Dossor and the terrifyingly challenging work with Van Load created an amazing grounding for me, and it was in fact *Funny Peculiar* that took me down to London and into the West End after a short season at the Mermaid Theatre in Puddle Dock. It transferred, in the spring of 1976, to the Garrick Theatre in Charing Cross Road, where Richard Beckinsale played Trevor, my husband, and Pete Postlethwaite replaced Kevin Lloyd as Desmond the baker in one of the funniest scenes ever to be staged: the aforementioned slapstick scene. Suffice it to say that a lot of real cream buns were involved and the two characters, after having words, embark literally on a bunfight, ending up with them both covered in cream. I have rarely heard laughter like it in a theatre since.

Funny Peculiar at the Garrick marked the first time that my mother came to see me in a play. She had rung up not long after we opened and both the show and I had been declared a hit by the critics. She said she wanted to come and see it, adding, 'I don't mind how you live,' meaning that she had guessed that I was living with Pete and she was giving her stamp of approval.

He and I had been living in a legalised squat in Whitechapel for a couple of months but had been thrown out because the dog had not only chewed through the wiring to the stereo system but had also left one too many little messages on the shag pile. To add insult to injury, the girl whose squat it was came home unexpectedly one weekend to find Pete and me in her bed. Worst of all, the dog had, unbeknownst to us, ripped the crotch out of her best knickers, a habit Babs never quite grew out of. Well, we had thought she wouldn't be home that weekend and it was a much better bed than ours.

So we found ourselves a new flat in Greek Street, Soho, with Babs, of course, in tow. It cost £25 per week and was on the second floor, with an office underneath us, an Italian restaurant on the ground floor and, in the tiny flat above us, a pair of over-friendly, slightly suspect girls, visited by a long succession of men traipsing up and down the stairs, throughout the evening and on into the small hours. Our flat consisted of one huge, L-shaped room with a large bathroom at the back, and the whole place was carpeted in deep purple, which also carried on into the bathroom and up the side of the bath. Its three tall windows looked down on to Greek Street. The first thing my mother saw when she walked in and went over to the window was the sex shop opposite with a neon sign that flashed 'The Soho Sex Centre'. She said nothing but laughed a little nervously. This just heightened my anxiety about her seeing the play, as it involved references to, amongst other things, oral sex and fellatio in particular, whilst the final scene of the play involved Trevor lying in a hospital bed with a cage over his legs and my character, Irene, putting her head down under the cage, to his obvious enjoyment. I was dreading seeing my mother afterwards, not knowing what on earth she would make of it. To my amazement she said, 'Oh, Julie, that *was* funny! You would keep looking under the sheets, wouldn't you?'

In this last scene, I would sit on one side of the bed and Trevor's 'mistress', played by Susan Cameron, would sit on the other, eating chocolates; she would put her head under the sheets after popping a chocolate into her mouth and come up again to say something, the chocolate having been eaten. Therefore specific chocolates were chosen, that is, ones with soft centres, so that she could eat one quite quickly in time to come back up and say her line. One night the wrong chocolate was put in the box, a hard caramel, and although she did her best to eat it, it was impossible so she had to spit it out on to the sheet. However, when Richard got out of bed for the curtain call it looked as if he'd had a terrible accident. His pyjamas were covered in melted chocolate from the discarded caramel, which was smeared all around his nether regions, and he, poor thing, had no idea, while the rest of us could barely bow for laughing.

I stayed in the play at the Garrick for a year, during which Pete, Babs and I settled into our version of domesticity in the flat at number 6 Greek Street. Life in Soho was peculiarly suited to life in the theatre, in that, like us, the place came alive at night. The street had two nightclubs, Le Kilt and the Beat Route, which only got going at about ten o'clock at night, so the flat had a constant thump, vibrating its floor and walls until about three in the morning. Spookily, and unbeknownst to me, on the door of the Beat Route at that time was a tall, dark, handsome doorman whom I was to marry some twenty years later. Grant must have seen me walk past on numerous occasions and I'm sure I must have clocked him.

Once the clubs closed in the small hours, it was the turn of the dustcart. Its engine alone created a huge amount of noise, plus there were all the mechanics at its rear end. Crate upon crate of assorted bottles from these clubs as well as the numerous restaurants, not to mention the one directly beneath us, would be hauled, smashing and clanging, into the back of the cart, an extremely loud and lengthy process lasting at least an hour, with the dustmen shouting to each other above the clamour. Throughout the night there would be various fracas, as people, the worse for wear, would turn out of the clubs and restaurants, and groups of drunks would descend on the many strip joints and brothels. Even when there was no fracas, they would rarely talk, preferring to shriek at the tops of their voices. So it was not until around three or four o'clock that any sort of peace would descend and we could go to bed. By day, which started for us in the early afternoon, the flat became a drop-in centre for any actor who happened to be in town for a voiceover or an interview, and we were continually running out of tea, coffee and other provisions. I longed for a bit of space of my own and frequently went to the theatre early to spend the afternoon down in my dressing room, reading, with a cup of tea and a chopped-liver sandwich, something I wouldn't dream of eating now, from the little café up the street. The dressing room was my home away from home. It was here in this one-room flat that I discovered a need for time and space alone, which I still have today and which I crave if I don't get enough.

Greek Street was not an ideal place to keep a dog and taking her out for a wee last thing at night on the streets of Soho was not a walk in the park, if you get my drift. Pete always did that whilst I took her out during the day and, even then, I was frequently pointed at by tourists and smirked at by office workers, who quite obviously thought that I was a prostitute. I suppose that walking through the streets of Soho, with no bag and a small dog, given my penchant for lots of eye make-up, could have given the wrong impression. More than once I heard someone say, 'Look! There's one.' Or on one occasion, 'How much do you charge, love? Is the dog thrown in for free?'

On several days during the week and on a Sunday, I would take Babs on the tube to Hyde Park. This was a massive risk as although Babs was intelligent she was pretty much a free spirit. One Sunday morning during that boiling summer of 1976, I had taken her to the park and decided on a bit of a sunbathe in a deckchair before it got too hot. At first Babs settled down underneath the chair but after a short time, and as more people began to arrive in the park, she staked out an area around the deckchair. Anyone who had the audacity to cross over her boundary was seen off with a barrage of yapping and a baring of teeth. Eventually she palled up with a Border collie type belonging to a man who was sunbathing just outside her designated protection zone. I watched, the proud mother, enjoying the sight of the two of them nipping one another playfully and bounding around with great joyous leaps into the air.

The game then seemed to heighten in intensity, culminating in the two of them chasing one another round and round this man's deckchair, each circuit getting faster and faster, and then just as they were becoming a blur they both stopped dead and peed with shivering excitement, one after the other, on the man's clothing, which lay in a pile next to his chair. I leapt up in a panic, got my things together and tried to catch Babs without waking the man. This resulted in my chasing her and the collie in circuits around his deckchair until, with a flattening rugby tackle, I pinned her to the ground. Just as I thought I'd escaped the man woke up.

'Oh hi! . . . I'm just catching up my dog. Time to go home now.'

'Oh yes,' he said, smiling sleepily at Babs. 'What's her name?'

'Babs . . . What's yours called?'

'Oh, I haven't got a dog.' The stench of dog

260

pee was already rising off his clothes in the summer heat. The collie was nowhere to be seen.

'Oh . . . ah . . . OK. See ya.'

Along with her free spirit, Babs also had, paradoxically, a rather strait-laced, disapproving side to her. She simply took against anyone who was different in any way and would randomly berate people for wearing, say, yellow socks or a panama hat, and on one occasion in a desperately embarrassing incident she started a horrible, almost howling attack on a black man, whilst I was at the pick-and-mix in Woolworth's. Everyone stopped and stared, first at her and then at me, with ill-disguised contempt for what they interpreted as my rampant racism, something that had clearly rubbed off on my dog and had possibly even been trained into her.

Once whilst I was taking her for a walk along Oxford Street, a girl dressed as a punk, with bright-pink hair glued high into a spiky Mohican and wearing very tight red jeans, minced her way past us in the crowd. Babs, without warning and employing a brilliant vertical take-off, leapt up and bit her on the arse. The girl screamed and rounded on me with a string of expletives, kicking out at the dog, which, straining at the leash, continued in a fit of frenzy to bark and growl at her. I think I probably didn't help matters by trying to explain that Babs didn't really approve of what the girl was wearing, because this seemed only to crank her fury up a notch, at which the expletives became totally unintelligible and froth started to ooze at the corners of her mouth. At last she teetered off on

261

high-heeled boots, looking back red-faced at the dog and rubbing her buttock angrily as she went.

We always took Babs with us when performing in the theatre, once foolishly taking her on stage at the Mermaid Theatre for the curtain call, where the sight of hundreds of people clapping, a sign that we used to indicate that she was doing something we disliked, caused her to evacuate her bowls there and then, in front of a rather bemused audience. Once in the theatre she would make the dressing room her home and then woe betide anyone with the temerity to enter. She had bitten more stage-doorkeepers than I care to think about, even cornering one poor dresser in my dressing room for the whole of the first act of *Funny Peculiar*. I came off at the interval to find her cowering up against the wall with Babs snapping at her feet, having lost her voice, the dog, that is, after an hour and a half of persistent barking.

I had Babs for seven years and was heartbroken when, having nowhere to live at the time and having exhausted the goodwill of all the kind people to whom I had farmed her out in the past, I was forced to give her away, albeit to a nice old pensioner who adored Jack Russells, and who I knew would find her odd little ways endearing — for example, not minding discovering the crotch missing from his underpants every now and then.

Directly across the street from the flat was number 59 Greek Street. It was built in 1883 as the Soho Club and Home for Working Girls; in the 1920s it went on to become the Theatre

Girls' Club, a home for women working in the theatre; by the time we moved in opposite it had become a hostel for homeless women. Whether it took on this last incarnation because the actresses housed there had been out of work for so long that they had been rendered destitute, I've no idea, but they certainly involved themselves in an inordinate amount of drama.

On our first night in the flat, after being woken by the sound of breaking glass and awful, unearthly-sounding wails and screams, we flung up one of our windows to find that some poor soul had thrown themselves, or had been thrown, from a third-floor window and was lying there lifeless on the pavement, her pale limbs stuck out at unnatural angles like a set of matchsticks. The paramedics were in the process of manoeuvring her on to a stretcher. The police were also there (which subsequently seemed to be the case every other day), trying to calm the situation, while hanging out of the windows above were a motley group of women in varying states of *déshabillé* and what seemed to be varying degrees of mental disorder.

It was like a scene from *Marat Sade*. One of the women was waving a carrier bag down at a young policeman whilst shouting something unintelligible. Then, getting no response as the policeman was otherwise engaged, she tipped the carrier bag upside down and emptied its contents down into the street, where it landed, not upon the policeman at whom it was aimed, but on what turned out to be one of the inmates who had been dodging about, generally getting in the way of the emergency services. Although it was both rainy and chilly the woman was dressed only in what looked like a thin, grey, ankle-length nightdress, which threw into relief her squat, Michelin-man frame. She instantly wheeled round on the spot, letting out an almost operatic scream. This scattered the little group of inmates who had gathered around the injured woman, as well as the police and the paramedics, and there were various cries of, 'Oh no!', 'Mind you don't step in it!' and finally from the woman herself, 'The dirty cow! Come down 'ere and say that!' Then from above came a booming voice, surprisingly cultured, if a little slurred.

'I won't be troubling myself, thank you very much, and I think you'll find that that mess belongs to you, as, following the stench, I found it in your bed.'

Much cackling followed from various quarters. Then a bucket appeared at the window and, before another word was spoken, it was emptied of a liquid, the identity of which can only be guessed at, on to the heads of the group below, narrowly missing the paramedics who were loading their patient into the back of the waiting ambulance. After a screaming match between the two protagonists, too tedious to record, people started to disperse.

'I don't know what she thinks she's looking at.'

It was a loud, rasping, cockney voice, roughened by years of drink, cigarettes and God knows what else.

'It's fucking rude to stare.'

At first we couldn't tell where it was coming

from or to whom it was addressed.

'Yeah, you, ya little tom!'

It then became clear that it was coming from one of the top-floor windows.

'Lady fucking Muck.'

In the corner, backlit, was the silhouette of a big, round woman, her arms and her tumescent, unsupported, but thankfully clothed bosom flopping out over the windowsill, her face, somewhat sinisterly, in complete darkness.

'What is she? Queen of all she fucking surveys?' And then rather mysteriously, but megaphone-loud, 'You are what you eat!'

Oh my God; like a member of an audience picked on by a comedian, I almost looked behind me to check that it really was me that she was shouting at, but as I was the only person that I knew of to be eating a banana in Greek Street at half past four on that particular morning, I pulled my head in so fast and pulled the window down with such a bang, that my banana got severed three-quarters of the way down and a small crack appeared in the corner of the pane.

We lived in Greek Street for two years and I don't think a single day went by without some comment from the woman opposite. It could be anything: 'How many fags have you had today?' or 'Look at the state of the place! What are the punters gonna think?' or 'You're not wearin' that, are ya?'

I never made any reply, for fear of encouraging her, and all in all her observations, some too close to home for comfort, forced us to keep the curtains closed an awful lot of the time.

There are three characters whom I recall with something almost resembling fondness from number 59 Greek Street: the first was the above commentator; the second was the posh woman who threw the turds down on to the pavement and who screeched out into the night such gems as 'Thou knowest not the day nor the hour!' and once, 'If you do not remove your enormous crack from my vicinity, I shall be forced to fill it with my boot!' The third was 'Yella-Bellied Brenda'.

Going by her accent, it seemed that Yella-Bellied Brenda came from Northern Ireland. She got her name because every so often, day or night, she would take to the streets, for no apparent reason, chanting the phrase, 'Ya yella-bellied bastards!' over and over again at the top of her not inconsiderable voice. God knows what had happened to the poor creature, or what hell she was reliving when this occurred, but it was generally met with reactions that were not steeped in the milk of human kindness. If the weather was inclement, she would actually shelter in the doorway of number 59 and shout her accusations from there, causing an absolute furore within. The bucket would frequently make an appearance on the windowsill above, the posh lady booming down with her own somewhat mysterious and particular kind of threats: 'If you do not cease from these incantations, I shall be forced to take a drink and you know what will happen then!'

This was followed by the bucket being emptied of the suspicious-looking and often steaming liquid on to the head of the hapless Brenda.

The commentator would be a little more blunt: 'Shut the fuck up!' Then with her huge, bare arms wobbling, she would close her window with an ear-splitting bang.

I am ashamed to say that this behaviour created huge entertainment for us opposite and, indeed, probably for our entire side of the street. It was like watching *Candid Camera* as unsuspecting office workers, passing by at the time, jumped in fright and darted out of the way, wondering what on earth they had walked into as the steaming urine cascaded down, often missing Brenda and splashing on to them in the process. I suppose, once back in the warmth of the office, with their clothes drying off nicely, they would soon be in no doubt as to what, in fact, they had wandered into. On one occasion a man wearing a chef's hat and whites, who worked in a nearby restaurant, came out and, quite clearly driven to the end of his tether by Brenda's incessant wailing, stood on the pavement, screaming at her to stop, a large butcher's knife in his hand. The police was called. The man was taken away, still angrily remonstrating, but Yella-Bellied Brenda was left to continue her refrain.

One night there was an incident in which the window of the sex shop opposite was smashed by a drunken man, setting off the alarm and also, unfortunately, Brenda. She came out almost instantly and began to patrol the scene with her usual rant. The police arrived ten or fifteen minutes later to find that the entire contents of the window

— which consisted of several giant dildos and a couple of sets of extremely uncomfortable-looking underwear, strung together with leather thongs and metal rings, and having holes where there usually aren't any — had been looted. The window-smashing culprit quite clearly hadn't taken them as he was still there, lying flat out on the pavement in an alcoholic stupor, although several ladies from number 59 had been bobbing about but had now gone inside. The police proceeded to manhandle the drunk up on to his feet, but on waking he became violent, thrashing out in all directions with kicks and punches, and shouting drunken abuse at the coppers.

Meanwhile, Yella-Bellied Brenda was reaching a kind of hysteria with her own rantings. Once the police had wrestled the drunk into the back of the Black Maria, either they had decided to teach him a lesson, or they thought that Yella-Bellied's insults were aimed at them, or quite possibly, like most other people, they couldn't take any more of her wailing, but whatever the reason they shoved poor old Brenda into the Black Maria too. For a short while after they slammed the back doors shut, there was a very welcome silence, and then Brenda started again with her 'Yella-bellied bastards'. The man joined in with some sort of shouted, drunken response, while the old Black Maria shook as if a rugby scrum were taking place inside.

In the meantime the police had gone across the street to the Beat Route Club to tackle some other altercation. By the time they returned, at least a couple of hours later, the Black Maria was completely motionless; the man had long since gone silent, but dear old Yella-Belly was still going at it full pelt. It was a marvel that this woman never came near to losing her voice. At this point they opened the doors and let her out, but just before they slammed them shut again, a slurred but plaintive cry of 'Merciful heaven!' was heard quite clearly from within.

After we'd been living in Greek Street for two or three months I had a clear-out and took a bag of clothes over the road, thinking the women might find them useful. A matter of hours later, I saw a massive woman waddling down the street in a pair of my shoes. I take a size three and a half and the woman barely had her toes wedged into them; a sleeveless cardigan of mine was also stretched tightly across the vast expanse of her back. I watched her as she wobbled off. There was something of the little girl dressing up in her mother's clothes, and something in the pleasure that she appeared to take in wearing her new clothes and her deluded sense of her own appearance, that I found immensely touching. After she'd got about fifty yards she stopped abruptly and pivoted around on the spot, looking directly up at our window as if she had known that she was being watched. I quickly stepped back, not wanting to be seen and therefore shouted at. I waited a minute or so and then took another look. She was still standing there and, on catching sight of me creeping up to the window, she placed a thumb in each ear, waggled her fingers and stuck her tongue out, and then with a girlish giggle she turned her back, bent over, wiggled her bum at me and pranced off down the street. Although I'd never been able to properly catch sight of her face when she was in her usual place at the window, I knew without a shadow of a doubt that this was the commentator. Even if the great wobbling arms — although they were a bit of a giveaway — had been covered, there was no mistaking the mixture of aggression, cheek and a surprising element of charm in the turn of her head and the swagger of her walk.

It appeared that the majority of the women housed there were mentally disturbed in some way and fell into a sort of no man's land between mental health care and prison. My husband, Grant, who had been a young policeman at West End Central, told me much later that number 59 Greek Street was well known to the police. They dreaded the inevitable call to go round and it was always palmed off on to the 'rookies', because no one else wanted the job. It seemed that the women used to get rather excited by the sight of these young men (Grant was then only eighteen) in their policemen's uniforms. Once inside the building with its dimly lit corridors, where the odour of unwashed bodies was all pervading and where haggard faces peered through the cracks of half-opened doors from the darkened rooms behind, the young men were subjected to harmless but nevertheless creepy catcalls, and a lot of exposing and propositioning went on. They were told back at the station that it was a home for old actresses. Grant finally admitted that he had laboured under that delusion until very recently. When I put him right he said he'd always wondered what it was about acting that had made so many women go round the bend. And as I said to him at the time, that is an entirely different matter.

Greek Street eventually got to be too much. Today Soho is much improved and less seedy than it was then, when it gave the impression of being a place in which people came to abuse both themselves and others. The lonely, disaffected and damaged gravitated towards it; you could hardly walk through the little garden in the centre of Soho Square for homeless winos and drug addicts. The detritus and paraphernalia of their lives were scattered around on the grass and in the flower beds: bottles and cans stacked under the benches; needles stuck into the trunks of trees. Above the mostly pleasant aroma of coffee and food cooking in the various restaurants, the traffic fumes and the generalised city smell, there was always the pungent stink of stale urine.

I used to think sometimes that people — and when I say people, I suppose I mean men, and when I say men, I suppose I mean drunks — came to Soho specifically to urinate. The door into our building was round at the side in Manette Street and it opened directly on to the road, above which was a Dickensian-looking arch linking us to the Pillars of Hercules pub. Being sheltered, fairly dark and out of the way of the main thoroughfare, it reeked, needless to say, of old piss and was forever being mopped and

271

disinfected by the restaurant on the ground floor. On a couple of occasions on coming home late at night after the show, I had trodden in something soft and with an unmistakable stench, only to discover that someone had crapped in the doorway. I suppose you could say that this was the last straw and one morning not long before I moved out, I returned home after doing a bit of shopping to find a man brazenly pissing up against the door. Boiling with rage and without a thought in my head, I took a run at him and kicked him with some force up his bottom, causing him to pitch forward and nut the door with his forehead. He spun around — tall, bearded and unkempt-looking — and I immediately felt sorry for him; in fact I was on the verge of apologising when he began a tirade of screaming, frothing abuse. I backed away, instantly regretting my actions, as he advanced on me, his flies still open and his penis half sticking out, while propelling out a string of invective on a cloud of stomach-churning breath becoming more agitated by the second. I retreated, terrified, one hand held up, palm out, in a conciliatory gesture, unsure as to whether I should let him know about his accidental exposure, but quickly coming to the conclusion that perhaps it wasn't such a good idea to bring his nethers into it. He proceeded to harangue me with a curious mixture of hell and damnation, added to the threat that he, himself, could rip my guts out and very much enjoy the experience. I was halfway up Manette Street in the middle of the road by the time I turned tail and ran, and it was a good hour before I returned, peering tentatively around the corner to make sure he'd gone. I spotted him in the crowd milling along Oxford Street a few weeks later and crossed over the road, lest he see me and recognise me as his one-time assailant, prompting the haranguing to start all over again.

When I finished in *Funny Peculiar* in the spring of 1977, I discovered to my surprise that I had lost three-quarters of a stone in weight, which took me down to just under eight stone. On the day that I left the Garrick, I looked at the poster-sized picture of me as Irene, the character that I played, at the front of house and wondered what had happened: the girl in the photograph had a rounded face and thicker legs and arms. This is a syndrome that has repeated itself throughout my career. Whenever I am engaged in a long run in the theatre, I gradually lose weight. Just recently in the sixteen weeks that I performed in *Acorn Antiques the Musical* I lost just over a stone and I wasn't exactly overweight to begin with, but no matter what I ate I couldn't seem to keep the weight on. It was suggested that it was due to the dancing, singing and general physicality of the part, which was true to a certain degree, but this weight loss occurred with any part that I played, regardless of the physical energy exerted, if it was played over a period of time. I believe it had more to do with the effort required for me to re-create the part every night, putting a huge pressure on myself to make the audience believe in and engage with it each second that I was on stage, and with the adrenalin rush that this produced.

Shortly after the run finished we tried to go down the same route with Willy Russell's hilarious play, *Breezeblock Park*, as we had done with *Funny Peculiar*, starting off at the Mermaid, with Wendy Craig in the central role, played brilliantly at the Everyman by Eileen O'Brien, but after a mauling by the critics we took it valiantly into the Whitehall Theatre, with Prunella Scales instead. Playing the very dim, lovable and funny Vera, I had a ball. The show was adored by the audiences and although the cast, myself included, were well received, the play was trounced once again by the critics, despite the fact that several of them were seen to be convulsed with laughter on press night. It came off after a few weeks with audiences roaring their approval to the last.

15

'We're Missin' *Brideshead* for This!' — Victoria Wood

The following year in the summer of 1978, after a stint at the Royal Court Theatre under the direction of Max Stafford-Clark in which I played a New York Jewish lesbian who was also a solo round-the-world yachtswoman in a completely unintelligible play by Snoo Wilson titled *The Glad Hand*, I took a job at the Bush Theatre, a tiny space above a pub of the same name on Shepherd's Bush Green in West London. It was, and still is — despite almost having its grant taken away this year in a disgraceful and ludicrous proposal by the Arts Council of Great Britain — a major force in the championing of new talent, especially writers. The proposal was withdrawn after a welter of opposition from actors and writers who had launched successful careers from that tiny stage. Our production was to be an evening of playlets — we were instructed not to call them sketches — written by such luminaries as Snoo Wilson, Nigel Baldwin, Ken Campbell, Ron Hutchinson, Dusty Hughes, who also directed, and a young woman I'd never heard of before called Victoria Wood.

The evening was to be titled *In at the Death*

and some would say that the audiences were, on most nights. Also in the cast were Godfrey Jackman, Clive Merrison, Alison Fiske and Phil Jackson, while Victoria, fresh out of BBC1's topical *That's Life*, was to provide musical interludes between each sketch — there, I've said it — one of which was the glorious 'Guy the Gorilla' ('died of chocolate, not usually a killer'), as well as writing a sketch of her own.

The sketches were to be based on small snippets from newspapers connected in some way with death: not major articles, but those little pieces tucked away in the bottom corners of the inside pages, probably best found in local papers. Ken Campbell took his from the *Malaysian New Strait Times*; Nigel Baldwin took his inspiration from the *Holyhead and Anglesey Chronicle*; and Vic used the tabloids. Ron Hutchinson's piece was set in Northern Ireland, based around a Ruby Murray lookalike contest. There was a brilliant sketch written by Dusty Hughes about 'ghouls', the people who turn up to gawp at road accidents, tube disasters and the like, but the hit of the evening was Victoria's piece, which was entitled *Sex* and involved a young woman, worried that she was pregnant, played by me, finding out from this other character, played by Victoria, that she hadn't even had sex. It brought the house down every night.

One line that I particularly remember as a rafter shaker was: 'Well, where are you in the menstrual cycle?'

' . . . Erm . . . Taurus.'

It was here at the Bush that our relationship was cemented, easily slipping into a friendship on the first day of rehearsals, when we discovered that we had Geoffrey Durham in common, he of the near facial hair-fire disaster, who had lived underneath me in Canning Street when I was at the Everyman. It turned out that he was Vic's bloke and so here was our first bond. The second, which Victoria informed me of over liver, boil (sic) and onions at the Bush café round the corner from the theatre, was that we had met before. It turns out that she had auditioned at Manchester Polytechnic School of Theatre when I was a first-year there. I had been drafted in to usher the auditionees into the theatre to do their pieces and had spent the entire time trying to entertain them with stories of my nursing days, previously recorded herein, and generally showing off from my privileged position of already having a place. At first I couldn't remember her being there and then the image of this shy little girl, wearing glasses and throwing up in a bucket, flashed before me.

There was actually a third thing that bonded us. One evening early on, after rehearsal, Vic and I were going somewhere or other in her newly acquired Mini van. Wherever it was, we somehow got lost in the back streets of Shepherd's Bush, God forbid. After about ten minutes we ended up in either a cul-de-sac or a 'no through road', so a three-point turn was necessary in order to get out. Victoria swung the car round with great aplomb and being a non-driver at this stage of my life I was hugely impressed by her skill and confidence. Then she backed up and I think we must have been talking because she reversed just a little too far. We heard a bit of a crunch and she pulled tentatively forward to reveal that she had knocked down an entire garden wall. Our escape from that street, apart from the paroxysms of laughter, that is, with the screeching of tyres and the smell of burning rubber, was worthy of a 1970s action thriller.

It was an interesting time, although I fear that we gave poor old Dusty Hughes rather a hard time, or at least I think I did. I just felt that I knew best. I had come from the great Everyman, a working-class hero; I ploughed my own furrow; and some London-based, middle-class, university-educated bloke was not going to direct me. In those days I still laboured under the misapprehension that certain types of direction were tantamount to slurs on my acting ability and had what you might call a wee chip on my already rounding shoulder. One day, frustrated by the lack of progress in rehearsals, Victoria and I hatched a devilish plan whilst down in the pub toilets. We rushed back upstairs.

'Dusty! What sort of car have you got?'

He told us.

'Where is it parked?'

'Why?'

'We think it's being broken into, it looked as if someone was trying to get into it!'

And off he shot. Then we put the kettle on and decided on what we thought was the best way to play the particular sketch we had been rehearsing with Dusty.

Dusty was a talented playwright, going on, two years later in 1980, to win the London Theatre Critics Award for Most Promising Playwright, and he took our undermining, prank-playing and joke-cracking at his expense in very good heart.

As ever, I was in my element fooling around, which took me right back into class-jester mode. One lunchtime whilst for some reason we were hanging out of the office window upstairs, we spied Harold Pinter standing at the bus stop in the street below.

'Harold! Hello, there! You write plays, don't you?' I called.

'Pardon?'

'You're a writer! We could do with one of those up here!'

Then a week after we opened we wrote 'H. Pinter (two tickets)' on the bookings list just for a laugh and scared the cast half to death, laughing our heads off backstage as we watched the other actors nervously upping their performances to impress the very absent Mr Pinter.

Backstage at the Bush consisted of an area approximately six feet by six feet and a set of stone steps leading down to the street. These were also used as the fire escape and, once the audience were in, the dressing room. The only toilet facility was downstairs in the pub itself and so this is where we rushed at the interval of an early preview, only to hear, whilst sitting on the lav, a middle-class voice intone loudly, 'Oh dear, could do better. Shall we bother with the second half?' After that, it was pint glasses and frequent cries of 'Don't drink that!' as thirsty actors reached for what they thought was their pint of Carlsberg in the dark. It was extremely cramped with six actors all trying to get changed in this space, and Vic and I had many a private joke about the slack nature of a certain actor's underpants.

It was also hazardous, not the slackness of the underpants, you understand, but the backstage space. One night we were all on stage, apart, that is, from Victoria who didn't appear until the last few minutes leading up to the interval. During the course of these we heard a dreadful crash, accompanied by the soft thud of flesh on stone repeated several times, from backstage. When we finally exited we found Victoria covered in blood halfway down the stairs, where she had accidentally slipped and fallen whilst hovering over a beer glass and cut her hand. In doing so she had also knocked over a number of other glasses, splattering the costumes with their contents, and they didn't all contain drinks. What the second-half audience thought of the badly stained costumes one can only guess at and as for the smell as they dried under the stage lights in that tiny space, perhaps they thought that they were experiencing early Odorama.

The show did well, being well received on the whole, and it was on the final Saturday that David Leland walked in and asked to speak to Victoria. It turned out that he was running a young writers' festival at the Crucible Theatre, Sheffield, and he asked Victoria to write a play for it. She said she would write something for me. I thought this was very kind, but couldn't ever imagine it happening, and went off to have a not particularly happy time at the Bristol Old Vic, where at my audition to play Phoebe in Shakespeare's *As You Like It*, Richard Cotterell, the director, said, 'Come downstage, Julie, I want to see your f-f-f-f — '

'Erm, is this what they call the casting couch?'

'I want to see your f-f-f — '

'Blimey, Richard, what sort of production is this?'

'Your *face*!'

'Oh . . . fair enough.'

I got the part but hated it, unable to get to its centre. Looking back, I think I was trying too hard and expecting too much from it. Perhaps I'd have done better if I had shown my f-f-f —

It was here at Bristol that I was told the tale of an actor being on that very stage, playing Macbeth during a matinée. He had started the famous speech, 'Tomorrow and tomorrow and tomorrow . . . ', when an aged voice from the stalls was heard to say, 'Oh, that'll be Wednesday.'

And it was here that I read Victoria's wonderful new play *Talent*, which she had, indeed, written for me. My character was called Julie and my character's boyfriend was called Dave Walters. The play centred around a talent contest in a seedy Northern nightclub. Julie was entering the contest and Maureen, her best friend, played by Victoria, had come along for support. It fitted me like a glove, the extreme opposite of the experience I was having with Phoebe. I knew this girl exactly, what she would wear, how she would speak, how she would smoke, cry, laugh, and when she would breathe. And I wasn't free! It had to go ahead without me and I was mortified. The part was played by Hazel Clyne, but the show was seen by Peter Eckersley, a Granada Television producer, who picked it up to be adapted for television. This meant I had a chance to audition for the part.

It was a play with songs, two of which I was required to sing, one of my own choosing (Stevie Wonder's 'Isn't She Lovely?') plus one of the numbers from the show. The latter was a gorgeous, sardonically nostalgic song titled 'I Want to Be Fourteen Again'. When it came to my turn to sing, Victoria played it in my key, a privilege I'm not entirely sure the rest of the auditionees enjoyed. In fact at the end of the audition, just as I was leaving the room, she said, under her breath, 'Don't worry, I'm going to play it in a really high key for everyone else!' I took it as a joke, but I'm not certain to this day whether it was.

Anyway, as history will confirm I got the part and there began a working friendship where Victoria gave me brilliant gift after brilliant gift. We followed *Talent* with a sequel the following year titled *Nearly a Happy Ending*. This featured the same two characters, Julie and Maureen, who had appeared in *Talent* and involved Maureen's attempts at losing her virginity at some awful sales conference in a dreary hotel. Again it was both hilarious and touching, and an amazingly generous vehicle for me. It was followed fairly quickly by another one-off comedy drama titled *Happy Since I Met You*, in which Victoria didn't star, and I played opposite

Duncan Preston, my character being a drama teacher and his a struggling actor. It was a gorgeously bittersweet comedy.

Peter Eckersley then decided that Victoria and I should have our own series and so *Wood and Walters* was launched. Even though Victoria was doing all the writing, she insisted on the use of both our names in the title of the show. Sadly Peter Eckersley died suddenly in between the recording of the pilot and the making of the series, and we missed him hugely, not just as a producer but also as a man. It was never the same and we felt that the series, which was his baby, suffered enormously without him.

We recorded it up at the Granada Studios in Manchester every week on a Friday afternoon. The television studio audiences turned up with a ticket to see a show but had no idea which one it would be. As this took place in the middle of the day, it was mainly elderly people who were wheeled in and we would invariably go on set to be met by a bank of white heads, with comments that could only be attributed to the aged or the hard of hearing pinging out into the often deafening silence. 'Who are these girls?' and 'What did she say?' 'What's a boutique?' 'Is it a comedy?' and once, 'We're missin' *Brideshead* for this!' This last became a private catchphrase for Victoria and me. At my BAFTA tribute in 2003 Victoria was sitting next to me and just before she got up to make her speech, she handed me a scrap of paper on which she had written: 'We're missin' *Brideshead* for this!'

Getting through the show was often like

wading through cold porridge and to whip the oldies into a frenzy of mirth a warm-up man was employed at the top of the show. Most of his jokes failed miserably, and Vic and I would wait backstage, hearts sinking as we listened to the wind blowing the tumbleweed across the vast empty space in between each gag. On one occasion when the audience was particularly ancient, with the sound of beeping hearing aids and the clack of false teeth filling the air, the warm-up man, after straining to get a laugh out of them and not succeeding, resorted, in a fit of frustration, to dropping his trousers and showing them his arse. You could have heard a pin drop.

In 1984, Victoria asked me to join her, Duncan Preston, Celia Imrie and a host of other good actors in her new series *Victoria Wood as Seen on TV*. This could not have been a more different experience to the one at Granada. It was expertly and slickly produced by Geoff Posner, and was recorded on a Saturday night as if it were a live show. There was a sketch set in a shoe shop where I played a rather batty sales assistant and Vic played a customer. She had said beforehand that she wasn't sure whether it would work because it was so off the wall, and I wasn't sure how I should play it, but because the whole evening had a live-theatre feel to it, it put a creative edge on everything. Just as the lights went up for the sketch to begin, I decided on the spur of the moment to stumble about in the shop window, creating havoc and knocking shoes everywhere, and we were off; it was like the old Everyman days. The sketch was brilliantly written and would have worked anyway, without my cavorting about, but what was so gratifying for me was finding the character there and then, during the show itself. The studio audience had a ball. In one sketch, involving a very old waitress taking ages to serve soup to a couple, I thought we might have to stop the sketch, as the laughter went on and on and on, with people doubled up, and I could see Celia and Duncan, who were also in it, twitching with suppressed laughter.

As far as sketch writing is concerned, Victoria is in a league of her own. Her sketches are intelligent, brilliantly observed and, without exception, immensely funny. The soup sketch came out of the two of us ordering soup from an ancient waitress in a restaurant on Morecambe sea front. This small incident was the launchpad for an iconic sketch which, knowing her speed at writing both sketches and songs, probably took her a matter of minutes. Often when we were rehearsing *As Seen on TV*, Geoff Posner, who also directed, would ask her to write some extra material. She would go off to the corner of the rehearsal room and ten minutes later would be back with something utterly hilarious.

It was in this series that my favourite character of all time was born: Mrs Overall. 'Acorn Antiques' was a sketch based on a badly made soap, inspired by the early *Crossroads*, in which, much to our amusement, Duncan Preston had played the part of a character called Ginger Parsons very early on in his career. It was set in an antiques shop situated in a fictional town called Manchesterford, run by the snobbish and imperious Miss Babs (no relation), played brilliantly by Celia Imrie. Mrs O was the cleaner and what a gem of a part she was. We always filmed that particular sketch the day before the show, without an audience and thus without the consequent nerves and pressure. It was heaven. I can remember the first time, as I waited to make my entrance, realising that I could see the monitor and therefore I could make sure that my tray, upon which I had tea and macaroons for Miss Babs, could poke out into shot before I was due on. The whole crew joined in, making their own similar cock-ups: the boom being in shot; Mr Clifford (played by Duncan who is six-foot five) jumping up suddenly and banging his head on it; shots being slightly out of focus and clumsily positioned. People would come from all over the BBC to watch when we were recording.

The very first time we were to record, all the elements of Mrs Overall came together at once. I was being made up, which consisted of a bit of base and a bit of lipstick making a tiny, pinched, dark-red cupid's bow; I was also meant to be wearing a wig from the BBC wig department. Victoria and I had gone up there to sort through and see whether there was anything we wanted for the show. In the process we tried on every-thing in our path, including beards, once discovering that the small goatee I was trying to stick to my chin was what was known as a merkin.

'A what?' I asked innocently.

'A pubic wig.'

'Oh blimey! I wondered what the hole was for! Oh, eugh!'

Finally we came across a quite severe-looking grey bun and thought that this would do fine. So there I was, sitting in front of the make-up mirror with the wig on, a wig stand next to me and my hair flattened down in preparation, restrained by a hairnet that made my head look rather small and pealike. I looked at myself in the mirror and then looked at Victoria. We both laughed, having the same thought at the same time: 'I don't need a wig, do I?' And so she was born. The public loved 'Acorn Antiques', a fan club was formed and twenty years later people are still coming up to me in the street and firing Mrs Overall quotes at me. 'What was it, muesli?' or 'Oh, I am pleased'. So when in 2004 Vic decided to set it to music for a production to be directed by Trevor Nunn in the West End, 'Oh, I was pleased.'

In 1994 we did our second television film together, *Pat and Margaret*. The last one had been *Happy Since I Met you*, back in 1980. In some ways the two characters, Pat and Margaret, mirrored those of Julie and Maureen, in that both Julie and Pat, whom I played, were strident, verbose and ambitious, while Maureen and Margaret, played by Victoria, were shy, genuine and unambitious. In *Pat and Margaret*, Pat was Margaret's famous older sister, from whom she had been separated at a young age. In the intervening years Pat had become a famous actress and had made it in America in a successful, *Dynasty*-style television series, whereas Margaret worked in a motorway service station café, shovelling out chips all day long. In the story, the two sisters, unbeknownst to one another, are brought together in a 'surprise, surprise'-type show and from there the drama unfolds. As Pat, I believe I had some of the funniest speeches ever written. She was a bitch and a very angry bitch at that. If only I could be that funny when I was that angry. However, my favourite line wasn't one of mine; it belonged to Pat and Margaret's mother, played by Shirley Stelfox, who also played my friend in *Personal Services* and is now a current regular in the soap *Emmerdale*. She said, on being confronted by her two daughters about her shortcomings as a mother, 'I didn't know what love was until I bred my first Afghan.'

I have played so many parts written by Victoria and every one has been of the once-in-a-lifetime variety. After reading them for the first time, every one has made me laugh out loud and left me gagging to slip into their shoes and get tottering. And Petula, in the comedy series *Dinnerladies*, has got to be up there with the very best of the best. *Dinnerladies* was set in a works canteen. Victoria played Bren, one of the said ladies, and I played her somewhat eccentric mother. We had scene after scene together, where she gave me all the best lines and simply stood there more or less as a feed.

She has been unutterably generous in her writing, more often than not giving the best lines to me or whoever it might be that she is sharing the scene with, and I have frequently said that, had I her talent for writing, I wouldn't be giving those punchlines to anyone else. But that's Victoria.

16

Ecstasy with Mike Leigh

Meanwhile, returning to London from Bristol in 1979, my relationship with Pete having come to an end, I embarked on what I consider to be another of the jewels of my acting life: a play at Hampstead Theatre Club to be written and devised by Mike Leigh.

It was for me the ultimate acting experience. To begin with, the actors, Sheila Kelly, Jim Broadbent, Stephen Rea, Ron Cook, Rachel Davies and myself, all worked on their own with Mike. First we made lists of the characters who had peopled our lives, many of them in this book, discussed them with him. Then a shortlist was drawn up and discussed again, and finally Mike picked a person from this list as a basis or springboard for the character that would eventually appear in the play. For several more weeks we worked individually with Mike, doing solitary improvisations, and gradually he started to put the actors together in group improvisations. In the course of these, I found that my best friend was to be Sheila Kelly and then that I was going out with Stephen Rea, whom I subsequently married and with whom I eventually had three children. For sixteen weeks overall, often until late into the night, we improvised continually so that these people became unutterably real, the fabric of their lives and the world in which they lived true and vivid. Now, thirty years later, I still can't go past the Catholic church on Quex Road, Kilburn, without thinking, Oh, that's where Mick (Stephen Rea) and I got married.

The play was set in Kilburn in London and so most of the improvisations outside the rehearsal room took place in seedy pubs up and down the Kilburn High Road, with Mike tucked away in a corner listening and watching the goings-on. He had instructed us not to come out of character unless blood was drawn. I played a very rough, feisty, loud-mouthed woman called Dawn, whom I had based on someone who went to my school. On one occasion I rounded, in a Dawn-like way, on a very heavy-looking navvy who was leering at me as I crossed the bar to go to the lavatory.

'Wharra you looking at?'

'Sometin' that needs a good seein' to.'

'You should be so bleedin' lucky! Get fucked!'

'Exactly my thoughts.' And then into his pint, 'Scrubber!'

'What did you call me?'

'I called you what you are — a scrubber!'

He was now looking pretty menacing and my heart, that is, Julie's heart, was pounding in my throat, whereas Dawn was up for a fight. There had to be a compromise here. I turned on my heel, throwing a loud '*Cunt!*' over my shoulder, and disappeared into the Ladies' with as much of a swagger as I could muster, whereupon I dashed into a cubicle and locked the door, fearful that the navvy might be in hot pursuit. Once inside I collapsed on to the lavatory, shaking and hardly daring to breathe, as I listened to pub customers coming in and out. Eventually Jean (Sheila Kelly) came to see where I was and as Dawn I had to concoct a story involving constipation to explain my absence.

On the first night of the show, which was titled *Ecstasy*, at Hampstead, about twenty minutes into the first half a woman stood up at the back and declared in a loud, very middle-class voice, 'Who are these people? They're not actors!' and walked out. Mike was thrilled, indeed we all were, and of course highly amused. It was a compliment as far as we were concerned, a tribute to the realism of the piece.

On another occasion, halfway through the second half, Jim Broadbent suddenly declared, 'Oh God! I don't feel very well!' The audience giggled knowingly at this, obviously thinking they were into an *Abigail's Party* scenario, where one of the characters has a heart attack. However, on stage we were in panic mode.

'Am yer all right, Len?' I said, staying in character, to which Jim mumbled something unintelligible.

We tried to carry on with the play, each of us trying to ascertain how ill he was by asking questions in character, none of us taking our eyes off him, until suddenly he stood up and blurted out, 'Oh God, I'm sorry, I think I'm having a stroke!' and blundered off the stage.

For just a few seconds the place went deadly silent, all of us, actors and audience alike, reeling from being yanked out of Leigh world and plunged shockingly and confusingly into the real one. Sheila Kelly then stood up and said, 'Is there a doctor in the house?' About twenty-nine people put their hands up. It was Hampstead after all. There ensued a polite discussion:

'Well, you go then . . . '

'No, please, you go . . . '

'No, really, I think this is more your sort of thing . . . '

Finally one of them came backstage and tended to poor Jim, who was by now lying flat out on the floor of one of the dressing rooms, in extreme discomfort. It turned out to be a very nasty virus from which he recovered in a few days, but more importantly, it was something for us all to dine out on for months — did I say months? no, years — to come.

During the play the characters spent a lot of their time drinking and on the last night, the prop drinks, which were supposed to be vodka and tonic, beer and bottled Guinness, were replaced by the real thing. I'm pretty sure it was Stephen Rea who was responsible, as I seem to remember him confiding in me before the show and swearing me to secrecy lest Mike should find out. But what I remember clearly was the mutual private glee we shared as Sheila and Jim discovered that their normal beverage was rather more warming than usual and that it went straight to the spot. A great deal of near-corpsing took place as Stephen, with the devil in him, insisted on constantly filling up everyone's glass, with Sheila, ever the professional, realising she was fast getting drunk and trying to stop him, and all of it conducted whilst remaining steadfastly in character. All I can say for my own part is that Dawn liked a drink and Julie was well and truly plastered by the end of the show.

17

Rita on Stage and Screen

In the spring of 1970, whilst appearing in Victoria Wood's play *Good Fun* at the Sheffield Crucible Theatre (which was set in an arts centre up north, where a group of its employees prepare for a cystitis sufferers' rally), I was sent a script of a new stage play titled *Educating Rita* by Willy Russell. It had been commissioned by the Royal Shakespeare Company, with Mike Ockrent set to direct, and was to be put on in their studio theatre, which at that time was the Donmar Warehouse in Covent Garden.

I was immediately attracted to the character of Rita, a working-class hairdresser who realises there is more to life than the narrow horizon she sees before her. She wants it broadened, and she wants an education, so she embarks on an Open University course. During the course of the play she finds herself marooned between her own working-class roots and family, on the one hand feeling that she has somehow left them behind, and the middle-class life she craves on the other, sensing that in essence she is an outsider. Although her marriage to her husband Denny breaks down because he does not understand and is threatened by her aspirations, all comes good in the end when she grasps that, through education, the most important thing she has gained is choice. There was not a scene in the play that I didn't identify with and, without wanting to sound like a complete pill, just like *Talent* before it, it felt a little like destiny.

At the time *Good Fun* was rumoured to be going into the West End and I really couldn't face a long run, even though every night was a riot on stage and my character, Betty, a cosmetics saleswoman, brought the house down. Her opening line after knocking on the door and being told to come in was: 'I'm sorry . . . I never lay my hand on a strange knob.' One night the hysteria grew to such a pitch that we simply couldn't continue with the scene and everyone, the cast included, just collapsed with laughter that went on and on. Nevertheless a nice, short, three-month run, in repertoire, which meant playing only half the week, with another production taking the other half, was a far more attractive deal than a run in the West End with eight shows a week for nine months, even though the difference in money would be huge. So I plumped for *Educating Rita*, thinking it would be all over by the autumn . . . How wrong could I be? I'm glad to say it was never to be over.

In the summer of 1980 I was renting a room in the flat of my friend, the actress Rosalind March, in Oakmead Road, Balham, along with Babs, my Jack Russell terrier. We had both come out of long relationships — that is, Ros and me as opposed to Babs and me — and we spent a lot of evenings, armed with a bottle of wine, vindicating ourselves of any blame, while heaping it instead on the hapless men involved, and celebrating our freedom. We had met originally through the acting agency, Actorum, a couple of years earlier.

Actorum was an agency run by and for actors, with a tiny office in Tower Street, and when members were unemployed they were expected to come into the office to man the phones, ring round for work and negotiate contracts. Although it worked in principle, in practice some members were rarely, if ever, in the office and others were never out of it, which at times gave rise to a degree of, shall we say, bitterness. Whilst there were people who were wonderfully efficient in the office, there were others who put only themselves up for parts, plus one or two who suggested themselves for parts that were completely wrong for them. One such individual, who at this time was most certainly middle aged and not what a girl would describe as good-looking, put himself forward to play Romeo in a production of *Romeo and Juliet* at the Royal Shakespeare Company, no less, when actually, were it being cast at the time, *The Hobbit* would have been more appropriate. Needless to say he wasn't called for an audition. Also problematic was the fact that no deal could really be negotiated without close consultation at every stage with the actor for whom the deal was being struck. This resulted in situations such as the one that occurred when I was filming *Nearly a Happy Ending*.

It was our last evening in the studio and for some reason we were very behind with the recording. It may have had something to do with the director coming down and saying, 'What's happened? You were funny in rehearsal . . . Be funny!' This, as any actor will tell you, is the kiss of death. Anyway, in those days if you hadn't finished in a television studio by ten-thirty they would simply pull the plug, so the pressure and tension were already fairly high when suddenly I was summoned up into the director's gallery to take an urgent phone call. I couldn't imagine what it was; thoughts of my flat burning to the ground or my mother being ill or worse shot into my head as I picked up the receiver. To my surprise, on the other end was the chirpy voice of a fellow actor.

'Julie! Good news! I think I've got Sheffield Crucible over a barrel! Shall I go for the extra fiver?'

Just before rehearsals for *Educating Rita* were to start I decided to take a little holiday. Ros was about to do a commercial in Amsterdam. The filming would be spread out over five days or so, with quite a bit of free time, and we thought it would be fun if I went along too. We checked into a hotel that had been booked by the production company. It was on the Heerengracht, one of the three main canals that run through the centre of the city. The name means Gentleman's Canal, the appropriateness of which was completely lost on us, at least to begin with. The hotel, one of those ornate-looking, tall, thin houses, was cosy and friendly. After unpacking in our respective rooms, which were at the top of a narrow creaky staircase, we went down to the little bar for a drink. The bartender, a good-looking chap with bright blond hair, was wearing a kilt. He was chatty and friendly, speaking very good English, but he was definitely not Scottish. We spent the evening talking to him and another rather dapper man in his fifties who had just checked in and who, it turned out, was a consultant neurologist from Canada. Both of us being tired and Ros having to get up at some unearthly hour, we decided to get an early night.

The next evening we ended up again in the little hotel bar. This time, there were just two or three young men, standing around quietly having a drink. As the evening went on and the bar started to fill up, we began to notice a distinct lack of women. It was only later, around midnight, when the consultant came back into the bar after a night on the town, that we began to cotton on as to what kind of hotel it was. With him was a huge and very beautiful black man dressed from head to toe as a cowboy, including leather chaps and spurs. I innocently asked whether they'd been to a fancy-dress party, a question that was mysteriously met with peals of laughter from the assembled group.

As the night crept on towards the small hours, the cowboy, enlivened by drink, began to remove his clothes and show us his piercings. I thought I was daring, having two in one earlobe, but these were simply eye-watering to behold; there were little rings and studs glinting and gleaming from folds and crevices that a person simply does not associate with jewellery, and all I could think at the time was what a terribly uncomfortable impediment some of them would be to certain activities.

Anyway, dear reader, as you may have guessed long before I did, it was a gay hotel and the production company presumably thought it was a nice safe place for a woman on her own, as Ros was initially going to be. It was either that or, when she asked them whether they would also book a room for her friend, they got the wrong end of the stick. I really don't know which it was but it was all very educational and, more importantly, it made us laugh, starting a friendship that has lasted to this day.

When the Royal Shakespeare Company commissioned a play from Willy Russell, apparently they were expecting a big modern musical like *John, Paul, George, Ringo and Bert*, which had enjoyed a massive success, here and in the States. What they got was a two-handed play with one set and no idea how to cast it. It remained on the shelf for some time, after which it was decided to cast it from outside the company, leaving Willy and Mike Ockrent to their own devices. So we started rehearsals in June 1980.

Mark Kingston was to play Frank, the Open University lecturer, and the two of us hit it off immediately. Although I had identified with the character of Rita on just about every level, when it came to act her I had real difficulty in finding her core and agonised through rehearsals about who she was, trying different approaches and using different characters from my own life as inspiration. At one point Willy suggested that if I wanted, I could play her as a Brummie. That night when I went through the script I was fascinated to find that the timing and rhythm of Rita's one-liners were at odds with the Birmingham accent and its kind of dry, downbeat music, which has utterly different cadences and humour. It simply did not fit the sparky Liverpool tempo. I never truly found Rita until the first preview at the Donmar where somehow, through sheer terror and the life-or-death need to survive in front of an audience, she clicked gawkily into place. I thought that I would most certainly fall flat on my face as soon as I stepped out on to the stage. On that first night Mark and I stood holding hands in the darkness backstage, waiting to go on, shaking with fear, both feeling that the critics would dump on us from a great height and that a blanket of humiliation was waiting to smother us.

How wrong could we be? I remember during the first-night interval Mike whooshing through the dressing rooms, making an O with his thumb and forefinger, kissing it, thrusting it into the air and calling to the gods with a huge smile on his face, 'Prima! Prima! Prima! Prima!' whilst Mark and I just stared at one another, thinking: Is he deluded? No, he was right; the next day the papers were full of praise and you couldn't get a seat. After its three-month run we transferred to the Piccadilly Theatre, a great barn of a place, made more intimate by shutting off the upper tiers.

One day during the course of the run I received a phone call from a man who introduced himself as Lewis Gilbert. He told me that he was a film director and that on the recommendation of his wife he had come to see the play and had absolutely loved both it and me. He was going to make a film of it and said that he wanted me for the part but could not offer it to me just then as he had yet to raise the money. He would be in touch.

Approximately three months later he rang again. He had been in America where potential investors had talked of Paul Newman and Dolly Parton in the roles of Frank and Rita. Well, I could think of two very good reasons why I couldn't compete with her. It seems that because I was an unknown I would be required to do a screen test, the very thought of which sent me into paroxysms of panic. I would have to prove myself all over again to people who knew nothing about me.

It seemed an exhausting task, in which the stakes felt ridiculously astronomical: a tiny unreliable pivot on which my life might turn and move into another league, where I was to star in a major motion picture or, alternatively, where I would fail to make the grade and then have to live with that and the rejection therein — not an easy one for me (remember the fiasco of the walking race? And the hoohah over eleven-plus, where failure was just about equal to death?) — and I would then have to watch someone else take the part that I had created. I would be too nervous! I wouldn't be relaxed enough to be really inside the character, and what if I was just too nervous to perform at all? The Americans wouldn't think that I was good-looking enough

301

and what if, what if, what if . . . It felt like a test to see whether I was good enough to be on this earth instead of right for a part in a film and a part that I knew inside out at that.

However, salvation was at hand; a month later I was put out of my misery when Lewis rang again.

'It's all right, darling, we've got Michael. You won't have to do a screen test now.'

At first I couldn't make any sense of this; I thought he could only be saying that I had not got the part.

'Oh . . . '

'OK, dear . . . ? Happy?'

'What?'

'You've got the part.'

'*Oh my garrrrrrrd!*'

'Yes, dear, now that we've got Michael, we don't need a star to play your part.'

' . . . Sorry? Michael . . . ? Michael who?'

'Caine, darling, Michael Caine is going to play Frank.'

'M-Michael Caine . . . ? Michael C — Alfie? Alfie is going to play . . . Rita?'

'No, dear, he's going to play Frank.'

'Yes, no, yes, no, I knew what you meant. *Oh my gaaaaaaaard!*'

I rang everyone I knew, including Duncan Preston. So when a few minutes after my last call the phone rang and a deep Texan drawl said, 'Hi, am I speaking to Julie Walters?' I answered suspiciously, 'Yeeees?'

'My name is Herbie Oakes. I am the producer of your movie *Educating Rita* and — '

'Stop before you start! Yeah, great name, Duncan, very good, but I know it's you and do you know how I know it's you? Because your Texan accent is soooooo bad!' And cackling manically I put the phone down.

About five minutes later I decided to ring Duncan back. He completely denied having just called me and, what is more, I believed him. *Oh my gaaaard!* I'm already off on the wrong foot. In fact, I'm off on the most terrible of feet. But the producing person with the 'great name' rang back and, in an obsequious, faltering way, I tried to explain and apologise.

'I'm so sorry, erm . . . Mr . . . Mr Hoax, er, no . . . I'm sorry, Mr Mr Mr Mr Mr Mr . . . Oakes.'

'Please call me Herbie, yes, I thought I had the wrong number.'

Oh, if only you had. But, even though I'm not sure that he had understood, he was charming and friendly, going on to explain that he had simply called to introduce himself and to invite me round to his place for drinks so that I could meet Michael as well as some other people whose names went immediately in and out of my head. All I heard was *Michael*, Michael (*The Ipcress File, Get Carter, The Man Who Would Be King, Zulu, Alfie* and millions of other films too numerous to mention) Caine.

He was, as you might imagine, funny, friendly and direct, with a working-class down-to-earthiness that put me at my ease straight away. When I was leaving, Shakira, his wife, whose vivid beauty was even more arresting in the flesh than it was in print, said, 'You are so lucky it's Michael.'

I mentioned this to Lewis.

'Oh yes, darling, when you think who else it could have been, she's absolutely right.'

I have spent the last twenty-five or so years trying to work out who on earth he might have been referring to.

We started shooting some time around the beginning of August 1982 in Dublin at the university. The play was set in northern England and in reality the university would more than likely have been some red-brick monstrosity, but Willy and Lewis wanted it to be intimidatingly other-worldly for Rita and remote from the probably sixties-built secondary modern that she would have attended. So the beautiful, photogenic Trinity College, Dublin, was cast, with its imposing eighteenth- and nineteenth-century architecture, and its sense of ancient academia.

The Friday before we were to start on the Monday, I was due to have a make-up and hair test, in which I would be made up as the character, wearing my wig and costume, and they would shoot some film of me in order to see that the whole thing worked. Unfortunately, a week or so earlier I had been bitten by a horsefly and Mount Vesuvius had erupted on my cheek, large, red and glowing. I stood there in the glare of the lights, feeling rather awkward in the wig, make-up and costume, as it was very different from the stage production, where I had worn my own hair throughout and where Rita's clothes reflected the fact that from the very beginning she had already moved away from her working-class contemporaries towards the middle-class student identity she craved. In contrast, in the film she looked the antithesis of a student, to begin with at least, when she was still very much a hairdresser in a little suburban salon. Lewis wanted the cinema-going audiences to see her transformation clearly displayed in her choice of dress and general demeanour. So I stood there in my pink-and-black-striped pencil skirt, pink blouse, black fishnet tights and staggeringly high heels, as Lewis, Freddie Williamson, the make-up artist, and Candy Patterson, who did my costumes, discussed me in stage whispers from behind the camera.

'Less eye make-up, Freddie, that's too much, she looks as if she's done three round with Muhammad Ali.'

No, Freddie, I like tons of eye make-up, I was well pleased with that.

'Well . . . the thing is, she's got such small eyes, perhaps we just go without.'

Noooooooooo!

'Yes, that's probably best.'

Nooooooooo!

'The natural look.'

God, *nooooooo!*

'Exactly, now what's that on her face?'

My nose?

'I don't know, I presumed it was just a spot. I've done my best to cover it up.'

What do you want? The George Cross?

'Well, let's hope it's gone by Monday. What do you think?'

'Well . . . '

'It could be a bite.'

Oh my God!

'Hello, helloooo, excuse me, I say, hello! Please allow me to put you out of your misery: *I've been bitten by a horsefly, everyone.* I know this to be the case because I was actually there when it happened.'

Luckily they laughed. The bite was gone by the Monday, well, more or less, with the help of a trowel and a whole container of concealer, that is.

The filming lasted nine weeks and with the very gorgeous Lewis Gilbert at the helm it was an unstressed, light-hearted pleasure. He was delightfully absent-minded and legend has it that once, after filming for some time at Pinewood Studios, he drove the twenty miles to Shepperton Studios by mistake and berated the security man on the gate for not recognising the name of the film he was directing. On one occasion when everyone had assembled to start filming after lunch, the entire crew and I decided to play a trick on Lewis, who had not yet returned. Hiding behind vehicles and round corners, we all watched as he approached the set and stood there for several seconds with an open-mouthed, slightly baffled smile on his face. He then turned round slowly in a jerky, flat-footed little circle, muttering puzzled half-words as he went: 'Oh . . . thought . . . Ha . . . mm.' We jumped out at that point and surprised him; he laughed at the fun of it all but claimed that he knew we were hiding all along. He had an appealing clumsiness and would frequently walk on to the set knocking lamps this way and that, leaving cries of 'Relight!' in his wake, and once when not quite concentrating he crossed his legs and fell off the dolly. (This is a platform on wheels for the camera and not something that you blow up, dear reader.)

Michael was completely unstarry, managing to my surprise to walk around Dublin without any fuss and without being recognised to a troubling degree; he rarely stayed confined to his trailer, preferring rather to be out on the set chatting to the crew. He loved good food and treated us to lavish meals in some of Dublin's and the surrounding area's finest eateries. He also gave me one of the best pieces of acting advice ever, which was: 'Save it for the take.' It may sound obvious, but there is a great temptation to do a scene at full pelt in rehearsal, if only to make sure that you actually can, but often there are, for technical reasons, lots of rehearsals and you can kill the freshness and spontaneity of the thing by constant repetition.

This happened on the day when we were shooting the scene when Rita comes back to tell Frank why she hadn't turned up to his house for dinner. It was meant to be tearful and from the moment I woke up on that morning, I was preparing for it, even gulping my breakfast down whilst on the verge of tears. By the time I got to the set I was already drained and the first shot was of Rita standing there crying through the rain-lashed window. So in the very first rehearsal, I let it all out and then struggled to achieve any tears through the next five or six rehearsals, until Michael pointed out that it was not that close a shot and that they couldn't really see whether I was crying or not anyway. Another filming lesson: check the size of the shot before launching into your performance of performances. By the time it came to my close-up I had absolutely nothing left and it was then that Michael said: 'Use the rehearsals for yourself, and save the special stuff for the take.' It has rung in my ears many, many times since.

The whole experience, being my first film, was a steep learning curve. I had performed the role innumerable times on stage and that performance was in itself like an old film playing in my head, something that needed to be got rid of rather than utilised. It was a performance designed to reach people sitting in the back rows of the Piccadilly Theatre, while I was now required to give a performance for an audience that for a lot of the time was just inches from my face. However, Lewis was always at hand with his inimitable style of direction: 'Too big, darling, it's not the Albert Hall!'

No one could have been more surprised than me by the success of the film. When I first went to see it in a little screening room in Soho, I was appalled by my performance, thinking it over the top and amateurish, and again, as with the play, I thought both it and I would be dumped on from a great height by critics and public alike. I wanted to run and hide, so when Lewis mentioned that Columbia Pictures had bought it for release and that on top of that there was talk of Oscar nominations, I thought he had gone completely off his rocker with optimism when the film would probably not even make it in the 'straight to video' category. Of course it did go to video but before doing so the play enjoyed a huge, worldwide, theatrical distribution and success.

The film opened in London first, in the spring of 1983, with a royal premiere at the Odeon, Leicester Square, attended by the Duke of Edinburgh. He sat in the row in front of me and when the film finished he turned round to give me a huge thumbs-up and a wink. My mother came down from Birmingham and, unable to get through the crowd in order to get into the cinema, she called to a policeman for help. Pointing up at my name on the hoarding she told him in no uncertain terms that that was her daughter up there in lights and could she please come through or else.

The following autumn the film was to open in the States and that August Columbia Pictures' mighty publicity machine was set in motion. I flew with my friend Ros Toland to New York and was booked into a huge corner suite at the Plaza Hotel, looking directly out over Central Park. One of my fellow guests was the King of Morocco, who had taken the entire first floor of this enormous hotel, together with his massive entourage and his three hundred items of personal luggage. Ros, who had been the publicist for the film of *Educating Rita* in Britain, had a refreshingly irreverent attitude towards the Hollywood establishment as well as a wicked sense of humour, so I had asked her to accompany me, both as a friend and as a personal publicist to help stave off the worst excesses of the publicity demands. I fell for New York instantly and even today the first sight of Manhattan, lit up as you drive across the midtown bridge from the airport, makes my skin prickle. I think it one of the most beautiful sights in the world. Everywhere I turned seemed to be a movie location; in fact the whole place felt like a film set. It was buzzy, neurotic, with an ambient sense of excitement and danger. There were warnings back then that to veer off the beaten track was not advisable and ending up in the wrong street in the wrong neighbourhood could spell disaster for a bumbling tourist. I was enthralled by the city and still am.

Waiting for me when I arrived at the hotel was a script that had been sent to me by Burt Reynolds, whom I instantly confused with Burt Lancaster. It seemed he had seen the film and wanted me for his next project. I thought: This is it! I've arrived! Look out, Hollywood, I'm here! Then I read it. It was not only awful but I was being asked to play an upper-class New York stockbroker type: why? So I duly turned it down, and in any case I wanted to do the publicity tour that was to take me in some style around America, Australia and Europe. However, Burt wasn't taking no for an answer and sent a message, saying that even if I didn't want to do his film, he would like to meet me. This I couldn't resist. He flew Ros and me down to his home town of Jupiter, yes, Jupiter in Florida, where as we drove through the town we noticed several buildings emblazoned with the letters BR. We were booked into an hotel and that very night we were to meet Burt over dinner at the Burt Reynolds Dinner Theater where a production of *The Hasty Heart* by John Patrick was playing, starring the woman who played the eldest daughter of the Von Trapp family in the film of *The Sound of Music*. We were very excited. When Ros informed me that the man we were meeting was in fact not Burt Lancaster of *From Here to Eternity* and *Elmer Gantry* but Burt Reynolds of *Smokey and the Bandit* and *The Cannonball Run* fame, I was thrilled. Then I recalled an interview that I had seen on television in the recent past with Dolly Parton, who had just done a film with him, and she said that they had two things in common: they both had forty-inch chests and they both wore wigs; the latter comment Burt was apparently not too pleased about. So as we were being driven to dinner in our stretch limo through the streets of Jupiter City, I regaled Ros with this story, adding that above all else we must not mention the wig or refer to it in any way, however obliquely.

'Hi, Julie, Burt Reynolds, welcome to Jupiter!'

He was quite short, wearing built-up shoes, and had gorgeous, dark, twinkly eyes. I kept my own directed straight at them, never letting them stray north to the unnaturally dark thatch lurking at the top of his conker-brown forehead.

'Thank you, WIG!' It just came out, exploding out of my mouth without a thought. Well, there was a thought; it was *don't mention the wig*! I then scrabbled about trying to recover, with verbiage spilling everywhere: 'Yes, yes . . . thank you . . . wig . . . ' Oh God, there it goes again!

311

'Wig . . . ' Please, brain, stop it . . . Try to engage, please! 'Wig . . . wig . . . wiggoing to enjoy this . . . our . . . selves . . . tonight. It's, it's so . . . let . . . jet . . . lagged . . . I am so get-lagged . . . erm.'

Burt instantly came to the rescue, ushering us through with loads of bonhomie and a joke that made us laugh, but which I cannot for the life of me remember now.

We were seated for dinner in a private box at the back of the theatre, with a huge black bodyguard who according to Burt had been something high up in the Miami State Police. The first half of the evening was a little strained, mainly because we were forced to sit through the first half of a rather turgid production of a play long past its sell-by. Then when the interval came along like a cold drink in the desert, Burt pressed something and a soundproof glass screen glided across the front of our booth, thankfully remaining there for the rest of the night. Once we were released from the coma-inducing show, the evening bubbled into life with Burt getting more laughs and engaging our interest in a way that *The Hasty Heart* could never hope to do. His parting shot was, 'Look, I'm not going to try to force you to do it, although I know you'd enjoy yourself, and I'm not going to try to force you to do the movie either!'

The next day we were taken by limo to his house and watched as his helicopter landed on the lawn in the back garden to take us to Miami airport. Burt gave me his phone number and said that if there was ever anything I needed that he could help with, I was to give him a ring. We were then whisked up and out of Jupiter to land on the runway a matter of yards from the aircraft that was to take us back to New York. What on earth the planeload of gawping, bemused travellers thought of these two young, slightly scruffy girls getting out of a helicopter and straight into first class, I dread to think. All I can say is I'm glad it was Burt Reynolds of *Cannonball Run* fame and if I am to believe the numerous people whom I have met since who have worked with him, I missed out on that film and a whole lot of fun.

Back in New York the press junket began with twenty television interviews, one after the other, followed by a seemingly endless round of newspaper interviews. Michael, Lewis and I were each ensconced in a separate room at the Plaza, visited in turn by individual journalists. That evening Michael took us to Elaine's, a famous restaurant frequented by celebrities of different types. The walls were covered in their photographs, personally signed to Elaine with some chatty message usually followed by a lot of exclamation marks. So when on arrival I asked Michael where the Ladies' was and he instructed me to turn left at Woody Allen, I went along the wall scanning the photos for Woody's little elfin portrait and ended up tripping over the real man's feet. We sat in the corner, with Michael pointing out anyone famous as they came in, with all the fresh excitement of a boy actor. 'That's Henry Mancini . . . You know, 'Moon River'.' The charming thing about the whole experience was that Michael was more famous than any of them.

Ros and I had a ball in New York; she had friends there and we were out most nights, painting the town some colour or other. On my last morning I woke up inexplicably wearing a New York City Department of Sanitation T-shirt. I never quite worked out where that came from but perhaps after the painting I'd done a bit of mopping and dusting.

Next stop was Los Angeles; the drive in from the airport there, of course, is a completely different kettle of fish. It is a massive, sprawling suburb, which is all sub and no actual urb, acre upon acre of tatty, low-rise housing, with no character whatsoever. We were checked into the Beverly Hills Hotel, a pink palace of a place set in the heart of the not-at-all-tatty and highly manicured Beverly Hills, which is known for its celebrity clientele and its famous Polo Lounge, dubbed by Bette Midler the Polio Lounge.

It was Labor Day weekend, which gave us time to ourselves, so we headed to the pool. We were shown to our loungers by two tanned, athletic-looking young men, sporting Ray-Bans and dressed in blindingly white singlets and shorts. Ros, with her wonderfully dry, irreverent wit, and I sat there agog, chortling at the assembled clientele. I had never seen so much gold in one place. There was enough there to solve Third World debt. When one woman dived in I checked the muscular young men to see whether they displayed any signs of concern; they didn't, but it was a wonder she ever came up again. She was covered in what is nowadays referred to as bling and so, it seemed, was everyone else there: great lumps of the stuff hanging from earlobes, necks and wrists, not pretty or delicate or subtle. In fact, a block of gold just strapped to a person's front or perhaps a bank statement made into a sunhat would have been more aesthetically appealing, whilst creating a similar impression.

Just before we left I appeared on the *Tonight Show* with Johnny Carson and regaled him with stories of the Beverly Hills Hotel, such as how we were not allowed into the Polo Lounge with its snobby old dress code because one of us was wearing denim, and that in fact the most smartly dressed people in there were the hookers, but that was apparently absolutely fine with the management because they looked right. I also told him that, after staying there, 50 per cent of my luggage was now towelling. Johnny loved all this and invited me on the show twice in one week to talk about it further; the only other person ever, at that time, to have appeared on the show twice in one week was, strangely enough, Burt Reynolds. Unfortunately the hotel didn't see the funny side of it, and I was never booked in there again.

I had always had a fascination for Los Angeles. For as long as I can remember, every Christmas we received a card from my mother's second cousins who lived there. The card was in the form of a photograph of the entire family beaming festively and somewhat glamorously at the camera. They were called the Takahashis and, yes, as you have no doubt surmised from the name, they were and indeed are Japanese, or at least Japanese-American.

My great-aunt Margaret had gone to California from Ireland in the 1920s and worked as a waitress on a train. One day she was taken ill and a Japanese doctor tended her. The result was that even though neither could speak the other's language, they nevertheless fell in love and subsequently got married. They settled in the Japanese quarter and their children in turn married Japanese-Americans. During the Second World War they were interned in a camp, even though they had never been to Japan, knew very little about its culture and, to all intents and purposes, saw themselves as American. It was when my mother was a child at home in Ireland that her cousin Margaret first got in contact via the local post office. They were both aged around eleven at the time and she had been writing to them, never having met them, ever since. So it was with great excitement that I contacted the Takahashis and told them I was in Los Angeles.

I was invited to dinner at their home downtown and felt instantly at ease with them. There was something strangely familiar that I couldn't quite name: something in a turn of phrase, a knowing glance, the tone of someone's laugh, the set of someone's mouth, my mother's eyes surrounded by an Oriental face, the features of a distant cousin. They looked Japanese but there was a liberal, if subtle, sprinkling of O'Brien genes. They joked that they thought their small eyes were down to being Japanese, but that now, having met me, they could see that

316

they were in fact Irish eyes. I booked tickets for them for the Los Angeles premiere and enjoyed watching the Columbia Pictures representative who, after ushering them in, turned to a colleague and mouthed silently, but with the pronounced articulation of someone communicating with the deaf, 'Her *cousins?*'

Just as I was about to leave Los Angeles, a call came for me to appear on *Good Morning America* with the famous television journalist, Barbara Walters (no relation). It was to happen live, the very next day in New York, so I was to fly there immediately that evening. I arrived at the airport in Los Angeles to find that the flight was delayed because La Guardia airport in New York was fogbound. The plane eventually took off well past midnight. When we arrived in the vicinity of La Guardia, an announcement was made to the effect that the airport was still fogbound and would we please be a little patient. They did not send Ros with me on this particular journey as it wasn't deemed necessary just for one night and so I was travelling alone in first class, seated next to a man who, as we circled the airport waiting to make a landing, was becoming increasingly nervous. Eventually the captain's voice came over the speaker system with the comforting announcement: 'Ladies and gentlemen, if I could just have your attention for a moment. It seems that this fog just isn't going to lift so we are proposing that we land at Newark instead of La Guardia as we are running out of fuel fast.'

With that the man sitting next to me jumped

up out of his seat and shouted, purple-faced, at the blank wall in front of him, '*You asshole!*'

We landed at Newark airport some twenty minutes later at about four o'clock in the morning. I hadn't a clue where Newark was, so it might just as well have been in Brazil. I couldn't remember where I was staying and, needless to say, the Columbia Pictures rep, for whom I had no contact number and who was meant to meet me off the flight about six hours earlier at another airport entirely, was not there. I had no dollars, as they were in my hotel room back in LA, and I had been assured at the time that not only would I not need any money, as I would be met and taken everywhere by a rep in a limo, but that I would be back within twenty-four hours. Stiff with panic, I wandered out of the deserted airport in the vain hope that at least there would be a car waiting for me. No such luck. I then went towards the taxi rank and heard a woman ask whether anyone wanted to share a cab into Manhattan. At exactly the same time the name of the hotel I was booked into popped inexplicably into my head and I took her up on the offer, along with another woman and a man. I had no idea how far we had to go and was shocked to see the familiar skyline within minutes of setting off; it seemed Newark was a lot nearer Manhattan than La Guardia. I sat in the back of the cab, desperately trying to think how I was going to explain my lack of funds, and then when the cab pulled up outside my expensive-looking hotel it just exploded out of my mouth, just as Burt Reynolds' wig had done only a few days earlier: 'Erm . . . I'm really sorry but I haven't got any money.' Absolute silence. 'Erm . . . Columbia Pictures were meant to be meeting me . . . I'm so sorry . . . '

'Oh, that's OK. Forget it.' This was the nice lady to my right.

'Oh, really . . . Columbia Pictures, huh?' This was the rather cross man sitting in the front and addressing me as if I were a halfwit claiming to be a brain surgeon.

'Yes, I've got a film opening here.'

'It's all right, really.' The kind woman again.

'Oh really? You've got a film opening and you have no money.' The cross man, now sarcastic as well as patronising.

'Yes, I'm an actress, I was just put on a plane last night. I'm on *Good Morning America* in the morning.' Me, squirming.

'It's fine, really.' The woman.

'You are a movie star appearing on *Good Morning America* and you can't pay for your cab ride?' The man.

'Yes, I know it sounds odd, but . . . I'm so sorry.' Me, squirming even more.

'Yeah, you betcha it sounds odd.' The man, very cross and sneery. He turned his head away and raised his palm towards me in a 'talk to the hand' kind of gesture. 'Yeah, whatever, lady. We'll pay.'

I skulked off into my very posh and impressive-looking hotel. It never crossed my mind that I could have got the hotel to pay the cab for me and saved myself the humiliation of trying to explain the unbelievable. A lesson was learnt that night. Now I always make sure that I have enough money on me for a cab, a contact number and an address, no matter who says that they have organised everything.

Next morning after about an hour and a half's sleep I was sitting in front of a make-up mirror at the studio, supposedly getting ready for the show. Even though there were magenta-coloured circles under my puffy, bloodshot eyes, which had virtually disappeared inside my head, I had for the first time in my life elected to wear no make-up, as the thought of touching my eyes, let alone trying to define them with eyeliner and mascara, was too much to bear. Never had the term 'red eye', the name given to the Los Angeles to New York flight, been more appropriate. Just before we went on air and the interview was about to start, I happened to mention to Barbara, who was sitting there in fully coiffured, beautifully dressed, perfumed splendour, that I hadn't bothered with make-up. Even beneath the powdered, orange perfection of her own freshly applied maquillage, I could see that she had paled at the thought of appearing bare-faced on national television and, indeed, when we went on air, she thought it so significant that she turned straight to camera and announced, 'She has no make-up on, everybody!' I saw a playback of the two of us afterwards and could see only too clearly why it is necessary to wear at least a modicum of slap in a situation such as this; not only because of the draining effect of the powerful studio lighting, but also because up against Barbara's extraordinary hue I looked positively green.

From LA we went on a nine-week tour, taking in San Diego, San Francisco, Seattle, Philadelphia, Boston, Washington, Chicago, Denver, Dallas, Atlanta and Hawaii. Then on to all the major cities of Australia, followed by New Zealand, and finally the Netherlands and Scandinavia. I saw mainly the insides of hotel rooms, but there were days off where we were treated royally; in Los Angeles, through a connection of Ros's, we went to visit Tippi Hedren's ranch. Tippi, famous for appearing in Hitchcock's *The Birds* and *Marnie* and for being Melanie Griffith's mother, lived on an amazing spread in California, where she kept animals rescued from the circus and the like. Amongst the elephants was one in particular, whose back I rode on, which spent its time obsessively walking round and round in circles, every so often rearing up on to its hind legs in a sad parody of its former days as a performer, continually doing the tricks that it had been taught to do long ago in the ring. There were lions lounging around on the tops of old buses, one of which I was able to sit down with and cuddle — admittedly he was ancient and had no teeth or claws, as these had been removed during his days as a circus performer — but even so when I got up to walk away the hair on the back of my neck stood on end as I was warned not to rush because he might just chase me and bring me down for fun. The most abiding image from that trip, however, was when we were sitting in the kitchen, having a cold drink at the end of the day, and a fully grown tiger, which had been bathing in a pond outside, jumped in through the window just like a domestic cat.

Nothing on the tour quite compared to this, although there were highlights: in Denver, we were taken on a special plane ride over the Rockies and through the Grand Canyon; in Sydney, I was put up in a penthouse suite looking out over the famous harbour, complete with a sunken bath and its own butler, the very suite that the Queen had occupied only weeks before; there we spent a day on a yacht, sailing around the harbour and going out to sea. Everywhere we went, we flew first class, which still epitomises luxury for me, and we stayed in the most exclusive of hotels.

In every city of every country that we visited, there was a Rita waiting to meet me: that is, an actress playing the part in a theatre somewhere. Today I still get people coming up to me in the street or writing to me to say how *Educating Rita* has influenced them, giving them the impetus to try further education and to make changes in their lives. I have often been asked whether I get fed up with being so associated with this part and I always answer that I am proud to be remembered for it, and that I would be thrilled to be remembered for anything, but to be remembered for this is a privilege.

Throughout my career I have continued to make a steady stream of films, good, bad and indifferent, since *Rita*, many of which I am very proud of and many that have been arguably more accomplished in the acting stakes, but none has matched that film or been met with the same warmth and recognition.

Mrs Weasley, in the Harry Potter films, probably comes close and does, of course, add a whole new audience, that of children, and I must confess I love to see the look of wonder on their faces when they discover that the woman fondling the vegetables at the supermarket, or trying to park her car on the High Street, is none other than Mrs Weasley. It's usually their parents who point me out and there is very often a fierce discussion as to how this person could possibly be Mrs Weasley, who as everyone knows is a rotund redhead. In the film, of course, I wear a red wig and padding; in fact my substantial bosoms were, for the first couple of films, stuffed with birdseed, which became a little worrying whilst filming at King's Cross station with the number of pigeons that there were pecking around on the platforms, and even more worrying when I thought I clocked an owl looking interested. I pictured the scene where I see Harry and the boys off on the Hogwarts Express turning into something out of Hitchcock's *The Birds*. However, without *Rita* I probably would never have been considered for the Harry Potter films, because it was *Rita* that got me recognition in the film world and, more importantly, in Hollywood.

I won my first film BAFTA for *Educating Rita* at a ceremony during which I got increasingly drunk. I was sat at a table separated from my friends with a group of people that I didn't know. I had no idea how much I had drunk, as waiters never allowed your glass to be empty, constantly hovering with a refill, and I was too nervous to eat the dinner provided. I had no real expectations of winning so when my name was called out by Michael Aspel who was hosting the evening, as usual I was unprepared. I tottered up on to the stage and by this time I was totally plastered. I stood there for several seconds, staring my BAFTA in the face, and then I said, 'Has anyone got a carrier bag? I can't go home on the tube with this.'

Muted laughter.

'Thank you . . . thank you . . . thank you . . . thank you . . . No, really . . . thank you . . . No, honestly . . . thank you . . . No, thank you . . . Thank you . . . Thanks.'

Then as I left the stage, thinking my speech to be cleverly ironic, Michael turned and said to a quietly embarrassed audience, 'Well, she might at least have said, 'Thank you',' and brought the house down.

After the ceremony I, along with fellow winners, was meant to be presented to the Princess Royal but this proved impossible as I could not be found. This was no wonder because I was, in fact, under the table, literally, discussing the state of the film industry with an actor who was quite clearly as drunk as me but whose identity has now been completely obliterated from my memory. Should he wish to make himself known and put me out of my misery, he can contact the publishers at any time.

Having played Rita on stage as well as film, I am often asked which of the two media I prefer and I have to say that the live theatre wins hands down. Nothing can compare with the adrenalin-fuelled excitement of theatre, where the actor tells the story and pulls the focus, and each performance is unique, as is the relationship with each audience. Film is much more technical, where the story is told more by the director and his editor. It is shot out of sequence in tiny segments lasting only a matter of minutes and once shot is set in aspic. It is not possible in film for the actor to experience the thrill of a story unfolding, in the way that the cinema audience does whilst watching the film, but in theatre the actor shares this with them. This is not to say that I don't enjoy film; it is far less stressful than theatre. You get a chance to do lines over and over again and you don't have to artificially project the character out over the stalls.

Even so I have had the good fortune to be involved in two great productions at the Cottesloe Theatre at the National: the first one being Sam Shepard's *Fool for Love* in 1985 and the second, more recent one, Arthur Miller's *All My Sons* in 2000. Because of the intimacy of the space in which they were performed, these two experiences, along with *Rita* at the Donmar Warehouse, managed to combine the intimacy of film with the heart-pumping excitement and shared experience of live performance. Also, if a film turns out to be a flop, unlike a bad stage production you don't have to keep acting in it until the end of the run; it's either straight to DVD or you keep your head down when you pass the only cinema for two hundred miles that is showing it.

325

18

The Two Alans

In the spring of 1982 I was offered a part in a BBC film written by Alan Bennett, titled *Intensive Care*. Unfortunately the actor playing the lead role was taken ill at the last minute and so Alan himself was drafted in to play the partly autobiographical role.

In the piece I was to play the part of a nurse who becomes sexually involved with his character and when the day of the read-through arrived we were issued with new scripts that contained certain changes. The chief one was during the bed scene. The two characters are about to get undressed and in the original they did so with some gusto. However, in the new script the lines had been changed; I now had to say how much I liked Alan's character's shirt: 'That's a nice shirt . . . keep it on.' When we actually came to shoot it, Alan was so nervous that Gavin Millar, the director, brought down a bottle of whisky to calm his nerves. After much ribbing on my part, with Alan standing there, pink from giggling, and me running around the set, screaming at him not to come into the bedroom yet while I mimed catching a just-lubricated Dutch cap that kept slipping from my grip like a wet bar of soap in a bathtub, all of which he endured with an excruciatingly embarrassed glee, we finally shot the scene. Afterwards, due to the release we both felt at the scene being completed, there was such a sense of post-coital relief that the two of us sat up in bed together and had a cigarette.

I have had the immense privilege and good fortune to work with Alan Bennett on five different occasions, including both *Talking Heads* series and a BBC play titled *Say Something Happened* with Thora Hird and Hugh Lloyd, and each production has had that familiar feeling of somehow coming home. The two *Talking Heads* that I did were another sort of acting heaven and the whole idea of talking directly to the camera appealed enormously to the storyteller in me. The volume of words was daunting, however, and although I had learnt both the scripts back to front, I elected to have a monitor on set with autocue, in case of a sudden loss of concentration or lapse of memory. It was more of a security blanket than anything else, because if I did feel wobbly on the lines it would mean that, however briefly, I was not in character, and I would therefore have to stop and go back anyway.

For my performance in *Say Something Happened* — where I played the part of a rookie social worker investigating an aged couple (Thora Hird and Hugh Lloyd) who had been put on the 'At Risk' register but ultimately finding that she, the social worker, was the one who was most at risk — I was nominated for my first BAFTA. The nomination was split between that and my performance in 1982 of Angie in

Alan Bleasdale's *The Boys from the Blackstuff*.

This was the first time that I had played such a dramatic role, and the first time that I had voiced, or at least recognised that I was voicing, my own angst through the angst of the character. I found Angie's outpouring of anger and pain powerfully cathartic and we all experienced the old Everyman feeling that we were involved in something ground-breaking and important. It is still a performance that is close to my heart. No one writes about the chaos and madness that runs through ordinary life like Alan Bleasdale.

As a writer he is a total maverick; who else would cast me in the role of Robert Lindsay's mother in a television drama series? But that's just what he did for the series *GBH* in 1991. It was a role I relished: an Irish grandmother! To begin with, we tried all sorts of prosthetics to age my face, including having a full cast of it made. This covering the whole of my face, including my eyes and mouth, with plaster of Paris, with a straw inserted up each nostril so that I could breathe. I am not a particularly claustrophobic person but came close to understanding what that condition is like during this procedure.

It took me back to when we made Greek masks back in my Manchester Poly days, where the plaster of Paris didn't cover our eyes, nose and mouth, and someone had to rip off the plaster halfway through in a frenzied fit. I can see it now, the student's arms flailing and strips of the stuff flying through the air, one piece landing comically on someone else's head, another sticking to the mirror, and tiny encrusted spots of it staying on the teacher's glasses for the rest of the academic year.

Well, that didn't happen to me, but the scene played itself over and over in my mind as I sat there waiting for the plaster of Paris to dry. In the end we decided that all the prosthetics looked artificial, creating a barrier between me and the audience, and becoming more of a distraction than anything else so that the viewer would be thinking: Oh, how did they do that?

I can recall saying at the time that everyone knows I'm forty and not seventy, and if we have to go through all that, with goodness knows how many hours in the make-up chair each day, to make me look the right age, you might just as well get an actress who is the right age; so let's just allow the wig, costumes and body language to do their stuff. And the excellent make-up artist — who could have had a field day with latex wrinkling and the like, the BAFTA Craft Awards flashing neon in her mind's eye — was the first to say it has got to be done through acting; no one is going to be fooled. And so that is what we did.

Inside my own head I was definitely the character but I still can't judge whether I got away with it or not. Who cares: I got to work with Robert Lindsay, who has got to be one of the funniest, most inventive, generous and versatile of actors, and someone for whom I not only had huge respect but with whom I felt an instant bond. For me, he was one of those people with whom, from the first moment you meet them, you feel a comfortable familiarity. We worked together again in 1994 on Alan's next project, the epic *Jake's Progress*, this time, more appropriately, playing husband and wife. We had a glorious seven months in Ireland, ending every week with a breakneck dash to Dublin airport on a Friday night, along roads that in those days made our Sussex farm track feel like the M1, in order to get home.

19

'I Love to Boogie' — Oscars and BAFTAs

When the possibility of an Oscar nomination for *Educating Rita* was mooted after the film's warm reception in Britain, I thought it a ludicrous notion, but nevertheless it happened and it was, to say the least, a shock. I guess the inordinate amount of publicity I had done around the States had paid off. I was first nominated for, and subsequently won, a Golden Globe. I was also asked to co-host the ceremony for this with John Forsythe, he of the blue-white hair who played the handsome patriarch in the American television series *Dynasty*. I thought that because of this I had probably not won, and therefore had not really thought of anything to say should the opposite be true. When my name was called out as the winner of Best Actress in a Musical or Comedy, all I could think of was a daft joke alluding to the fact that, as I was also running the show, it was a bit of a fix and that the cheque was in the post. This also happened to be rather topical as at the time there had just been a scandal involving a very bad actress whose billionaire husband had tried to buy her a Golden Globe. My joke went down like a cup of the cold proverbial and was lambasted in the press as tasteless.

The Oscars were a very different kettle of fish; in fact the Oscars were like nothing else. Unlike the BAFTAs, Britain's version of the Oscars, which were a fairly stuffy affair that people mainly read about in a smallish column on a fairly insignificant page of a newspaper the next day, the Oscars were like the Second Coming. During the week running up to them, it seemed that every daytime programme and every news show was running a feature on them. There would be indepth discussions of the various nominees' performances and whole programmes given over to what the nominees might wear on the night. I remember seeing a long, lacy, wafty thing being proposed as my possible number for the big night and thinking: God, are they going to get a surprise! I was in fact going to be wearing a knee-length, soft, black-leather number, given me by Elizabeth and David Emanuel, who only a couple of years previously had designed the wedding dress for the Princess of Wales. It was pronounced by one publication the worst outfit there, but, as this was Hollywood, I took it as a compliment.

My fellow nominees were Meryl Streep, Shirley MacLaine and Debra Winger, and according to the newspapers and the bookies I was the rank outsider at something like a hundred to one. We all knew that it would be Shirley MacLaine who would end up holding the golden phallus and thanking her Auntie Betty for being so supportive. She did, in fact, give a very funny speech, opening with saying that the interminable ceremony had felt longer than her entire professional life. Her amazing career had spanned thirty-odd years in which she had never won an Oscar, and her performance in *Terms of Endearment*, for which she was nominated, was rich and real and funny, and it deserved to be honoured. So I suppose I was fairly relaxed about the whole thing, knowing that I didn't stand a chance. It would have been much more tense-making if I had thought that there was a possibility of winning.

I was thrilled to be in the same line-up as Meryl Streep. Although we were more or less the same age, I felt like I had grown up being mesmerised by her on screen and that she belonged to some other rarefied and glittering stratosphere that bore no relationship to the prosaic, let's-have-a-cup-of-tea world that I inhabited. The last thing I expected, dear reader, was twenty-three years later to be sitting on my arse in the middle of an olive grove, on the beautiful Pelion Peninsula, in southern Greece, with my sprained ankle resting in the esteemed actress's lap while she shouted orders in a marvellously Brown Owl kind of way.

'Ice! Quick! Get it elevated!' — and almost like a group of twittering Brownies people were running this way and that, only too keen to obey, icing and elevating as if their lives depended on it. Someone obviously misunderstood and in the melée an ice lolly was shoved into my hand. Then sucking on my lolly and on Meryl's instruction I was carried through the streets of the village to my digs like a May Queen. This was done by the member of the crew most people fancied, which was a bit of a bonus and helped to counter-balance the humiliation caused by folk coming out of their houses and shops to stare and some of them to inexplicably cheer as if we were a newly married couple. The film was *Mamma Mia!* and when my agent rang to say I had been offered the part of Meryl Streep's friend in . . . I didn't wait for the rest, I screamed 'YES!!' it turned out to be a bit of a hit.

The day of the Academy Awards itself was a bit like a cross between Christmas, some kind of distant crisis and your wedding day; gifts arrived at my hotel room, of exotic beauty products that I had never heard of, and hand-made chocolates, champagne and flowers from film companies, agents and people wanting to advertise their products and services. A blur of masseurs, hairdressers, stylists and makeup artists came and went, until all that there was left to do was go. It was all strategically timed with military precision. We were told in no uncertain terms that, as a thousand limousines would be converging on the Dorothy Chandler Pavilion more or less simultaneously, we must leave our hotel at the allotted time so as to be on the red carpet at the right point. I was being accompanied by my agent and a friend of hers, Dan.

Just as we were about to leave, I heard a scream from her bathroom. It turned out that after much coaxing, the zip in her dress had given up, spitting out a couple of teeth as it went. We stood there for several seconds, staring at it, Sara pink with panic and perspiration, and Dan pulling the two sides of the overstretched zip together as if they might get the message and mend themselves. Eventually he remembered the sewing kit in the bathroom and did a sterling job of lashing the two bits together with some big loopy stitches in a contrasting but not altogether inharmonious colour, with back-up from a couple of safety pins. We were off.

When we arrived at the theatre, we were met by something that I had never experienced before. There were huge crowds of overexcited people, gawping and screaming, many of whom had camped for several days previously on the grass outside, and of course there was the red carpet. Then it was a rarity, reserved for enormous premières, but even so, this was in a league of its own. It must have taken us a good hour and a half to get up it, as we were waylaid by endless television crews and journalists who had travelled not only from all over America but from all over the world. After the ceremony, which may not have been quite as long as Shirley MacLaine's career but was probably longer than mine, there was a do with dinner and dancing. I was paraded round by a Columbia Pictures executive to meet various famous folk, three of whom stick out in my memory. The first was Michael Jackson, who was dressed in his then normal military gear and had a very little voice; the second was Mel Gibson, who was just very little. The third was Liza Minnelli, whom I had in fact met before.

Just before we were to start filming *Educating*

Rita, Michael Caine threw a party at his restaurant, Langan's Brasserie in London. In the small hours, as the party was drawing to an end, a lot of us went on to a club called Tramp where after a couple of hours I found that I could not stand a minute longer the blistering agony of my new cowboy boots, which I had purchased only that day from R. Soles on the King's Road, so I decided to go to the Ladies' to take them off. Because I was wearing no hosiery whatsoever and my feet, after at least a couple of hours of frenzied dancing, had probably swollen to twice their size, their removal proved nigh-on impossible. As I sat on a chair, veins popping in my forehead and face crimson with effort, the door opened and in came Liza.

'Hi.'

'Hello.'

'Need a hand?'

'Oh . . . yes please.' Whereupon she bent down and pulled my boot off.

'Oh, my . . . you're bleeding. Do you want the other one off?'

'Yes, of course, Liza and then fix me an ice-cold Martini, call me a cab and you may take the rest of the night off.'

No, that's right, I didn't say that; just, 'Oh . . . '

She whipped it off and said, 'Wait here, I'll be right back.'

I sat there, staring at my feet. They looked unsavoury and gross, and I thought: Liza Minnelli has just heaved my sweaty, blood-soaked boots off these. Within minutes she was back brandishing plasters, antiseptic and cotton wool; lifting the aforementioned plates on to her lap, she gently bathed and dressed them.

'Oh, you should throw these boots away. Nothing should give you that much pain.'

I was just wondering whether we were about to embark on a discussion about something more than blisters when she jumped up and lifted her skirt. I laughed nervously. I had read *The News of the World*, I knew what these Hollywood stars were capable of. She began to remove her tights. Oh my God! Liza, I'm not that way inclined, even when I had a bit of a crush on Mrs Banbrook in year seven; my fantasy never went past friendship, couldn't we just —

'Here, put these on. It'll make getting the boots on and off easier. And trust me, throw 'em away.'

So when I met her at the Oscar bash some eighteen months later, I felt as if we were old friends.

'Julie, hi! Congratulations!' I noticed then and since that Americans congratulate you after an awards ceremony, even if you haven't won, simply for being nominated. In Britain that doesn't happen; you've simply lost and people look sorry for you, avoiding all eye contact.

'Hi, Liza.'

She hugged me and whispered conspiratorially in my ear, 'Don't tell Shirley, but I voted for you.'

'Oh thanks, that's nice. No, I won't tell her.'

I don't suppose she'll ever read this; I mean, after all, I haven't read *her* autobiography.

Then as I was being dragged off to be introduced to yet another weary megastar, I managed to get in, 'I've still got your tights! Not on me, you understand, I splashed out on a new pair for tonight. Though I might have had more luck if I'd worn yours! No, I'm glad Shirley won, we can all sleep safe in our beds now.'

In 1984 the party to be at was Swifty Lazar's and directly after the rather sedate dinner and dance, Willy Russell — who had also been nominated for, but not won, Best Adapted Screenplay — and I set off to find it. We couldn't locate either of our limos, so we jumped into a cab and instructed the driver to take us to Swifty Lazar's, thinking it was the name of a restaurant. When the befuddled-looking cabbie said he had never heard of such a restaurant, we took him for a chancer and duly got out and into another taxi. Again, the driver had never heard of the place, so in frustration we went on to another party that we *had* heard of, but by the time we arrived there were just three people propping up the bar and, not knowing any of them we decided to call it a night. So we never made the big post-Oscar party. We found out the next day, when quizzed as to where we had got to the night before, that Swifty Lazar was not a restaurant at all but a very famous old Hollywood agent. The whole Oscars thing was a not-to-be-missed experience but it has to be viewed for what it really is, which is first and foremost a wonderful piece of hype and marketing for the film industry; many a brilliant film and performance has gone unnoticed over the years because, for whatever reason, there hasn't been the budget to sell it and distribute it properly.

On every Oscar night various parties are held around Tinseltown, all with varying 'must be seen at' ratings.

At my second Oscar experience in 2001, when I got the Best Supporting Actress nomination for Mrs Wilkinson in *Billy Elliot*, it was the *Vanity Fair* party that everyone wanted to get into and as a nominee you were sure of an invite. However, I chose Elton John's party instead because he'd asked me personally at the première and he's far too cuddly to turn down anyway, plus there's always the chance that he might play the piano and do a turn.

No one could have predicted the phenomenal success of *Billy Elliot*. We all knew that we had a really good script, a fabulous central performance from Jamie Bell, and a skilfully directed, funny and charming film from Stephen Daldry, but how were they going to sell to the general public a film about a miner's son who became a ballet dancer? And to which bit of the public would it appeal? Apparently no one knew how to approach it and things were looking grim until two people from Universal came to a screening and said, 'We like it.' From that moment everything changed. Once a big studio showed an interest, everyone else did too.

In 2001, my second film BAFTA was for *Billy Elliot*; this was a very different acting experience from *Educating Rita* as I was allowed to really create a character. Although it was already brilliantly written by Lee Hall, Stephen Daldry and I would get together and generate whole new scenes on the spot: something I have never been party to, before or since. All films, in my experience, are so schedule dominated that there is never the room for such a 'luxury', but somehow Stephen managed it. I had real fun with the character, taking away any maternal instinct that she might originally have had, as this would not only make her and her relationship with Billy more complex and thorny, but also steer her away from any sentimentality. Then the choreographer, the redoubtable Peter Darling, told me how his dance teacher had smoked and called out instructions to her pupils whilst perusing the *Daily Mirror*. Well, I couldn't resist that, could I? I pored over documentaries about the little dance schools that seemed to be particular to the North-East, where the film was set, and loved the fact that the majority of the teachers couldn't really dance themselves. This suited me perfectly as dancing — well, at least choreographed dancing — was something that scared me and I already had the ghost of my experience on *Stepping Out* haunting me.

In that film, which was shot in 1990, dear Lewis Gilbert, for it was he, told me that although it was a film about a tap-dancing class, it didn't matter a jot that I had never tap-danced and that I hadn't a clue how to do it.

'No, darling, don't worry about all that. We can shoot around all that, darling.'

Thank God I got Phil Collins' sister Carole to teach me a few steps and even then I found it virtually impossible to get the ins and outs of it into my forty-year-old brain, almost wearing out the kitchen floor and kicking several dents into my own shins and ankles in the process. Then once we got to Toronto to start a three-week rehearsal period prior to filming, I found that, apart from Andrea Martin, I was the only person in the cast who had never tapped before and in the course of the first day's rehearsal I was placed bottom of the class. The ancient Hollywood-style choreographer, who had the look of a scrotum in glasses, made us rehearse in a line-up that placed the most proficient dancer, which was, of course, Liza Minnelli, on the far right, with the dancers decreasing in skill as you moved left until you ended up with me at the other end. It was hell.

This was what was in my head as I went to my first rehearsal of *Billy Elliot*. No, Peter assured me, I wouldn't have to do anything that was out of my ability range.

'So . . . what? A bit of walking to the beat and perhaps a bit of skipping or something?'

'No.'

He was a man of frighteningly few words and again I found it headachingly difficult to learn the steps. There was something terrifying in the fact that the music waited for no man and it wasn't exactly music that had a nice sedate tempo. Unlike a play, where a momentary lapse of concentration could be covered by a dramatic pause whereby a girl could recover her equilibrium and then carry on, with dancing the music and the beat were relentless, and it was a lot harder and required a lot more skill than I possessed to cover any lapse of memory or

341

clumsy slip of the foot. After weeks of rehearsal I had sort of got it but had never really managed to get through it without some sort of slip-up. When the day came to film the dance sequence with Jamie Bell with whom I had yet to dance, I saw him in the corner doing some amazing-looking steps and asked him what scene they were from. He stared at me for slightly longer than is comfortable and then said, 'It's our dance sequence to 'I Love to Boogie'.'

I was dumbfounded; I didn't even recognise them as they were being so brilliantly executed and they bore no resemblance what-soever to the clumsy tangle of steps I'd been trying to get into the right order over the previous weeks.

It was a long morning, and that is all we had in which to film a sequence that should have taken several days. I was in the early stages of the menopause and it was a very fuzzy-headed day, where I felt heavy and bloated, starting the morning unable to get the steps right and then, embarrassingly, unable to prevent myself from crying, something I am not in the habit of doing in public, unless it's whilst acting a part. I went to a far corner of the room for a little privacy and to hide my emotions, and then wished that I hadn't as all it served to do was draw unwanted attention to my state, make me feel more isolated than I already did. It also meant that, at some point, I would have to turn around and face the assembled crew, who were all waiting for me, pawing the ground and kicking at bits of equipment, keen to get on with an impossible schedule.

Of course, when I did turn around, I was met with nothing but sympathy, friendly, understanding pats on the back and a cup of tea, which could have given rise to another blubbing session. Indeed, my lip did begin to tremble, but with a massive intake of breath and a feeling of it's now or never, I knocked back the tea, turned on my heel, the camera rolled and I went through the dance for the first time ever without a hitch. We had it. I noticed that very recently when I shot *Mamma Mia!* I was less afraid of the old dance and I think, along with that film's patient and understanding choreography team led by Anthony Van Last, that the conquering of that little sequence in *Billy Elliot* had a lot to do with it.

20

'Something There to Offend the Whole Family' — *Personal Services*

After the hoohah of the 1984 Oscars was over, I stayed around in Hollywood for a short time on the advice of a couple of executives from Columbia Pictures. I was introduced to a hotshot agent at Creative Artists Agency and was duly taken on. I did the usual rounds of casting folk and the movers and shakers of the film industry, and was even given a few scripts to peruse, but they simply didn't know what to do with me; the scripts were all a bit Rita-esque, with old-fashioned, cheeky, chirpy, 'cor luvva duck' characters, some American screenwriter's romantic and ill-informed idea of what a working-class English girl was like. How could I summon up the enthusiasm to work on things like these when I had had the privilege of the likes of Alan Bennett's, Willy Russell's, Alan Bleasdale's and Victoria Wood's characters to perform?

At a loss, they then sent me bland, generally written characters in romantic comedies of the sort that had been popular in the 1970s, where every line was predictable and clichéd, and could be said by a hundred characters in a hundred different ways, instead of the taut, precise and

344

brilliantly observed stuff I had had the good luck to have grown up with and grown used to. So in my heart of hearts, much as I loved the idea of Hollywood, I knew where I wanted to be. I felt that the roles that I wanted to play, and the projects that I wanted to be a part of and that would fulfil me, were tied to my roots, and that there was a cultural divide that I could not comfortably cross without living in America and soaking it up for some time. I wasn't prepared to do that when my real interest lay deep down in my own history and people. I also felt that the talent of British writers, technicians and directors was unrivalled.

So back home I came, travelling straight up to the Lake District on arrival, Eskdale to be precise, to start shooting a film titled *She'll Be Wearing Pink Pyjamas*.

This was a piece about a group of women on an outward-bound course, with an interesting script written by Eva Hardy that didn't quite live up to its potential when completed, but with a fabulous bunch of women, Pauline Yates, Paula Jacobs, Maureen O'Brien, Janet Henfrey, Alyson Spiro, Jane Evers and Penelope Nice amongst them. The film looms large in my memory because of an incident that occurred after we'd been marooned up there for two or three weeks.

One evening after filming we were all in the bar of the hotel, bemoaning the fact that in a day or so's time we would have to remove our clothes for a particular scene that was set in a shower. Being naked in public is not something that I seek out in life, or in work for that matter. I had

345

done it once before in Alan Bennett's *Intensive Care*, where his embarrassment was so extreme that it made me feel positively Gypsy Rose Lee, and I was to do it once again on stage in the West End in *Frankie and Johnny in the Clair de Lune* in 1989, but that was in a very dim light. And then finally — and when I say finally, I'm pretty positive that I mean finally — I was to strip off in 2003 for the film *Calendar Girls*, but this was a very brief shot, after a pep talk from Helen Mirren and the rest of the girls, plus a glass of champagne, plus a seniority that gave us women total dominance of the set on that day.

However, back in 1984, I certainly felt no such seniority and the thought of a fairly long scene with dialogue whilst you soaped your lalas in a naturalistic fashion was not on my list of things I must do before I die. Then someone — and I can't remember who, though I've often been given the credit — came up with the idea that we should refuse to do it unless the crew took their clothes off as well. Everyone, including the sound crew, who were in the bar that night, thought it was a gas and in the excitement the idea developed into us telling the producers that there had been some kind of recent ruling by Equity, the actors' union. Then Pauline Yates suggested that we get her husband, the actor Donald Churchill, to ring up pretending to be Peter Plouvier, the then general secretary of Equity, to inform our producers of the bogus ruling. The next day a message was left at the hotel reception, asking the producer to ring Peter Plouvier at Equity urgently, along with Donald

Churchill's telephone number, which, of course, he duly did.

The conversation went something like this:

'Yes, hello, could I speak to Peter Plouvier, please?'

'Yes, speaking.'

'Yes, hello, Peter, you left a message for me to call you. I'm working on the film *Pink Pyjamas*.'

'Oh yes. I'm sorry about this, but I believe you have a scene involving several actresses having to appear naked and . . . er, it's coming up this week, isn't it?'

'Erm, yes, that . . . that is correct, yes. Is there a problem?'

'Well, I'm afraid the Women's Committee have just passed a motion stating that should any female members of a cast be required to appear naked, then the same number of crew will have to appear naked too. This was passed . . . er, just yesterday morning and I'm afraid you are the first production that it applies to. Erm, I've spoken to Alan Sapper, the general secretary for the crew's union, and he is in complete agreement and will be instructing his members accordingly. I am sorry about this. I expect you could do without it but I'm afraid we are forced to comply.'

Nobody expected for a minute that the producer, whose name I have left out to spare his blushes, would believe a word of this. But, dear reader, he did.

On the day that the scene was to be shot, we arrived to find members of the crew in heavy discussion with the producers, some saying that they refused to undress.

'I'm not taking my clothes off! I have to bend down a lot . . . it wouldn't be right.' This was heard coming from one little huddle. Others were trying to negotiate a fee for revealing all.

'I'm not going to let a bunch of loony feminists ruin my film!' This was heard being screamed tearfully from the producer's caravan later.

By this time we were terrified, not of the impending scene but of the consequences of our prank once the truth was out. However, we felt that now we had to carry on until the bitter end. Inside the shower set the moment came for us to remove our dressing gowns in order to shoot the scene. As soon as we did so, true to their word the sound boys whipped everything off as well. Many a sound technician would have felt diminished by the size of his boom, but not our man, and may I say that he gave the boom, which was, after all, very large and hairy, a good run for its money. Next to follow was Clive Tickner, our marvellous lighting cameraman, sitting there on the dolly, looking ravishing in nothing but a set of headphones. Eventually, the entire crew, which I have to say was suddenly greatly reduced, were naked; all, that is, except the director, who refused and looked most uncomfortable into the bargain. I can't think why, dear reader, but thereafter a lot of people went round inexplicably lifting their little fingers behind his back, especially when he said anything that could be construed as a mite pompous.

This went on until the end of the shoot and is probably still going on today, for all I know. I am not saying he was an unpopular director, but I do have to say that the caterers offered to make a giant custard pie, with the proviso that some brave person would have the chutzpah to shove it in his face on the last day of filming.

It is amazing how respectful men become when they, too, are naked and in a position to be judged. I noticed it when on a nude beach in Greece; there was absolutely no leering and no comments, lewd or otherwise. Once the scene was over we made our confession with a case of champagne placed strategically between us and them, to ease any embarrassment, and it was all taken in good heart. It is a story that still follows me around the world today; in fact a friend of the very producer of whom I speak contacted him from Australia, only a short forty-eight hours after the joke was played, and reported having read about it in a Sydney newspaper. It turned out to be a publicist's dream but, even so, a box office disappointment, as was the film I did the following year in 1985.

This was called *Car Trouble*, in which I starred with my dear friend Ian Charleson, whom I had worked alongside in the play *Fool for Love* by Sam Shepard at the National Theatre. It was a huge success resulting in us both being nominated for Olivier Awards. We transferred to the Lyric Theatre in Shaftesbury Avenue for a limited run, and I adored him. We were attracted to the child in one another and shared a huge mutual affection as well as a certain wicked, camp humour. *Car Trouble* was a comedy that revolved around an awful couple called Gerald and Jacqueline Spong. He is the overproud owner of an E-Type Jaguar and, to cut a very long story short, Jacqueline takes a fancy to the dishy mechanic played by the dishy Vincenzo Ricotta, who happens to be servicing the said E-Type and predictably ends up servicing her. The climax, for want of a better word, occurs when they are at it in the car and inadvertently slip the handbrake off in a mid-coitus frenzy, sending the car careering through woodland down a bank. The two of them end up being stuck together, Jacqueline having gone into a trauma-induced spasm. I thought Barry Norman was going to spontaneously combust when he reviewed it on *Film '86* as he was so utterly furious. *City Limits*, which was then *Time Out*'s rival what's-on magazine, called it 'a sizzling turd of a movie'. The magazine has since folded but not before honouring me in the form of a garden gnome inscribed with 'The person you would most like to spend a day on Clapham Common with', and my awarding it with the honorific title 'The magazine I would most like to wipe my bottom on'.

However, *City Limits* was forgiven the following year when it gave me the award for Best Film Actress for my portrayal of Cynthia Payne, the notorious Streatham-based madam who famously issued luncheon vouchers to her clients, in the film *Personal Services*. David Leland had written a really affectionate, moving and funny script, and Terry Jones of *Monty Python* fame was to direct. David had told me that he was partly inspired to cast me, as well as being influenced in his writing of the part, by my performance as Betty in Victoria Wood's play *Good Fun*, which he had directed some six years earlier at the Sheffield Crucible. But even though I was his and Terry's first choice for the role, the producers weren't so keen and I was forced to read on camera on three separate occasions before being finally offered the part. A few days later there was to be a press conference, at which Madame Cyn and I were to be centre stage, to announce the forthcoming production, so David and Terry organised dinner in a now-forgotten location so that the two of us could meet. I remember the restaurant as being exclusive and not entirely empty, and it can only have been a matter of minutes before the sneaky sidelong looks, the sly backward glances and the behind-the-hand titters and whispers began.

'Do you like sex, Julie?' Cynthia has just sat down.

'Erm . . . Well, it depends . . . on who it's with.' I giggle and my cheeks start to burn.

'A lot of my girls can take it or leave it, but you get a girl who actually likes it and you've struck gold.'

Cynthia has quite a loud, strident voice. In fact she is talking to me as if I were sitting inside a cupboard with the door shut. The actress in me makes a note and a man at the next table has a coughing fit.

'Oh, yes . . . I . . . can see that.' My neck is

351

burning now as well.

'Yes, I couldn't be doing with it when I was on the game, I got too sore.'

A man and a woman have just entered the room, turned round and gone out again. David coughs.

'Erm, shall I order for you, Cynthia? I know what you're like when you get talking.'

David knows Cynthia well, having apparently spent the last two years in her company researching this film. I notice that he has gone grey around the temples since I last saw him and that his hairline has slightly receded.

'Yes, David, you order. I like a man who can take the lead. I don't meet many of those these days. All my lot want to be humiliated . . . here.'

She rummages in her bag and brings out several small black-and-white snaps. It takes me time to focus on the first one.

'He's a bank manager.'

There is a naked man lying, well, cowering, on the floor of what looks like a perfectly ordinary sitting room, covered in some dark substance.

'He likes to be covered in Hoover dust.'

Diners at the surrounding tables are now enveloped in total silence; there isn't even the scrape of a knife to be heard.

She produces another snap for my perusal. In it a group of elderly men are sitting round with cups of tea, being served biscuits by a couple of topless women in stockings and suspenders; one of them looks the spit of Mrs Raven who did our cleaning when I was a child.

'That's one of my parties.'

'Oh . . . The gentlemen are quite — '

'Yes, I know, I prefer them old. They're easier to handle; the young ones are too much trouble, I won't have young ones. I turn them away.'

There is now a waiter lurking by the doorway into the room; I can see his shoulders going up and down. A little droplet of perspiration has just run down his ribcage.

'A lot of mine are slaves.'

'Par — '

'Slaves.'

She then goes on to explain that she has several clients who simply wish to be totally servile and humiliated by a woman in high heels and the bonus is that they make no demands for sex. It is all about role-play, she says.

'It's marvellous, Julie, I have my house scrupulously cleaned once a week by a man wearing nothing but a suspender belt and stockings. He cleans my kitchen floor on his hands and knees with a toothbrush held between his teeth and as long as I kick him up the bum every so often he's fine. I've got another pair who do my garden, I just have to shout at them from time to time, tell them they're bad and make them cut the lawn with a pair of nail scissors, and they're as happy as Larry.'

'Gosh . . . '

'Yes, so if ever you need a cleaner I could easily find you someone and the beauty of it is *they* pay *you*!'

'Right.'

There are now two waiters in the doorway, quite openly enjoying the show. Cynthia, in the meantime, has moved on to regaling us about a man who wants to be dominated, frightened and humiliated, and she tells us how she and a friend took him out to a lonely spot in the countryside, where they ordered him to undress, tied him to a tree and then left him for a couple of hours.

'Yes, we just gave him a slap and then went shopping in Brighton. He used to love it, except one time we forgot all about him and went home. We had to go back for him in the dark and we couldn't remember where we'd put him. We had such a laugh.'

More photos then appear, one of a huge man wrapped up in a blanket with a dummy in his mouth and a ludicrously large baby's bonnet on his head.

'He's a High Court judge.'

Another photo is of a scrawny, bespectacled man sitting on a large, apparently naked girl's lap at what was obviously another of Cynthia's parties.

'He's a Justice of the Peace and this one, he . . . he is a very high-up policeman.'

This last is of a tall, lanky-looking man dressed in a schoolgirl's uniform complete with gymslip, white, knee-length socks and a blond wig tied up in pigtails.

'You should come to one of my parties, Julie, you'd love it.'

I managed to avoid this. Cynthia visited a couple of locations whilst we were filming, both times holding court on the pavement opposite. Having gathered a little group of onlookers around her, she then set about telling them how whatever it was that we were filming really happened.

'No, it wasn't like that. No, you see . . . etc.'

Eventually the locations were kept a secret. The shoot itself was an education, I think for one and all, but obviously more so for some than others. The sets were generally littered with sex toys of various types and an eye-watering selection of pornography that was continually being pored over by members of cast and crew alike.

'But her nails are chipped!'

This was from my mightily posh but lovely make-up artist as she stared horrified at a photograph of a woman holding a huge disembodied phallus, which might easily have belonged to a donkey, as if she were posing for an advert for Wall's Cornetto.

The film was moderately successful in a cultish sort of way, but I knew it wasn't going to be huge at the box office when I came out of an early screening and heard a woman say, 'Well, something there to offend the whole family.'

The following year I was offered the role of another real person, the wife of Buster Edwards who was one of the key players in the Great Train Robbery. Although in some ways it makes the job easier, having the character already in existence to draw upon whenever necessary, playing a real and living person also brings with it a huge responsibility to do them justice and even though in both these cases I was not attempting an impersonation of any sort, I was still required to find the essence of each. Unlike

Cynthia, June was a very private person and so I felt my responsibility to be even greater, as she was not the sort of person who was likely to stand on the pavement opposite a location and shout the odds about how authentic or not the portrayal of her life was. I was excited to hear from Norma Heyman, the producer, that Phil Collins was set to play the lead and in September 1987 we started rehearsals for *Buster*. We had been at it only a couple of days when I discovered that I was pregnant. About eighteen months previously, in December 1985, the fourth to be precise, I had met a very handsome man from the Automobile Association, the AA, in the Fulham Boulevard, in a bar on the Fulham Road.

I had just returned home after playing Lady Macbeth opposite Bernard Hill as the lead in Nancy Meckler's production of the Scottish play up at Leicester Phoenix. It had been a huge success for me on many levels, not least because it was the first time that I had not employed an accent of some sort to play a part and had spoken Standard English, but it was also a role I found profoundly moving. At the time I felt that the current prime minister, Margaret Thatcher, was a very good model upon which to base my interpretation of the character. Lady M's vaulting ambition, whatever the human cost, seemed to be a perfect parallel to Thatcher's mode of leadership but during rehearsals I discovered the frail creature beneath the character's driven exterior — the soft, vulnerable bit of her that breaks down and reveals itself in the 'mad scene'. It is the only part I have ever wanted to play again, apart, that is, from Mrs Overall of course.

I have always been fascinated by, fearful of and drawn to the subject of mental illness, feeling, I suppose, that we all tread a very fine line between what is seen as insanity and what is supposedly normal. I later felt compelled to write about it in my novel *Maggie's Tree* and although this was, in essence, a fairly dark story, I derived huge joy from writing it, partly because it dealt with a subject that I found disturbing, but also because of the element that is key in my desire to act, which is the monumental power of storytelling. Here in the novel-writing process I was the creator of all things; I decided where the characters came from, both physically and emotionally. I built them from scratch. It felt very akin to acting, but, of course, much lonelier and I do love the social, team-spirit nature of being part of a company or being surrounded by a film crew. So my experience at Leicester Phoenix covered most of the bases and was hugely fulfilling.

Once home in London, I went to the aforementioned bar to catch up with my best buddy, Ros March. A weekly session of talking through our lives to date was, and is, a requirement that I consider vital to the healthy running of my life and this particular one was rather lengthy as I had been away for some weeks. We had met at the Fulham Boulevard for tea at four o'clock in the afternoon and were still there by nine o'clock in the evening, by which time the place was awash with so-called 'Hooray Henrys', and Ros and I were three sheets to the wind. At some point I staggered up to the bar for yet more refreshments and, hearing all the over-privileged 'Yah-yahing' going on, I announced at the top of my voice to Ros, but also for the benefit of those around me: 'I bet nobody here is a member of the Labour Party!'

With that a big, deep voice next to me said, 'I am, actually.'

I looked up and that was it: love, dear reader, or, most likely at that particular juncture, lust. We struck up a conversation, about what, God alone knows, and then after saying goodnight he apparently spotted us staggering about outside, with me dropping ten-pound notes all over the place. Fearing for our safety he decided to walk us home. On reaching my door — at this time I lived a matter of minutes away, in St Dionis Road — I insisted on his coming in for a cup of tea, asking at the same time whether, as he was a man, he would mind taking a look at (a) my shower, as I could read a novel in between each drop of water that came out of it, and (b) my washing machine, which for some reason I had been unable to empty and which therefore had been full of soaking washing for several days.

The house was open plan so that the sitting room ran straight through into the kitchen. As I stood at the far end of the room watching, as my mother would have called him, this 'fine figure of a man' get down on to his haunches to inspect the faulty machine, I was overcome with an overwhelming sense of exhilaration. When he dropped on to all-fours for an even closer look and said, 'I think you probably need a pump,' I mistook his meaning, not realising that he was referring to the appliance, and I ran the full length of the room towards him, propelled by an irresistible urge, and leapt, laughing with drunken glee, on to his back.

'What the — !'

He shot to his feet and began to pivot round in an attempt to shed my limpet-like grasp, obviously thinking that this was an attack.

'No! No! I want you to have my children!' I cried reassuringly but round and round he spun. 'No, no, honestly, I'll give you reasonable access!'

Anyway, to cut a very long story short, we have at this point been together for twenty-three years. He was right about the pump, in all senses; he mended the washing machine that night and never really moved out, and a short and passionate eighteen months later we decided that we would, all things being equal, have a baby.

Only a couple of months later, in the run-up to the film *Buster*, we realised that we had in fact achieved our goal, if a little quicker than anticipated. When I broke the news to her, Norma H. decided that for insurance purposes it was probably better that it went no further than her. This was all very well, but I was suffering not just from morning sickness but from morning, noon and night sickness, and every so often during rehearsals, which were mainly with Phil, I would have to inexplicably get up and rush to the lavatory. This reached a crescendo of discomfort when one of my quick exits occurred with unfortunate timing and I rushed from the room just when Phil, as Buster, was telling me that he loved me and we were about to get into a clinch. That morning, my driver, Jeff, had asked me whether I was happy with his driving as he was concerned with the way I dashed, green faced, from the car at the end of each journey. Then Norma H. grabbed me later after rehearsals and said that Phil was wondering whether I had a problem with him, as my behaviour was so odd, so she was forced to spill the beans. There was much relief all round.

21

The Arrival

I was thrilled to be pregnant. It felt right in every sense. I had begun to feel empty on occasion during the couple of years prior to meeting Grant, wondering what my life was for. What was the purpose, apart from earning money, of rushing, in a whirl of stress, from project to project, never standing still long enough to really take a lie-in?

A few months before I met him, I was shooting the series *The Secret Life of Adrian Mole*, in which I played Adrian's mother. I came on to the set one day and, whilst waiting around to start filming, I picked up a copy of *Punch* magazine. Just inside the front cover, on page one above the list of contents, was a cartoon. In it there was a man sitting in front of a television set, with a newspaper in his hand, shouting to someone in another room: 'Oh, look! There's something on television tonight that hasn't got Julie Walters in it!'

I was stunned and although I joked with my fellow actors about it, I felt hurt and upset. The point of the cartoon was punched painfully home as I raced off that night, heavy with exhaustion, into the West End after filming, to appear in Sam Shepard's *Fool for Love* at the

Lyric Theatre, Shaftesbury Avenue. I began to question my life of constant work, the gaps filled with wild socialising that too often was fuelled by too much drink. It suddenly felt shallow, selfish and somehow fairly meaningless. I knew that cramming my life with work was partly due to the actor's insecurity about never working again, and the drinking was a simple blotting out, and that both meant that I didn't have to think about anything, but it was getting tiresome. I knew there was more and that night in the Fulham Boulevard, even through the fog of too much champagne, I knew somehow that I had found it.

Once the morning sickness, with its unpredictable bouts of throwing up — one of them on the bonnet of a Ford Fiesta whilst crossing the King's Road — was over, with textbook timing at spot-on three months, I felt wonderful. For the first time in my life I was suffused with calm and sailed around in a luxuriously protective, fuzzy cocoon. I loved the way I felt, everything seemed to be in perspective and I loved the way I looked: the ever-growing pod of my body, my skin rosy, my hair lustrous. Even my eyes were different, seeming to have taken on a new intensity of colour and depth.

'I've had a premonition!' This is Nora, a big Irishwoman and one of the dressers on *Buster*. She is hovering in the doorway of my trailer with a bit of a smug smile on her face.

'Oh . . . what . . . What's that, then?'

She has caught me halfway through getting into my costume, in which I am trussed up in a big pointy 1960s bra with a huge pair of matching knickers, not also pointy, you understand, and I am trying to cover my modesty. The reason for this modesty is that we are parked on a residential road and curious members of the public are gaping in through the open door behind her as they pass by.

'You are going to have a boy!' The smirk stretches into a big toothy grin.

'Oh . . . '

'Yes, oh definitely! It came to me in a flash.'

'Excuse me, are you Tracy Ullman?' This from a small, ginger-haired woman standing on the pavement outside and looking up at me from underneath Nora's armpit. She is staring in that crazed, hungry way that people often have when they think they've spotted someone off the telly.

'No, no, I'm not. Sorry.'

'Are you sure?'

'Yes, yes, I'm pretty sure I'm not Tracy Ullman.'

Nora now moves into the caravan so that the woman can enjoy an unimpeded view of me standing there in my bizarre-looking underwear.

'Of course she's not Tracy Ullman! This is Julie Walters!'

'Who?'

I'm thinking: can this get any more humiliating, when the woman does not even wait for my name to be repeated and walks off. Just as Nora is closing the door, she pops back.

'Oh yes! You do that show with Dawn French.'

'Yes, that's right, dear, and now we have to get on, we've a film to make and if Dawn catches her standing here gossiping, she'll be for the high jump!' And with that Nora closes the door so swiftly that I just catch a glimpse of the resultant draught lifting up the woman's thin red fringe to reveal a high freckled forehead. Nora cackles wickedly into the palm of her hand, then says, 'Yes, it's a boy! Here, let me hug you!'

I was shocked by this news and somewhat discombobulated. I had always felt that it would be a girl. Long before I got pregnant, I had thought that, if I ever were to have a child, no matter what, I would have a girl. This wasn't a longing, or even a preference for a girl as opposed to a boy, but I suspect that somewhere at the back of my mind the thought lurked that because I had had a bit of a prickly relationship with my mother, a daughter would help me understand and heal this to some extent, so Nora's news threw me completely. I began to imagine tiny boys with Grant's face running around the sitting room in St Dionis Road and every time I did so I found it so unbearably moving that I would want to cry.

However, these odd little crying sessions soon came to an end because two weeks later an amniocentesis test proved that Nora was talking out of her considerable backside. I was definitely, beyond a shadow of a doubt, having a girl. The consultant had asked whether we wanted to know what the sex was, or whether, like a lot of couples, we preferred to be surprised at the birth. This I simply didn't understand; for a start, I imagined the birth was going to be enough of a surprise all by itself, and second, the thought of a doctor and some laboratory technician somewhere knowing my baby's sex when I hadn't a clue seemed both ludicrous and out of the question. I felt that refusing to know was like refusing to accept that the baby was a valid entity until it was born, and that surely it could only be an advantage to know, as the unborn baby had more of an identity with which we could relate.

The little bump that was now starting to kick had lost its anonymity; it was now a 'she' instead of an 'it', and we were thrilled, as it was what Grant wanted, so we set about discussing names. Clea came up, but put together with Grant's surname, Roffey, we could see that it didn't perhaps work. I suggested Anya; he said over his dead body; he suggested Kelly and I said over mine and then some! I then went out on a limb and suggested Coco; Grant went quiet on this one, but a friend talked me out of it, saying that to name a child after a nighttime drink was almost tantamount to abuse.

Then, some months down the line I came across a reproduction of a Victorian music-hall poster and in the corner was the name Maisie. At last, after endless car journeys with each of us pinging out names only to have them roundly rejected, and months of us suddenly screaming something like 'Tallulah!' during some entirely unconnected task, such as feeding the cat or cooking the dinner, we had happened upon a name that didn't put Grant in mind of a female wrestler with a moustache and didn't remind me of some rough, scraggy-arsed girl from down the end of our road who, as my mother would have said, 'had gone bad'.

During the latter part of my pregnancy, partly as an antidote to all the serious and alarming books on the subject — such as those by Penelope Leach and Sheila Kitzinger, to name but two, which I had previously devoured and which mainly left me feeling that I'd already got parenthood wrong and she wasn't even born yet — and also because I wanted this precious and unique period not to be lost and clouded by time, I decided to keep a diary. This turned into a small and slightly daft tome titled *Baby Talk*. It helped hugely to keep everything in perspective and through it I discovered the joy and power of writing.

While I was writing it, lots of friends recounted their birth experiences, which I duly recorded. There follows two of my favourites.

21 December 1987

Our cleaner has become a Jehovah's Witness. She announced this startling fact only this morning. I say startling, because Benita is an Italian Catholic and her grasp of the English language is slight to say the least. It happened, she claimed, a few weeks ago when a couple of Jehovah's Witnesses, neither of whom spoke Italian, came and knocked on her door. They left her with a huge, leather-bound tome printed in English and I would rate at zero her ability to read the language, because she ignores all the notes we leave her, and the ones she leaves for us are for the most part, unintelligible; for instance, 'A cup I crack. Don't bless you with this. Sorry!'

She talks about her conversion in a very offhand way, as if it were from electricity to gas, which makes me think that she may well have misinterpreted what it is she has become caught up in, and now thinks she belongs to some club, or that she is now a representative of Freeman's catalogues. However, I didn't want to get too involved for fear that she might take it into her head to convert me, so I steered the conversation towards my own obsession, which, of course, was my condition.

Benita then said that her own daughter had been an enormous fourteen pounds at birth and had broken her pelvis. I think I'd rather be converted.

15 January 1988

G was calm as she felt the ache in the small of her back come and go. She had mastered the breathing techniques that had brought about vital relaxation. She felt that now, after months of concentrated yoga, relaxation was at her beck and call, to be summoned at the very mention of the word 'contraction'. For the first time in her life, she knew what being relaxed meant. She had prepared for the day and now that day had come. There had been a little blood, she had been sick, but using her newly found knowledge she had achieved calm. She timed her contractions and even managed a light meal.

The contractions soon became very painful, but she steadily got her things together. Her nightie, some joss sticks, a collection of tapes of Indian sitar music, and some fruit juice that she and her husband might sip during the forthcoming proceedings. Eventually the contractions were coming every five minutes and had become almost unbearable. It was time to leave. They bundled their belongings into the van after notifying the hospital that they were on their way, with G exercising supreme control over the pain. On arriving she could hardly resist a little smile in between contractions — a smile of total pleasure. Her first child would be born at any moment and she was handling it with practised serenity.

The midwife examined her and in a loud, matter-of-fact voice said, 'Well, you're so tense I can't even see your cervix, let alone see if it's dilated!'

She was put in a bath for two hours, after which it was discovered that her cervix had dilated half an inch. She gave birth some twenty-four hours later with pain that made the aforementioned contractions seem like mild discomfort in comparison. Not a joss stick had been lit, not a note of Indian sitar music played — they were still in the back of the van.

In fact the only sound to be heard, apart from human voices, was the ward clock, which had so jangled their nerves in the small hours with its incessant ticking that G's husband had ripped it from the wall.

G told me this story over lunch today. I joined

her in her laughter as she remembered, and as we resumed our meal I found my appetite had quite disappeared.

★ ★ ★

The story of my own daughter's birth turned out to be far less traumatic. It was and is the most important event of my life and as it cannot be topped, the telling of it will round off this tale. I was to have a Caesarean section a couple of weeks prior to the due date. This was decided by the consultant obstetrician because I had suffered high blood pressure in the last week or so of the pregnancy and it was also discovered that I was diabetic, so for the last couple of weeks I was forced to have insulin injections every day; both conditions miraculously disappeared at the moment of birth. The consultant was concerned that I would either have a big baby, due to the diabetes, or a small one, due to the high blood pressure. Added to his concerns was the fact that Maisie was in a frank breech position, meaning that not only was she upside down and refused to turn — he had tried to turn her manually, a procedure that had the effect of making me feel like a kind of bizarre glove puppet — but also that her legs were up over the back of her head. When she was born the paediatrician unwrapped her from her blanket and gently flattened out her legs, but when he let go of them they sprang straight back up around her ears. He said I would be relieved to know that this would go in a day or two, adding that, after all, it was not the sort of habit you would wish her to have as a young woman.

On the Sunday night before she was to be delivered at approximately eight-fifteen the next morning, I sat on the bed of my hospital room, overcome with inexplicable sadness. I ran a bath and soaked in it for a good hour. I tried to picture what my life would be like from eight-fifteen onwards the next day, but, as anyone will tell you, nothing on this earth prepares you for life after birth, no matter how many stories you're told. The sadness continued as I lay there and I began, as I had so often done, to gently rub my distended abdomen and talk to the little person inside. After a couple of minutes of explaining to my unborn daughter that in a few short hours her world would be opened up, she would be brought out into this one, and that it would be all right, that we couldn't wait to meet her, my sadness was suddenly thrown into focus. We had already bonded, and knowing her sex and giving her a name had made that bonding much more intimate. We were now on the eve of a kind of parting; she would be no longer physically part of me and it was a forced and unnatural parting at that. Somewhere, I guess, I felt I had failed her by not giving birth to her naturally, which seemed to be the root of my melancholy.

That night I slept fitfully and woke in the small hours to go to the loo. As I walked into the bathroom, I thought that I was wetting myself and then realised that, in fact, my waters had broken. I stood there for several minutes, in wonder, catching the liquid on my fingers and marvelling at the clear, pure nature of the drops. I had a huge desire then to be holding her and I said, 'You're coming! You heard me! You clever girl! Yes, now is the time, we're all waiting for you, with loads of love.' And I cried and then the sobs turned into little giggles of pure joy, and the sadness that had sat, leaden in the pit of my stomach, floated up and out on the laughter, and I knew that what was happening was meant and was perfect.

As I lay there in the cosy glow of the nightlight, hooked up to a machine that measured her heartbeat and my contractions, I had a brief, heart-soaring moment when I got the notion into my head that, now that she was on her way, I might just be able, with a little help, to give birth naturally, but it was not to be; the Caesarean was to take place as scheduled and I would be taken down to theatre at eight o'clock. But at least now I was excited about the prospect.

Epilogue — Another Beginning

Five years ago today . . .

I can hear my mother's voice, so close in note and tone to my own that they are one.

'Ten years ago today . . . ' I am calling up the stairs, 'Dad and I went down to the theatre.' I think I hear her yawn. I'm glad. 'I had my epidural and I noticed your dad had disappeared.'

Grant laughs, he knows what's coming.

'Then I looked round and everyone else had disappeared as well, nurses, doctors!'

I've got her now, I can hear her listening.

'Don't exaggerate.' Grant is still laughing. He is sitting in his overalls at our big farmhouse table in the kitchen, reading his *Farmer's Weekly*, surrounded by Soil Association bumpf and farm orders. He is drinking a cup of tea and eating toast.

'A nurse came back in and I said, where is everyone? And she said, oh, your husband went a bit green, we had to take him out.'

I hear her go 'Ahhh . . . ' Her sympathy is genuine.

'One minute, he's sitting there with a J-cloth on his head, looking concerned; the next he's out cold, surrounded by nurses.'

Grant stops laughing.

'I never could stand hospitals.' He feeds his crusts to the dogs and goes back to his *Farmer's Weekly*.

'No, it was a typical act of upstaging on your part.' Now I'm making myself laugh. 'You were so beautiful,' I tell her, 'so perfect.'

And she laughs and she is.

Film and TV

A Short Stay in Switzerland (TV, 2009)
Harry Potter and the Half-Blood Prince (2009)
— Molly Weasley
Mamma Mia! (2008) — Rosie
Filth: The Mary Whitehouse Story (TV, 2008)
— Mary Whitehouse
Harry Potter and the Order of the Phoenix (2007)
— Molly Weasley
Becoming Jane (2007) — Mrs Austen
The Ruby in the Smoke (TV, 2006)
Acorn Antiques: The Musical (2006) — Bo
Beaumont/Mrs Overall
Driving Lessons (2006) — Evie Walton
Wah-Wah (2005) — Gwen Traherne
Ahead of the Class (TV, 2005) — Marie Stubbs
Mickybo and Me (2004) — Mickybo's Ma
Harry Potter and the Prisoner of Azkaban (2004)
— Molly Weasley
The Return (TV, 2003) — Lizzie Hunt
Canterbury Tales, *The Wife of Bath* (TV, 2003)
— Beth
Calendar Girls (2003) — Annie Clarke
Harry Potter and the Chamber of Secrets (2002)
— Molly Weasley
Before You Go (2002) — Theresa
Murder (2002) (TV) — Angela Maurer
My Beautiful Son (2001) (TV) — Sheila Fitzpatrick
Harry Potter and the Sorcerer's Stone (2001)
— Molly Weasley

Billy Elliot (2000) — Mrs Wilkinson
 dinnerladies (TV, 1998–2000) — Petula Gordino
All Forgotten (2000) — Princess Zasyekin
Oliver Twist (TV, 1999) — Mrs Mann
Wetty Hainthropp Investigates (TV, 1999) — Agnes
Titanic Town (1998) — Bernie McPhelimy
Girls' Night (1998) — Jackie Simpson
Jack and the Beanstalk (TV, 1998) — Fairy
 Godmother
Talking Heads 2 (TV, 1998) — Marjory
Melissa (TV, 1997) — Paula Hepburn
Bathtime (1997) — Miss Gideon
Brazen Hussies (TV, 1996) — Maureen Hardcastle
Intimate Relations (1996) — Marjorie Beasley
Jake's Progress (TV, 1995) — Julie Diadoni
Little Red Riding Hood (TV, 1995) — Little
 Red Riding Hood/Grandma
Sister My Sister (1994) — Madame Danzard
Pat and Margaret (TV, 1994) — Pat
Requiem Apache (TV, 1994) — Mrs
Bambino mio (TV, 1994) — Alice
Wide-Eyed and Legless (TV, 1993) — Diana
 Longden
Clothes in the Wardrobe (TV, 1993) — Monica
Just Like a Woman (1992) — Monica
All Day Breakfast (TV, 1992)
Julie Walters and Friends (TV, 1991)
Stepping Out (1991) — Vera
GBH (TV, 1991) — Mrs Murray
Mack the Knife (1990) — Mrs Peachum
Victoria Wood (TV, 1989)
Killing Dad or How to Love Your Mother (1989)
 — Judith
Buster (1988) — June Edwards

Victoria Wood: As Seen on TV (TV, 1985–1987)
— Mrs Overall
Prick Up Your Ears (1987) — Elsie Orton
Personal Services (1987) — Christine Painter
Talking Heads (TV, 1987) — Lesley
Acorn Antiques (TV, 1986) — Mrs Overall
The Birthday Party (TV, 1986) — Lulu
The Secret Diary of Adrian Mole Aged 13 3/4
(TV, 1985) — Pauline Mole
Dreamchild (voice, 1985) — Dormouse
Unfair Exchanges (TV, 1985) — Mavis
Car Trouble (1985) — Jacqueline Spong
Love and Marriage (TV, 1984)
She'll Be Wearing Pink Pyjamas (1984) — Fran
Educating Rita (1983) — Rita
Objects of Affection (TV, 1982) — June Potter
Play for Today (TV, 1978, 1982) — Debbie
Boys from the Blackstuff (TV, 1982) — Angie
Todd
Wood and Walters (TV, 1982)
Happy Since I Met You (TV, 1981) — Frances
Screenplay (TV, 1979, 1981) — Frances
BBC2 Playhouse (TV, 1981) — Mrs Morgan
Nearly a Happy Ending (TV, 1981)
Talent (TV, 1979) — Julie Stephens
Me! I'm Afraid of Virginia Woolf (TV, 1978)
Empire Road (TV, 1978) — Jean Watson
Second City Firsts (TV, 1975)

Picture Credits

The author and publishers are grateful to the following for permission to reproduce photographs:

We do hope that you have enjoyed reading this large print book.

Did you know that all of our titles are available for purchase?

We publish a wide range of high quality large print books including:
Romances, Mysteries, Classics
General Fiction
Non Fiction and Westerns

Special interest titles available in large print are:
The Little Oxford Dictionary
Music Book
Song Book
Hymn Book
Service Book

Also available from us courtesy of Oxford University Press:
Young Readers' Dictionary
(large print edition)
Young Readers' Thesaurus
(large print edition)

For further information or a free brochure, please contact us at:
Ulverscroft Large Print Books Ltd.,
The Green, Bradgate Road, Anstey,
Leicester, LE7 7FU, England.
Tel: (00 44) 0116 236 4325
Fax: (00 44) 0116 234 0205

DEAR FATTY

Dawn French

With a sharp eye for comic detail and a wicked ear for the absurdities of life, Dawn French shows how an RAF girl from the West Country rose to become one of the best-loved comedy actresses of our time. Here Dawn French invites us into her most personal relationships with, among others, her mum and dad, her husband, her daughter and her friend Jennifer. Dawn reveals the people and experiences that have influenced her and that helped shape her comedy creations. She describes the experience of losing her beloved dad and later finding a tip-topmost chap in Lenny Henry. From raging about class, celebrity and bullying to describing the highs and lows of motherhood and friendship, *Dear Fatty* reveals the surprising life behind the smile.

FATHERS & SONS

Richard Madeley

Seven years before the Great War, ten-year-old Geoffrey Madeley was travelling to Liverpool with his family to take the ship to Canada to start a new life. But after their overnight stop on his uncle's farm, Geoffrey woke up to find that his mother, father and siblings had gone. In a heartbreaking betrayal, he'd been left behind. This child was Richard Madeley's grandfather. Shock waves would reverberate through the generations of Madeley boys, each struggling to cope with a tangled emotional inheritance. Starved of paternal affection, Christopher, Geoffrey's son, swore that for his son things would be different. But were they? And what kind of father did Richard become? *Fathers and Sons* is a journey into fatherhood in the most rapidly changing centuries in history.